¡Ay Tú!

JOE R. AND TERESA LOZANO LONG SERIES IN LATIN AMERICAN
AND LATINO ART AND CULTURE

¡Ay Tú!

Critical Essays on the Life and Work of Sandra Cisneros

EDITED BY SONIA SALDÍVAR-HULL
AND GENEVA M. GANO

UNIVERSITY OF TEXAS PRESS   TEXAS

Figures 2.1, 2.2, and 10.2 are used by permission of Stuart Bernstein Representation for Artists, New York, NY, and protected by the Copyright Laws of the United States. All rights reserved. The printing, copying, redistribution, or retransmission of this content without express permission is prohibited.

Copyright © 2024 by the University of Texas Press
All rights reserved
Printed in the United States of America
First edition, 2024

Requests for permission to reproduce material from this work should be sent to permissions@utpress.utexas.edu.

♾ The paper used in this book meets the minimum requirements of ANSI/NISO Z39.48-1992 (R1997) (Permanence of Paper).

Library of Congress Cataloging-in-Publication Data

Names: Saldívar-Hull, Sonia, 1951– editor. | Gano, Geneva, editor.
Title: ¡Ay tú! : critical essays on the life and work of Sandra Cisneros / edited by Sonia Saldívar-Hull and Geneva M. Gano.
Other titles: Joe R. and Teresa Lozano Long series in Latin American and Latino art and culture.
Description: First edition. | Austin : University of Texas Press, 2024. | Series: Joe R. and Teresa Lozano Long series in Latin American and Latino art and culture | Includes index.
Identifiers: LCCN 2023049620
    ISBN 978-1-4773-2989-4 (hardback)
    ISBN 978-1-4773-2990-0 (paperback)
    ISBN 978-1-4773-2991-7 (pdf)
    ISBN 978-1-4773-2992-4 (epub)
Subjects: LCSH: Cisneros, Sandra—Criticism and interpretation. | Cisneros, Sandra—Interviews. | LCGFT: Essays.
Classification: LCC PS3553.I78 Z56 2024 | DDC 813/.54 [B] —dc23/eng/2023
LC record available at https://lccn.loc.gov/2023049620

doi:10.7560/329894

CONTENTS

List of Illustrations   vii

Preface. ¡Ay Tú! ¡Sí Yo! Nosotrxs: The Sinvergüenza Collective   ix

Introduction. Her Fabulous Career: Sandra Cisneros's Lifework   1
    Sonia Saldívar-Hull and Geneva M. Gano

PART I. ¡AY, QUÉ RICO! CLOSE READINGS

CHAPTER 1. Lingering with Complicity in *Caramelo*   15
    Mary Pat Brady

CHAPTER 2. The Racial City: Navigating Chicago's Racialized Space in *The House on Mango Street*   31
    Olga L. Herrera

CHAPTER 3. Telenovela Feeling in Sandra Cisneros's *Loose Woman*: "I Think of Me to Gluttony"   47
    Adriana Estill

CHAPTER 4. "You Were Telling *Cochinadas*": Performative Metaphors for Storytelling in Sandra Cisneros's *Caramelo*   63
    Shanna M. Salinas

CHAPTER 5. Mapping the Decolonial: Community Cartography in Sandra Cisneros's *Woman Hollering Creek*   81
    Teresa Hernández

PART II. LOVE, SHAME, AND SINVERGÜENZAS

CHAPTER 6. "Love the Only Way I Know How": Cultivating Erotic Conocimiento in the Work of Sandra Cisneros   101
    Belinda Linn Rincón

CHAPTER 7. From Marginal to Sin Vergüenza: Overcoming School-Inflicted Shame through Transgressive Literary Aesthetics in Sandra Cisneros's Life and Writing   119
    Georgina Guzmán

CHAPTER 8. The Loose Woman and the Men of Ill Repute 137
Richard T. Rodríguez

CHAPTER 9. Wild, Wicked, and Crazy Brave Tongues: Locating the Collaborative Origins of Sandra Cisneros's and Joy Harjo's Poetic Voices 155
Audrey Goodman

CHAPTER 10. "Hay Que Inventarnos / We Must Invent Ourselves": The Impact of Norma Alarcón and Sandra Cisneros's Friendship on Chicana Feminist Literature 173
Sara A. Ramírez

CHAPTER 11. Faxes, Friendship, and the Rise of Chicana Literature: Examining the Archive of Letters between Sandra Cisneros and Helena María Viramontes 195
Linda Margarita Greenberg

PART III. ¡ADELANTE! SEEING AND LISTENING WITH CISNEROS

CHAPTER 12. La Sandra como Artista: The Visual Cisneros 217
Tey Marianna Nunn

CHAPTER 13. Sin Vergüenza: A Plática with Sandra Cisneros 237
Macarena Hernández

Acknowledgments 251

Contributors 253

Index 257

LIST OF ILLUSTRATIONS

FIGURE 0.1. Sandra Cisneros's personalized Texas license plate viii

FIGURE 1.1. José Agustín Arrieta, *Interior de una pulquería*, 1850 16

FIGURE 2.1. Sandra Cisneros, diary entries, May 14 and 15, 1968 38

FIGURE 2.2. Sandra Cisneros, diary entries, April 5 and 6, 1968 40

FIGURE 8.1. Ángel Rodríguez-Díaz, *The Protagonist of an Endless Story*, 1993 145

FIGURE 10.1. Letter from Norma Alarcón to Sandra Cisneros, February 1, 1985 177

FIGURE 10.2. Letter from Sandra Cisneros to Norma Alarcón, May 18, 1982 179

FIGURE 10.3. Sandra Cisneros with Chicana/Latina writers and artists outside Guadalupe Cultural Arts Center 186

FIGURE 12.1. Sandra Cisneros, *A Room of Her Own: My Mother's Altar* 230

FIGURE 12.2. Detail during installation, Sandra Cisneros, *A Room of Her Own: My Mother's Altar* 231

FIGURE 12.3. Detail of photos with writing, Sandra Cisneros, *A Room of Her Own: My Mother's Altar* 232

Figure 0.1. Sandra Cisneros's personalized Texas license plate. Image courtesy of the Sandra Cisneros Papers, Wittliff Collections, Texas State University.

PREFACE

¡AY TÚ! ¡SÍ YO! NOSOTRXS
The Sinvergüenza Collective

¡Ay Tú! This collection's title came directly from the pen of Sandra Cisneros, by way of her good friend and "spiritual brother," the incredibly creative South Texan writer and artist Ito Romo. She chose these "very Tejano and chistoso" words for her Texas-issued vanity plate in the early 1990s (see figure 0.1). It playfully and seriously captures what Sandra Cisneros's lifework has meant to us, the contributors to this collection, as readers, friends, and colleagues.

The phrase "Ay tú" has been traditionally used to silence those, especially girls and women, who transgress cultural boundaries within Latinidad. In many of our own upbringings, the phrase was usually followed by the rhetorical "¿Quién te crees?" (Who do you think you are?). Although it can be deployed in a teasing manner, the phrase nonetheless singles out the auditor for daring to step out of line by behaving in ways that differentiate *tú*, you, from the others: those "good girls" who are more obedient, compliant, or unpresuming. It implies that the auditor has an inflated sense of self, no sense of shame, and the familiar *tú* cuts her back down to a more appropriately modest size.

When we reflect on Sandra Cisneros's lifework and her choice of this phrase to label her vehicle (always a metaphor for movement and power in her narratives), we find its resonance with the Cisneros we have found in her work. Unwilling to be cowed, confronting those who would shame her into conformity, playfully dishing back as good as she has been served, Cisneros deploys the familiar in a new and maybe surprising way. Through her words, she not only reclaims her own dignity but also offers the language of reclamation to others who have also been made small, so that they may stand large and proud.

The phrase's negative connotations can undoubtedly call forth an ambivalent pang of embarrassment or shame: the cultural scars of its usage are deep. Even among us, the contributors to this volume, there was notable disagreement on its usage and its suitability in the title of this book. However, we felt that such a strong provocation of responses reflected how Cisneros's lifework has defied stigmas around gender, sexuality, class, and ethnicity while simultaneously risking controversy and disagreement. Ultimately, we felt that there was immense value in the opening up of the possibility of transformation from pain to pride.

In this spirit, we build from Sandra Cisneros's most recent poetry collection, *Woman without Shame / Mujer sin vergüenza* (2022), in which she provocatively and playfully reimagines what it is like to embody Latinidad and the feminine *without* shame. For Cisneros, to be a woman *sin vergüenza* is to reclaim herself, as a Chicana feminist, from cultural stigma. In that spirit, many of us who have contributed to this collection took up, in a gesture of defiance and joy, the moniker the Sinvergüenza Collective.

The Sinvergüenza Collective aims to honor the intellectual legacy and genealogy of those *mujeres* who gave us the tools and inspired us to assemble this foundational collection on Sandra Cisneros's life and writings. Notable among these women is Sonia Saldívar-Hull—prominent scholar, *educadora*, professor, and editor—whose work on Chicana feminism, literature, and culture set the foundation from which we speak as a collective group of writers, but there are more as well. This book is for us, and also for y'all. Sin vergüenza.

¡Ay Tú!

INTRODUCTION

HER FABULOUS CAREER
Sandra Cisneros's Lifework
Sonia Saldívar-Hull and Geneva M. Gano

Sandra Cisneros, recipient of the National Medal of Arts, a MacArthur "Genius" award, and the PEN/Nabokov Award for Achievement in International Literature, is one of the major writers of her generation and one of the first Chicana writers to become recognized nationally and internationally. Her work spans the genres of fiction, nonfiction, memoir, poetry, and visual and performing art, and crosses linguistic, cultural, and national borders. *The House on Mango Street*, her first book, has been taught in schools everywhere, from elementary schools to universities, and has been translated into more than twenty languages. She is a popular and beloved author and speaker whose audience draws from all walks of life. As one of the most influential Latinas in the public eye, Cisneros has used her platform to advocate for peace, women's rights, and other social justice issues.

This interdisciplinary collection of scholarly essays is the first of its kind to attempt a synthetic, critical examination of the author's substantial body of work and exceptional career. It places Sandra Cisneros's writing in relation to her life and offers readers multiple pathways for navigating her vast and varied body of work. This volume not only considers each of Cisneros's full-length books individually, it also identifies and explores broader themes and topics that have punctuated her works throughout her career, including those of love, female friendship, sexual abuse and harassment, and the role of the arts in the lives of everyday people. This collection connects and weaves together the strands of Cisneros's oeuvre, picking up threads that tie her and her work to other writers and artists, social and aesthetic movements, and contemporary history. As these essays show, Cisneros's writing and activism reflect on important world and local events, trace her motivations and inspirations, and link her concerns with those of other writers, artists, thinkers, and actors. Together, the essays collected here, many of which draw deeply on previously untapped archival sources, personal interviews, and privately held papers, illuminate Sandra Cisneros's unique and significant position within contemporary American literature and culture. More broadly, these essays collectively trace a textured history of the establishment and expansion of an aesthetically innovative, politically engaged, and intellectually vibrant Chicana feminist literary world in the late twentieth century. Writing, speaking, editing, publishing, touring, and fundraising, Sandra Cisneros was at the very heart of this world as it emerged and grew.

"OF MYTH AND BULLSHIT": THE BIOGRAPHICAL FACTS

Thanks to the hundreds of articles, interviews, blog posts, podcasts, essays, theses, dissertations, and other assessments of Cisneros and her work over the forty years in which she has been prominent in the public eye, the biographical outline of her life is well known.[1] Sandra Cisneros was born December 20, 1954, to Alfredo Cisneros Del Moral and Elvira Cordero Anguiano, the third child and only girl of seven surviving children. Her father, who grew up in Mexico City, immigrated to the United States as a young man, eventually ending up in Chicago and going into business with his brother as an upholsterer. A consummate craftsman, he had little interest in book learning, though he had attended some college. Cisneros's mother was from a working-class Mexican American family from Chicago. She did not complete high school but was dedicated to her own (and her children's) education and self-improvement. Elvira managed the household and encouraged her children to read and appreciate the arts. Her family was not particularly religious, but Sandra and her siblings attended Catholic schools instead of public ones. In middle school Sandra began keeping a journal, a practice she maintained through adulthood. She attended the all-girls Josephinum Academy of the Sacred Heart for high school, graduating in 1972. She then followed her two older brothers to college at Loyola University Chicago, where she majored in English and education.

Cisneros's first poems were published in high school and college, and on the strength of these she was admitted to the Iowa Writers' Workshop, where she worked with Louise Glück, William Anderson, Bill Matthews, Donald Justice, and Marvin Bell.[2] Cisneros was awarded a teaching assistantship but declined it, instead working to put herself through the prestigious program by taking odd jobs and serving as a translator in the international studies program. Bell, who was "absolutely the best teacher" Cisneros had studied under,

INTRODUCTION

directed her MFA thesis, a volume of poems titled "My Wicked Wicked Ways," which she submitted in 1978.[3] The collection would eventually be expanded and published in 1987 as *My Wicked Wicked Ways*: her first full-length book of poetry. At Iowa, Cisneros knew poets Joy Harjo and Rita Dove, the only two other women of color then enrolled in the workshop. Although they were not close friends at the time, their mutual support endured beyond Iowa and throughout their careers. While at Iowa Cisneros also met writer Dennis Mathis, who would become her most important first reader, editor, and friend. During these years, Cisneros published a few poems and wrote some prose pieces that would later be incorporated into *The House on Mango Street*.

Upon the completion of her master's degree, Cisneros "reluctantly" moved back to Chicago.[4] There, she made connections to Chicago artists such as raúl niño, Reggie Young, and Beatriz Badikian through Movimiento Artístico Chicano (MARCH) and Mujeres Latinas en Acción. She also joined a radical and passionate faculty of "idealists and anarchists, romantics, and realists," including photographer Diana Solís, at Latino Youth Alternative High School. It was here that Cisneros's "proletarian ideology" was formed and where she found "direction and roots" for her work.[5] She taught Spanish, English, and creative writing, served as an adviser for a journal of student writing, *Un Verano*, and organized student readings and other events. Cisneros also served as an artist in residence for the Illinois Arts Council, leading poetry workshops in public high schools across the state; she later took on a similar role in the San Antonio public schools. One of Cisneros's poems, "Sir James South Side," appeared on Chicago buses, and she was actively publishing poems in regional, women's, and Latino journals. In 1980, Lorna Dee Cervantes and Gary Soto published Cisneros's chapbook of poems primarily set in and around Chicago, *Bad Boys*. At this time she was actively reading in local bookstores such as Women and Children First and Jane Addams Bookstore, art galleries (her brother's apartment, "Galeria Quique," for instance), and community centers, in addition to the Newberry Library and universities. As Cisneros became more actively involved in feminist circles and developed her consciousness as a Third World feminist, she established a connection with Chicana feminist Norma Alarcón, who became a lifelong friend, collaborator, and supporter. Cisneros was hired by Loyola University Chicago in 1981 as a recruiter for the Educational Opportunity Program, which was aimed at underrepresented students; with Reggie Young, she coordinated Chicago's City Songs, a community poetry workshop for adults. During these years, Cisneros was writing but much of her time was devoted to her activity in the community. When she received a National Endowment for the Arts (NEA) Creative Writing Fellowship in Poetry in 1981, she was able to concentrate on writing new poems, traveling, and finishing the manuscript of *The House on*

Mango Street, which had been accepted for publication by the Houston-based small press Arte Público.

The NEA grant made escape from Chicago, and a year dedicated to writing and living a writer's life, possible. In the summer of 1982, Cisneros traveled to New York City and Provincetown, Massachusetts, where she hoped to complete *The House on Mango Street* before traveling to Europe. The manuscript was not finished, though, and she brought it with her, completing it on the island of Hydra in Greece before backpacking through France and Italy. Cisneros continued her travels, writing poems and living in France and Yugoslavia. Cisneros returned to Chicago in 1983 to work as a live-in nanny for her older brother. However, Cisneros knew that she wanted to leave Chicago permanently and applied for a position as the literature director at the Guadalupe Cultural Arts Center in San Antonio, Texas. She was hired for the job, enabling what she intended as her final departure from Chicago.

The Guadalupe Cultural Arts Center, a newly established nonprofit devoted to the promotion and preservation of Chicano arts and culture, was transformed by Cisneros's hard work, energy, and skill in community organizing. She began her new role as the only woman in the organization's leadership in January 1984. She edited and wrote for *Tonantzín*, the center's literary magazine; created a monthly reading series that brought important writers to the center, including Ana Castillo, Pat Mora, Rolando Hinojosa, Cherríe Moraga, Helena María Viramontes, John Phillip Santos, Luis Omar Salinas, and Alberto Ríos; taught creative writing workshops for children and adults; supervised a poetry-in-the-schools pilot program; and, with Bryce Milligan, organized the first annual Texas Small Press Book Fair, which was a huge success. At the same time, Cisneros's book *The House on Mango Street* was published, and she traveled throughout the state of Texas—to Laredo, Victoria, El Paso, Austin, and elsewhere—giving readings at bookstores, community centers, shopping malls, public library branches, colleges, and universities. Overextended from her constant travels to support her book and chafing against what she felt was the organization's paternalistic, overly restrictive direction, Cisneros resigned from her position in April 1985. At this time, Cisneros's work was starting to be recognized with awards and fellowships, one of the first of which was the Before Columbus Foundation Book Award. Cisneros also took on visiting professorships at colleges and universities. The first of these was at Texas Lutheran College in Seguin, in spring 1985. Over the next few years while working in these short-term teaching positions, Cisneros moved frequently, living with family, friends, and lovers, house-sitting, and surfing couches. *My Wicked Wicked Ways* was published by Third Woman Press in 1987. That year, Cisneros took a visiting professorship at California State University, Chico.

INTRODUCTION

Despite this activity and success, Cisneros was going through a dark period: in her words, it was "the year of my near death."[6] Barely surviving her exodus in remote, rural Chico, a heart-wrenching romantic breakup, and a disheartening experience teaching within an academic setting, Cisneros nonetheless took on additional visiting professorships over the next few years, at Berkeley and Irvine in California, at the University of Michigan, and at the University of New Mexico. She returned to San Antonio in 1991. After this, Cisneros declined to have more than occasional relationships with academic institutions, though she continued to teach writing workshops in less formal settings. Cisneros's life and career changed dramatically when Susan Bergholz became her agent in 1988. She became the first Chicana to publish with a major press and was catapulted into the national and international arena. *The House on Mango Street* was reissued by Vintage in 1989 and went on to become an international bestseller. With Julie Grau as her editor at Random House, Cisneros published *Woman Hollering Creek and Other Stories* to great acclaim in 1991. In 1994 Knopf published a book of poems, *Loose Woman*, and a children's book, *Hairs/Pelitos*, which was illustrated by her friend Terry Ybáñez. In 1995 Cisneros was awarded a MacArthur Foundation Fellowship, which gave her long-term financial stability (and health insurance!) for the first time. She quit her day job and purchased her first home, a Victorian bungalow in San Antonio's King William Historic District. She decorated it to her taste, painting it an exuberant purple, and adopted a growing menagerie of animal companions that included cats, dogs, and a parrot.

Cisneros's social life involved human companions as well, many of whom were artists and performers who shared her vision of creating socially conscious art that would appeal to a wide swath of the population. These included Danny López Lozano and Craig Pennel of Tienda Guadalupe, Franco Mondini-Ruiz, Garrett Mormando, Terry Ybáñez, Joan Frederick, Ellen Riojas Clark, Rolando Briseño, Ángel Rodríguez-Díaz, Ito Romo, Lisa Mellinger, and Gertrude Baker. Cisneros read and performed her work across the United States and around the world. In and from her chosen home of San Antonio, Cisneros read in the public schools and libraries; became involved with community-based Jump-Start Theater, which was led by visionary director Steve Bailey; and participated in vigils for peace, protests, and marches, alongside comrades and leaders including Emma Tenayuca and Dolores Huerta. Her connections to other artists and writers, including filmmaker Lourdes Portillo, visual artist Ester Hernández, and author Dorothy Allison, extended far beyond the local as well. In 1997 Cisneros founded the Latino MacArthur Fellows, Los MacArturos, an annually expanding group of geniuses that met for community workshops and presentations. She also originated the Macondo Foundation, an association of socially engaged writers who meet annually in

San Antonio for workshops and artistic exchange, and the Alfredo Cisneros Del Moral Foundation (named in memory of her father), a grant-giving institution that served Texas writers.

Throughout this period, Cisneros widened the scope of her activism. She remained engaged with the local community, reading and speaking at public schools, libraries, and community-based events to inspire others to dream big and take practical steps to achieve their goals. She also wrote and spoke out about events of national and global significance, a call she heeded as she became more spiritually engaged with Buddhist practices of making and living peace. Cisneros's conviction that war is wrong prompted her to *testimoniar*, to use her voice, to raise the consciousness of her audience as war and state violence raged around the world.[7] The war in Bosnia (1992–1995), which caught up her friend Jasna Karaula, marked an important moment in Cisneros's career as a public speaker, as she deliberately used her national platform to call for peace. Most prominently, she did this by writing letters to the editors of major newspapers, including the *Los Angeles Times*, the *Baltimore Sun*, the *New York Times*, and the *San Antonio Express-News*, to circulate Jasna's despairing letter from Sarajevo, call attention to the *matanza* (massacre) in Acteal, Chiapas, and declare her opposition to the US war in Iraq. Cisneros also took advantage of international interviews and major award ceremonies that were intended to highlight her literary accomplishments, transforming them into opportunities to speak directly to the public about the atrocities and violence of war.

The next decade saw the publication of Cisneros's multigenerational, epic novel *Caramelo* (Knopf, 2002) and numerous prizes and awards. Cisneros was awarded the Texas Medal of Arts in 2003 and won the Premio Napoli in 2005. In 2004, on the twentieth anniversary of the publication of *The House on Mango Street*, a definitive collection of the author's short works, *Vintage Cisneros*, was published. *Bravo Bruno!*, illustrated by Paris-based artist Leslie Greene, was published in Italy by La Nuova Frontiera in 2011. Cisneros's final work to be written and set in San Antonio, *Have You Seen Marie?*, was a collaboration with an old friend, the celebrated Chicana artist Ester Hernández. The book, a love letter and going-away present to her adopted hometown, was published in 2012.

The following year, Cisneros moved from San Antonio to San Miguel de Allende in Mexico. There, she completed an award-winning collection of nonfiction stories, *A House of My Own: Stories from My Life* (Knopf, 2015). Cisneros was awarded the National Medal of Arts by President Barack Obama in 2016. *Puro Amor*, a story set in Mexico and illustrated by the author, was published in 2018, and *Martita, I Remember You / Martita, te recuerdo* was published in 2021. Both of these books were published in bilingual editions, with longtime

INTRODUCTION

collaborator Liliana Valenzuela translating the English to Spanish. A new book of poems, *Woman without Shame / Mujer sin vergüenza*, was published by Penguin Random House in 2022. She has more books in the pipeline.

AQUÍ ESTAMOS: THE CRITICAL RECEPTION AND THE GROWTH OF CHICANA CRITICAL STUDIES

Scholarship on writings by Sandra Cisneros emerged with and as an integral part of Chicana critical studies. The first generation of this scholarship appeared in print during the 1990s, although Cisneros's work had been discussed by scholars in national and international contexts since at least 1985, when Sonia Saldívar-Hull presented a paper on *The House on Mango Street* at the National Association of Chicano Studies Conference. In 1986, Erlinda Gonzáles-Berry and Tey Diana Rebolledo published "Growing Up Chicano: Tomás Rivera and Sandra Cisneros" in *Revista Chicano-Riqueña*. The first Spanish-language essay on Cisneros's work, a study of *The House on Mango Street* by Pedro Gutiérrez Revuelta, appeared that same year in *Crítica*.[8] These essays were the first of many in English, Spanish, and other languages to be published on Cisneros's work.

The first academic conference devoted to Chicana literature and literary criticism was held at the University of California, Irvine, in 1987. Cisneros did not attend the conference, but her work was discussed by attendees, including María Herrera-Sobek, Julián Olivares, and Yvonne Yarbro-Bejarano. These papers were later published as *Chicana Creativity and Criticism: New Frontiers in American Literature*, edited by Herrera-Sobek and Helena María Viramontes, in 1996.[9]

The first full-length study of Chicana literature, *Women Singing in the Snow: A Cultural Analysis of Chicana Literature* by Tey Diana Rebolledo, was published in 1995; it included discussion of both Cisneros's prose and poetry. Sonia Saldívar-Hull's *Feminism on the Border: Chicana Gender Politics and Literature* (2000) and Mary Pat Brady's *Extinct Lands, Temporal Geographies: Chicana Literature and the Urgency of Space* (2002) argued for Cisneros's centrality within a politically engaged Chicana feminism, established Chicana literary criticism, and remain vital contributions to the field today.[10]

The thirteen critical essays in this volume continue the intellectual lineage of critical inquiry that the first generation of Cisneros scholars established. These original essays reflect careful analysis, sustained reading and thinking, and fresh insights by scholars who have spent years—and, in some cases, lifetimes—considering and reconsidering her work and life. Many of these critics have written some of the definitive work on the author. Here, they reconsider, expand, and see anew the author's oeuvre. Others are approaching the writer from a scholarly standpoint for the first time, bringing to her work new perspectives, visions, and ideas.

The essays in part 1, "¡Ay, Qué Rico! Close Readings," argue for a rereading of some of Cisneros's most discussed and debated writings. To begin, the essay by literary scholar Mary Pat Brady, "Lingering with Complicity in *Caramelo*," discusses the complex racial politics explored in Cisneros's turn-of-the-century epic novel. Arguing that the novel flirts with the long tradition of Spanish and Mexican celebration of typicality, at turns curating "types" while reviling their deployment to denigrate people, "Lingering" argues that the novel's form and plot draw readers into the uncomfortable position of recognizing the intricate way in which models of self depend on racialized logics.

Olga L. Herrera's "The Racial City: Navigating Chicago's Racialized Space in *The House on Mango Street*" examines the role of race, ethnicity, and segregated urban space in constituting the community of Mango Street. Drawing on new archival research, Herrera places Mango Street in the context of Chicago's neighborhood geography, Chicago's history of race relations, and Cisneros's 1968 diary.

Adriana Estill's "Telenovela Feeling in Sandra Cisneros's *Loose Woman*: 'I Think of Me to Gluttony'" emphasizes that *Loose Woman*'s aesthetics of excess can be understood as an extension of Cisneros's interest and investment in the telenovela as a potentially subversive genre. Estill argues that telenovela feelings, in their violent excess, counter social norms and challenge patriarchal demands on women's bodies and languages. Ultimately, telenovela feelings allow the speaker to reconceptualize and remake her body.

In "'You Were Telling *Cochinadas*': Performative Metaphors for Storytelling in Sandra Cisneros's *Caramelo*," Shanna M. Salinas utilizes critical race narratology to analyze Sandra Cisneros's deployment of the rebozo as an extended performative metaphor for storytelling in *Caramelo*. Salinas emphasizes how and why the performativity of the metaphor enhances meaning and amplifies the importance of storytelling for her narrator, Lala Reyes, as she reveals sources and sites of willfully repressed shame. In centering this subject matter, Lala negotiates the inherited narratives that inform and prescribe how she should view herself in order to fashion a self-created meaning of, and *for*, her own body.

Teresa Hernández's essay for this collection, "Mapping the Decolonial: Community Cartography in Sandra Cisneros's *Woman Hollering Creek*," explores Cisneros's positioning of space, place, and community within her celebrated short story collection *Woman Hollering Creek*. In particular, it guides readers through Cisneros's social and spatial orientations in "Tepeyac" and "Woman Hollering Creek" by exploring how these *cuentos* (stories) reposition

INTRODUCTION

border women's writing as a type of communal mapping. Ultimately, this essay considers how Cisneros's writing emerges as a type of "community cartography" that makes legible the decolonial possibilities within Latinx literature.

Part 2, "Love, Shame, and Sinvergüenzas," puts Cisneros's work in conversation with that of others, from Gloria Anzaldúa to Joy Harjo, as well as with disciplines that stretch far beyond literature, including queer studies and art history. Belinda Linn Rincón's "'Love the Only Way I Know How': Cultivating Erotic Conocimiento in the Work of Sandra Cisneros" posits that Sandra Cisneros's erotic writing emblematizes erotic conocimiento, which is knowing the self and others through, with, and from the body. She exposes how body ignorance is perpetuated and how "sucia love" can challenge heteronormativity's institutions. Erotic conocimiento is the foundation for a humanizing project where sucias become validated epistemic agents capable of personal and social transformation.

Georgina Guzmán's "From Marginal to Sin Vergüenza: Overcoming School-Inflicted Shame through Transgressive Literary Aesthetics in Sandra Cisneros's Life and Writing" proposes that shame is a powerful and recurrent theme in Cisneros's life and writings, and examines how she posits school as a primordial site of shame and injury for working-class students of color. Cisneros's writings elaborate on the long-lasting traumas shame can inflict, but also the healing powers of storytelling, which can enable us to reclaim our lost voices and self-esteem.

In his essay for this collection, Richard T. Rodríguez looks specifically at connections between Cisneros and gay men. "The Loose Woman and the Men of Ill Repute" traces the bond between them with respect to their outsider status as outcasts from the normative institutions of marriage and heterosexuality. Elaborating on Cisneros's well-known refusal of an identity cast within the terms of the heteronormative family ("she is nobody's mother and nobody's wife") and embrace of "loose woman" status, Rodríguez shows how Cisneros's feminist and sexual politics facilitate deep attachments between "the queen bee" and "her drones" on the page and beyond while simultaneously serving as a motivating force for Chicano gay male cultural expression. Rodríguez discusses how Cisneros's work has inspired a younger generation of artists and writers, using Lorenzo Herrera y Lozano and his poem "You Bring Out the Joto in Me" as a key example.

In "Wild, Wicked, and Crazy Brave Tongues: Locating the Collaborative Origins of Sandra Cisneros's and Joy Harjo's Poetic Voices," Audrey Goodman explores the generative potential of the intimate contact zones in which Sandra Cisneros and Joy Harjo worked and developed formative relations with their teachers, from their first encounter at the Iowa Writers' Workshop to the present. Goodman identifies elements of both poets' creative networks, arguing that such extended, deep relationships infused not only their physical encounters also but their imaginative lives and poetic production.

Sara A. Ramírez's essay, "'Hay Que Inventarnos / We Must Invent Ourselves': The Impact of Norma Alarcón and Sandra Cisneros's Friendship on Chicana Feminist Literature," explores how Norma Alarcón and Sandra Cisneros shaped the field of Chicana/Latina feminist literature through their publication and promotion of *Third Woman* and the establishment of Third Woman Press. Ramírez argues that the women's archived correspondence reveals a transformative friendship and the principles that have sustained not only the friendship but also the Chicana/Latina feminist literary field.

In "Faxes, Friendship, and the Rise of Chicana Literature: Examining the Archive of Letters between Sandra Cisneros and Helena María Viramontes," Linda Margarita Greenberg focuses on the relationship between two major Chicana writers, Sandra Cisneros and Helena María Viramontes, during a pivotal moment in their careers. Over the course of the 1980s and 1990s, these two authors exchanged a long series of letters and faxes with each other and with other emerging Chicana writers. Greenberg examines these letters to show how they reveal the interior struggles and empathetic crosscurrents that underlay the Chicana feminist literary community through its journey from newly established ethnic and feminist presses and homegrown journals until its emergence within the Latin boom of the mid- to late 1990s.

Part 3, "¡Adelante! Seeing and Listening with Cisneros," offers readers ways into Sandra Cisneros's lifework through a close look at her engagement with and practice of visual art in literary and extraliterary forms and by way of a new, extended interview with the author. Tey Marianna Nunn's "La Sandra como Artista: The Visual Cisneros" is the first study to place Cisneros's visual production in an art historical context. It explores the written clues Cisneros has left us as to her talents as a visual artist. Nunn addresses the significance of color and artistic components throughout her many publications and details her collegial affinity for and support of other visual artists. This chapter highlights the importance of collecting visual art and the impact of museums and, finally, examines Cisneros's production as a visual artist by sharing images and descriptions of her portraits, drawings, and installations.

The last contribution to this book finds journalist Macarena Hernández sitting down with her friend of two decades, Sandra Cisneros, for an extended interview in order to probe some of the less well-known areas of her life and work. In "Sin Vergüenza: A Plática with Sandra Cisneros," the pair talk about Cisneros's experience growing up in a house full of men, her earliest writing memories, and her discovery of the voice for *The House on Mango Street*. They delve into Sandra's undergraduate and graduate school experiences. Sandra

INTRODUCTION

tells us that she has yet to write the book she wants to write. "Like the book that I would say, 'Okay, now I can go!' I don't feel I've done that book yet."

This first book-length collection of critical essays on Cisneros offers new scholarship on her vibrant, magisterial, lyrical writings in multiple contexts. The essays, as well as Hernández's interview, reveal Cisneros as *la maestra*, someone who, alongside a few others, activated the field of Chicana feminist writers with her sharp focus on the local but with internationalist, interconnective impulses. Sandra Cisneros has been crucial to the development of Chicana feminist literature and Chicana feminist studies. As the essays that follow avow, Cisneros inaugurated a lineage that, while firmly based on a US Chicanx/Latinx space, opens up borders between the United States and Mexico and traverses the globe in solidarity with women, marginalized people, and sin vergüenzas in their struggle for gender equity, peace, and social justice.

NOTES

1. The section title is quoted from Sandra Cisneros, "Loose Woman," in *Loose Woman* (New York: Alfred A. Knopf, 1994), 113.

2. Michelle M. Tokarczyk, *Class Definitions: On the Lives and Writings of Maxine Hong Kingston, Sandra Cisneros, and Dorothy Allison* (Selinsgrove, PA: Susquehanna University Press, 2008), 215.

3. Quoted in Wolfgang Binder, *Partial Autobiographies: Interviews with Twenty Chicano Poets* (Erlangen, Germany: Palm and Enke, 1985), 65.

4. Quoted in Binder, *Partial Autobiographies*, 67.

5. Quoted in Binder, *Partial Autobiographies*, 67.

6. Katie Salzmann, finding aid, 9, Sandra Cisneros Papers, Wittliff Collections, Texas State University.

7. Sonia Saldívar-Hull, "*Mujeres Testimoniando*: No Neutral Position," *Western American Literature* 40, no. 3 (Fall 2005): 332–341.

8. Erlinda Gonzáles-Berry and Tey Diana Rebolledo, "Growing Up Chicano: Tomás Rivera and Sandra Cisneros," *Revista Chicano-Riqueña* 13, no. 3–4 (1985): 109–119; Pedro Gutiérrez Revuelta, "Género e ideología en el libro de Sandra Cisneros: *The House on Mango Street*," *Crítica* 1, no. 3 (Fall 1986): 48–59; see also Erlinda Gonzales-Berry, "Unveiling Athena: Women in the Chicano Novel," in *Chicana Critical Issues: Mujeres Activas en Letras y Cambio Social*, ed. Norma Alarcón et al. (Berkeley, CA: Third Woman Press, 1993), 33–44.

9. María Herrera-Sobek and Helena María Viramontes, eds., *Chicana Creativity and Criticism: New Frontiers in American Literature* (Albuquerque: University of New Mexico Press, 1996).

10. Tey Diana Rebolledo, *Women Singing in the Snow: A Cultural Analysis of Chicana Literature* (Tucson: University of Arizona Press, 1995); Sonia Saldívar-Hull, *Feminism on the Border: Chicana Gender Politics and Literature* (Berkeley: University of California Press, 2000); Mary Pat Brady, *Extinct Lands, Temporal Geographies: Chicana Literature and the Urgency of Space* (Durham, NC: Duke University Press, 2002).

PART I

¡Ay, Qué Rico!
Close Readings

CHAPTER 1

LINGERING WITH COMPLICITY IN *CARAMELO*

Mary Pat Brady

José Agustín Arrieta's 1850 painting *Interior de una pulquería* portrays an idealized pulquería as if it were a stage set (see figure 1.1). Five men sit around a long table while a gray-haired woman, sitting on the floor, makes tortillas and a young woman serves drinks. On the wall of the pulquería, as if looking over the younger woman's shoulder, is a reproduction of Diego Velázquez's *The Triumph of Bacchus* (1626–1628). The mythical figures in Velázquez's painting seem to peer down on the scene, just as the young woman's posture echoes Bacchus's twisted shoulders and extended forearm. The presence of the Spanish artist's celebrated painting signals the Mexican artist's playful meditation on the way the Spanish colonial empire impressed itself on Mexico's visual repertoire and shaped its imaginary. Here Arrieta offers a visual echo and perhaps a critique of the decadent effects of imperial violence. Playing a slightly jokey game of relay—the "high art" of the palace decorating the "low space" of the pulquería—Arrieta provides a genealogy for his own art and the genre in which it claimed a place: the costumbrista paintings of the nineteenth century. Yet this genealogy, as posited by Arrieta, denies costumbrismo's more immediate, more local ancestor, the eighteenth-century genre of *casta* paintings.[1] Like Arrieta, Sandra Cisneros also engages with these traditions, evoking and critiquing them in her celebrated 2002 novel *Caramelo*.[2]

Arrieta's reference to the famous painting snickers at art criticism as well. Nineteenth-century Mexican intellectuals, like their European counterparts, sneered at the quotidian scenes of homegrown costumbrismo, which, with its celebration of types of people, costumes, labor, and customs, came up against the supposedly more rigorous academic tradition of art that featured depictions of history, myth, and the storied elite. By re-placing Velázquez's *Triumph*,

Figure 1.1. José Agustín Arrieta, *Interior de una pulquería* (1850). Reproduction authorized by the National Institute of Anthropology and History.

Arrieta offers a counteraccount of art's proper locale and expected audience while also forging a different context for his own composition. In other words, Arrieta offers both an example of costumbrismo and a satire of the intellectual elite's framing of costumbrismo as banal and déclassé: upending the hierarchical relations the elite requires, by substituting the palace for the pulquería. The composition further reinforces this effort because it features the edge of the pulquería floor as if it were actually the edge of a theatrical stage, highlighting the work of costumbrismo as a self-conscious representation of typicality. By staging the pulquería scene, Arrieta references the way *casta* paintings emphasized each image's edges as a part of their logic of typecasting and boundary-making. For both Arrieta's painting and the *casta* genre from which it grew, the frame mobilizes the process of containment and comparison and inserts itself into that process as both instrument and instance. The frame as stage also signals one of the Spanish Empire's principal ideological tools: scale. Scalar logic forms the substructure for not only *casta* systems and their visualization, but also the celebration of customs more generally. Scalar legacies also subtly structure Western imaginaries.

Literary heir to Arrieta and to costumbrismo more generally, Sandra Cisneros's turn-of-the-century novel *Caramelo* similarly stages and references the long reach of Mexican cultural engagement with genres and types. It too rehearses Mexico's tradition of celebrating types, and, like Arrieta's painting, it also satirizes that tradition. But while the text is published as a novel, *Caramelo*'s celebration of myriad types and Cisneros's own performance of the novel in audio format reveal that rather than understanding the text as a novel, per se, we might better understand it, like Arrieta's painting, as a *stage* for the rehearsal, performance, and critique of this long, colonial tradition of celebrating types. Across the novel Cisneros compares storytelling to embroidery, weaving, and photography. She plays with the furniture of authoritative writing, moving footnotes into the novel to disrupt the expectations of what counts as either novel or work of scholarship—and then footnotes interrupt footnotes with jokes, references, and recommendations for further reading. Cisneros cares about form, and she cares about the way form shapes expectations. Such attention to form, to the impact of form on readers' expectations, dovetails with the novel's ambivalent relation to types and traditions as well as to its subtle, perhaps ambivalent, maybe radical critique of Mexico's long history of raciality. Put differently, in a novel filled with jokes and references to various celebrated types, it can be a bit confusing to ascertain the novel's own stance on these types, given *Caramelo*'s apparent critique of the habit of forming types—a habit it calls attention to through the numerous ways it reminds readers of the expectations we may bring to the reading of a novel, of what constitutes a novel and what counts as fiction or history. Such a playful and ambivalent deployment of types suggests that the novel is attempting to undermine the very logic underpinning raciality (and its castagories) altogether.

Arrieta's and Cisneros's celebration of typicality has its roots in scalar thought, which emerged at the dawn of the Spanish colonial effort, when Hernán Cortés's confessor and apologist, Francisco López de Gómara, justified empire building by arguing that "the world is one and not many."[3] With this pronouncement López sought to shift away from a plurivocal multiverse in order to erect an empire and form a monovocal, monofocal (Spanish and Catholic) universe. His proclamation rationalized abstraction (the world is one), transforming and authorizing indistinction while locating such homogenization and indistinction within intricately nested hierarchies. Refining and making practical their use of scale, Spanish colonizers embedded it into the quotidian through a scalar imaginary; such scalar thinking is especially evident in the *casta* system (legal devices for controlling privileges, exacting tribute, and rationalizing social relations), which deployed a set of castagories that folded into a homogenization of the world, producing abstracted notions of space and being within a nested hierarchy of abstraction and homogenization.

Elaborately differentiating the supposed combinations of Spanish, Indigenous, and African peoples, the *casta* system ultimately produced a sort of static purity at its edges by homogenizing a multitude of philosophies, languages, and aesthetic practices into the castagories "Indio" and "Negro," thereby flattening and thinning complexity into a scaffolded narrative of being, hedged and bounded by seemingly opaque purities. During the eighteenth century, dozens of artists sold hundreds of depictions of *castas*, spectacularizing them as an enumerated system of combinations. Yet in visualizing these homogenized castagories of "Indio" and "Negro," painters also celebrated aesthetic difference: crucial to their apparent appeal were the paintings' display of *different* clothing traditions, different vegetation, and different hardscapes, producing a visual repertoire of types. These displays of kinship wedded castagories to labor, markets, objects, and costumes, subtly weaving all of these into a scaffolded hierarchy. This grid of intelligibility taught people to understand themselves as knitted into a hierarchy, to see the work of racialization on display through the depictions of work and in the terms of an order governed by a scalar imaginary. Working the constant refrain—a relay of same-if-different—the paintings also depended on the triadic display of two parents and at least one child. This triad, with its subtle emphasis on the child at the center, figured the child as a project, promise, and threat and folded that child (those children) into a scaffolded, hierarchical narrative of being and (not) belonging. The figure of the child not only offers a sign of the effort to manage racial encounters, to racialize children in the service of an imperial violence, but also shapes the logic of scale itself. The child is both scale and the mechanism for establishing the scalar imaginary, the nested hierarchy of relations used to reinforce Spain's claim to superiority. The child materializes the very narrative establishing a scaffolded logic, helping scale hold a lien on an emerging Western, imperial imagination.

The *casta* painting genre fell out of favor after Mexico severed its colonial ties with Spain; in its place, and consonant with European efforts to celebrate the folk in the service of a nascent national, secular sensibility, was costumbrismo, introduced by European travelers and adapted by Mexican writers and artists. Mey-Yen Moriuchi argues that costumbrista art and costumbrismo more generally were the work of a nationalizing project meant to solidify a notion of Mexican unity by celebrating the typical figures that populated a highly racialized national imaginary.[4] Costumbrismo turned that process into the stuff of a nascent nationalist pride that attempted to rescue mestizaje from colonial denigration by reimagining it as aesthetically unique and inviting, knitting people together as exemplum. That is, costumbrismo suggested that one could "know" Mexico by recognizing its types: the vaquero, the china poblana, the *aguador* (water carrier), the *atolera* (beverage seller), each typified a mestizaje to be celebrated as distinct and visually compelling. This complex dynamic, like the *casta* system and costumbrismo, turns on recognition. People could be recognized as belonging to a cluster of relations while also being obliged to another cluster of relations. In locating people within this system, this dynamic reduced the world to singularities, to a rationalized logic of recognition and misrecognition. It is this project of recognition that Cisneros's novel examines. *Caramelo* considers the work of recognition within the grammar of social relations as well as that system's corruption and costs.

The *casta* system built the stage on which Arrieta's painting, costumbrismo in general, and, finally, *Caramelo* could depict types by celebrating or mocking them. The novel, however, brings the legacies of the *casta* system forward while offering an example of how to deny the seductive demands of scale. Building on the legacy of casting the child as the figure of empire and raciality, Cisneros thinks from the portrayal of the child and the absence of such portrayals to consider the legacy of idealized casting, which effectively scaled the quotidian understanding of sociality, of the relationships necessary to sustain life. Her trick of memorialization, in which the novel serves as substitute for the two daughters missing from a family photo but also as palimpsest for the legacies of racialized subjugation, helpfully anatomizes the ongoing work of scalar thought. If the novel rehearses type after type, it also offers ways to think differently: without scale and against the spatialized/racialized nested hierarchies that scale naturalizes as the only way to describe the real. Instead, Cisneros offers density, a textual texture that undermines the scaffold imaginary and signals alternative concepts of connection, relation, and belonging. Moreover, by messing with the form of the novel, Cisneros also undoes the genre's historical loyalty to a scalar logic via its expression in the bildungsroman, making her novel both an inheritor of this *casta*/costumbrismo tradition and a stage on which its legacies and performances are rehearsed and opened to critique. If such legacies include the ominous presence of the cast-out child, the unacknowledged daughter denied her place in the nested hierarchy, Cisneros ultimately leaves it to the reader to decipher the implications of this critique and to dwell with the figure, Candelaria, who seems to serve as a kind of remainder, the symbol of what/who has been lost to the castagorical maw.

Cisneros signals this legacy of traces and types in the novel's opening "Disclaimer":

> To write is to ask questions. It doesn't matter if the answers are true or *puro cuento*. After all and everything only the story is remembered, and the truth fades away like the pale blue ink on a cheap embroidery pattern: *Eres Mí Vida, Sueño Contigo Mí Amor, Suspiro Por Tí, Sólo Tù.*[5]

In this rich "Disclaimer" Cisneros signals her interest in popular culture, in textiles, and in the romantic narratives that we wrap around ourselves as protection from the harsher experiences of vulnerability and brutality. Challenging the authority claimed by truth, Cisneros, as a writer ensnared by the pleasures of her craft, celebrates the vibrancy of story as that which is shared and dwelled upon, as the remainder that shifts past the traces of truth claims. History, the passage suggests, is fabricated; it too is made, its narratives provide the fabric that warms us, yet it is stamped by the logics of market romance and in its faded ink we see the markers of what Maria Lugones astutely identifies as the ongoing "coloniality of gender."[6] This chatty disclaimer also reminds us of the traces of colonial systems and of the efforts to replace those systems, to repurpose them and find a different path forward even when that path simply paves over the old colonial road and thereby often leads to the same truncated set of (im)possibilities. What is more, the theme of the *dichos* (sayings) fading away travels across the narrative of *Caramelo* itself, just as references to the fading embroidery ink occasionally reappear, signaling both the impermanence of such sentiments and the continuity of traces across various forms and materialities. In this way the novel suggests the appeal of sentimental nostalgia, the extent to which such nostalgia can shape choices as well as its embeddedness in market economies.

With such an opening gesture, the narrative subtly nods toward the way these mass-produced crafts for homemakers serve as bittersweet cousins or fabricated counterpoints to the sturdy rebozos dyed, woven, and tied by Soledad's parents and grandparents. If the faded blue embroidery ink dates the narrator—it is hard to find stamped pillowcases for home crafters these days—it also opens a tension between commerce, craft, and raciality that the novel swerves toward and away from. The rebozo reminds us of the way Indigenous artisans took a Spanish item and transformed it, utilizing skills extant long before the Cortesian era; the rebozo endures as the ink fades; the fabricated and stamped *dichos* are nimble reminders of the market's variegated efforts to regulate affect, to produce individuation.[7] The rebozo and the manufactured, fading ink cloths, dictating *dichos* to be covered over with dyed thread, work in tension not just as aesthetic forms but as forms that name differing relations and differing approaches to understanding relationality. The local and communal history has been supplanted by a mass-produced effort to orchestrate social life.

Amid these conflicting forms, Celaya narrates her story of growing and discovering the buried histories and ties within her own family. As a narrator whose historical knowledge precedes her birth and who in her chatty and vivacious way laces serious accounts with jokes and diatribes that splice open puffed-up histories, Celaya reluctantly tells her Awful Grandmother Soledad's story while also offering a portrait of Soledad as a cast-out child who, when grown, casts into oblivion yet another vulnerable child: her granddaughter and Celaya's half-sister, Candelaria. This aspect of the novel is crucial to its critique of a social system mired in hypocrisy, even as it leaves the reader wrestling with the complexity of complicity. Cisneros offers a portrait of a social system reliant on exclusion.

Celaya, sometimes victim of the sentiments the *dichos* promote, wrestles with Soledad, who becomes the spokesperson for the fading blue ink on Mexico's colonized social fabric, the mouthpiece that names the remnants of the *casta* system, her racializing language set to structure decisions, connections, choices. That the novel pressures the system by exposing its costs can't be doubted, given its ambivalent portrayal of Soledad. Nor can its attention to the costs of recognition and the duplicities involved in maintaining certain systems of kin recognition be denied, given that the novel's entire plot careens toward the revelation of a refusal of recognition—the refusal of Celaya's father to take responsibility for his own first child, Candelaria.

Cisneros illustrates the legacy of this dynamic early in the novel as Celaya describes her aunt and uncle hustling to fund their annual trips to Mexico: "Uncle says what sells is *lo chillante*, literally the screaming. —The gaudier the better, says the Awful Grandmother. —No use taking anything of value to that town of Indians."[8] In order to contextualize the callous abandonment of Candelaria, Cisneros details the intensity of racial logics, the vibrancy of methods of instantiating raciality in a midcentury Mexican diaspora. Celaya's Tío laughs at the elaborate if cheap items he finds at flea markets, but it is his mother who racializes the aesthetic values his customers may hold. She means to denigrate them, to signal her disregard for what she considers the unrefined taste of those who cannot claim to be "gente de razón" and therefore have no place among the "civilized." It is a legacy of Spanish colonial practices, which excluded Indigenous peoples and Africans from that category.[9] She thereby deploys the *casta* system's method of *in*differentiation, where "Indian" names a denigrated, flattened type. The Awful Grandmother wishes to distinguish herself from the "Indians" and to do so via a reference to aesthetic sensibilities. And none of her children protest. Soledad may be the most rigorous spokesperson for raciality, but the novel slowly builds a case for the family's complicity with the system as well.

Nor is her characterization of "Indian" aesthetic preferences the only marker of Soledad's effort to shore up a scalar sociality. She tells Celaya's mother, "My son could've done a lot better than marrying a woman who can't even speak a proper Spanish. You sound like you escaped from the ranch. And to make matters even more sad, you're as dark as a slave."[10] Soledad references the peonage system that stitched the Mexican ranching system to the legacy of Spain's reliance on slavery to build its vast empire. She signals the color hierarchy that is a legacy of coloniality and that continues to serve as an agent of the coloniality of power. Yet if Soledad is the loudest proclaimer of anti-Indigenous and anti-Black sensibilities, the narrator too traffics in its legacies.

For example, Celaya notes that her great-grandmother Regina had

> the same face you see in the Mayan glyphs and everywhere in the Mexican Museum of Anthropology. Snarled lips and slanted jaguar eyes. Often this face is seen even now driving an M&M-colored taxicab or handing you a corn-on-the-cob on a stick. This face, ancient, historic, eternal, so common it doesn't startle anyone but foreigners and artists. . . . It must be remembered that Soledad was a Reyes too, although of that backward, Indian variety that reminded Regina too much of her own humble roots, a peasant Reyes from the country filled with witchcraft and superstition, still praying to the old gods along with the new, still stinking of *copal* and firewood.[11]

If Soledad and her mother-in-law, Regina, are quick to interpret Indianness through what Arturo Escobar has called the discourse of developmentalism, the narrator also associates the inhabitants of Mexico City with a homogenized account of an Indigeneity now relegated to the museum display case, its presence visible on the faces of the working-class inhabitants of the region.[12] Yet the specificities of contemporary Indigenous peoples have also been disappeared. It is *this* reenactment of the *casta* system and costumbrismo that *Caramelo* displays as if the novel too were a museum.

Across the novel one finds repeated comments such as Araceli's question, "How can you let that Indian play with you?," or Soledad's warning, "Don't you know a lot of Indians hang out at el Banquita?"[13] If these comments are meant to be degrading, the narrator also signals the seemingly contradictory nationalist pride with the comment that Benito Juárez was "the only pureblooded Indian to rule Mexico." Such language, the novel illustrates, is also internalized: "She, on the other hand, thought herself homely because of her Indian features."[14] Readers are also given a glimpse of the generations of racialized assessments, "Say what they say, their blood was Spanish, something to remember when extolling their racial superiority over their mixed-blood neighbors. . . . The family Reyes was still *española*, albeit mixed with so much Sephardic and Moorish ancestry, all it would have earned them in an earlier Mexico was a fiery death at the Plaza del Volador." Or, after a hard day's work Narciso Reyes sighs, "Today I worked *como un negro*," and the narrator explains that this "is what they say in Mexico when they work very hard."[15] *Caramelo* repeatedly underscores how imbricated racializing language is within a quotidian sense of sociality. It is this structure of racialization that frames people's understanding of themselves and sets the stage for their own efforts to navigate (and perpetuate) the nested hierarchies of racial scale.

The novel similarly illustrates how often skin tones are discussed and how interlinked colorism is with social standing even as, continuing in its curatorial vein, it comments on the broad range of "looks" one finds across the giant landmass known as Mexico:

> There are green-eyed Mexicans. The rich blond Mexicans. The Mexicans with the faces of Arab sheiks. The Jewish Mexicans. The big-footed-as-a-German Mexicans. The leftover-French Mexicans. The *chaparrito* compact Mexicans. The Tarahumara tall-as-desert-saguaro Mexicans. . . . The wide-as-a-Tula-tree Zapotec Mexicans.[16]

In pointing to the profusion of types, here noted because she feels aggrieved that Tejano high schoolers refuse to acknowledge her Mexicanness, Celaya also reveals how the process of cataloging is imbricated in the process of scaling. Note, for example, that the two Indigenous peoples referenced, the Tarahumara and the Zapotec, are offered as naturalized—compared to vegetation—while others are linked to nation-states. Through this flattening, arranging, and (here subtle) hierarchical scaffolding of difference, *Caramelo* signals the very cataloging tradition that *casta* and costumbrista paintings also relished.

The habit of thinking of *castas* as a social process did not disappear when the newly decolonized Mexican government abolished *castas'* legal import. Instead, the discourse of mestizaje actually maintained crucial aspects of the *casta* logic, aspects that *Caramelo* illustrates as actively in use. If mestizaje developed as an answer to the cruder formulations of the *casta* system by valorizing or celebrating Indigenous history as having made substantial additions to the emerging nation-state, its purveyors frequently presumed that Indigenous people were culturally "primitive."[17] Similarly, as Ben Vinson explains, the celebration of mestizaje "signaled that the qualities of scorned populations" were ultimately "salvageable" while also "rationaliz[ing] what had been largely an ad hoc process [of narrating racialization], providing substantive meaning and direction."[18] The celebration of Indigenous contributions to Mexican national culture required, in other words, the disappearance of Indigenous specificities and thereby their claim to sovereignty over languages, cultural practices, territories, and their own futures. The derogatory references to Indians that Soledad utters name that process of disappearance—a process that began when Spaniards separated those communities that accepted Catholicism from those that didn't (*Indios barbaros*) and via slaughter, trade, and coercion forced many to become detribalized, "freed" to become "peons" on Spanish haciendas. Despite Indigenous communities' support for the war against Spain, the Mexican state largely continued its anti-Indigenous practices in the name of liberal rationalism. *Caramelo* doesn't provide a chance to grapple with this history of violent detribalization or the effort to strip dozens of Indigenous communities from the Mayo to the Yaqui to the Opata to the Zapotec of their languages, cultures, histories, and control of their own socialities. Yet this history haunts the narrative, even as Soledad participates in this national project, if passively, through her dismissive language, and even as the novel itself, through its attack on a scalar imaginary, attempts to undermine the conditions that produced Soledad's sensibilities in the first place.

What is important to consider, then, is that even as the novel offers multiple moves away from a scalar logic by lingering with a jumbled-together density that cannot be sorted and ordered, it also offers a disturbing limit to that density. It does this even within exquisite lists that partially counter scalar abstraction. On her first trip to Acapulco, a young Celaya scans the landscape:

> Churches the color of flan. Vendors selling slices of *jícama* with chile, lime juice, and salt. Balloon vendors. The vendor of flags. The corn-on-the-cob vendor. The pork rind vendor. The fried-banana vendor. The pancake vendor. The vendor of strawberries in cream. The vendor of rainbow *pirulís*, of apple bars, of *tejocotes* bathed in caramel. The meringue man.[19]

A dying Soledad begins to feel absorbed into the materiality of all being:

> Puddle of rain and the feather that fell shattering the sky inside it, votive candles flickering through blue cobalt glass, the opening notes of that waltz without a name, the steam from a clay bowl of rice in bean broth, and the steam from a fresh clod of horse dung.[20]

And a disappointed, sorrowful, teenage Celaya returns to the neighborhood she had loved as a young child:

> The streets turned into trashy aisles of glow-in-the dark Guadalupes, Juan Diego paperweights, Blessed Virgin pins, scapulars, bumper stickers, key chains, plastic pyramids. The old cathedral collapsing under its own weight, the air ruined, filthy, corncobs rotting in the curb, the neighborhood pocked, overpopulated, and boiling in its own stew of juices, corner men hissing *psst, psst* at me, flies resting on the custard gelatins rubbing their furry forelegs together like I-can't-wait.[21]

The subtle virtuosity of lists like these bears great attention. It is not simply that Cisneros points to the poetry of dwelling attentively with juxtapositions, nor simply that the indexing and cataloging signal a vibrancy of sensual opportunity. Nor is it simply that Cisneros here celebrates the costumbrista tradition with an elaborately elongated series of types. Nor are the lists simply a clever way to remind readers of the mestizaje of a language that laps together Nahuatl and Spanish and English, alongside the inexpensive trinkets meant to catch a tourist's eye. Rather, it is that these lists suggest a reach for something outside of scale—a refusal of the scalar, organizing, categorizing, homogenizing imagination—not just through a celebration of density, but also through a suggestion of the interconnection of all forms of being, including those beings that have been relegated to the status of things. These unruly indexes exceed the ordered catalog, refuse the discreet abstractions of empire. Their playful qualities beg for the texture of sound, its feel; the repetitions tumble against one another so that a reader can get lost in the thick prose, linger in the flood of descriptions that catapult from image to image in defiance of prosaic realist prose. In keeping with her interest in deforming the novel, Cisneros challenges readers' patience with the seemingly innumerable lists. Her thick descriptions upend the possibility of a straightforward plot, slow it down, break what barely amounts to a plot into pieces the reader has to assemble, even as we may begin to wonder whether Celaya has been dissembling all along.

And yet, despite the novel's sallies against the linearity of a scaffolded hierarchy and standard novel plotline, scale still holds a lien on *Caramelo*'s imaginary; despite the poetry, despite the clever humor behind the combination of items and people indexed, despite the explosions of juxtapositions that make possible moments of beauty and humor, the text still seems caught in the legacy of the *casta* effort to flatten myriad Indigenous groups into a productive singularity, a homogeneity or indistinction that is rendered as "Indio." It even echoes the practices of colonial Mexico around scale: everywhere there is movement and definition, until one lands within the solidity of "Indio." There lies absence, perhaps opacity. Never does the novel acknowledge the contemporary Indigenous communities across Mexico, their vibrant cultures and languages, much less their struggles against nation-state and market. Even if used ironically, without counterpoints, *Caramelo*'s habit of slinging terms such as "Indio" around threatens to cast contemporary Indigenous peoples into the disappeared pot.

Oddly enough, the novel sets out to address the problem of the missing: "We're all little in the photograph above Father's bed. We were little in Acapulco. We will always be little." This gentle beginning, a nostalgic glance, changes suddenly when the narrator notes, "I'm not here. They've forgotten about me when the photographer walking along the beach proposes a portrait, *un recuerdo*, a remembrance literally. No one notices I'm off by myself building sand houses."[22] After this moment in which readers are asked to imagine a forgotten presence, the narrator, with a vision of herself as photographer, draws the figures in the portrait and the readers together: "Then everyone realizes the portrait is incomplete. It's as if I didn't exist. It's as if I'm the photographer walking along the beach with the tripod camera on my shoulder asking—¿*Un recuerdo*? A Souvenir? A memory?"[23]

Over the course of the novel, the narrator, Celaya, will fill in the gaps, take on the role of photographer, providing a series of textual snapshots, scenes, portraits, and, here and there, a still life. The titles of each subsequent chapter read like photo captions, the book as an album without specific connections between the snapshots. The grown Celaya draws from the material of her childhood to gift her readers with their own souvenir of a midcentury Mexico, a midcentury Chicago, a portrait of an evolving Greater Mexico. Yet, what at first glance appears to be a slightly naive, even obvious conceit turns out, after the novel's big reveal, to be a clever ruse. Only then do we learn that the family portrait is missing more than one daughter.

At the very end of the novel, as her father lies in a critical care unit, having suffered a massive heart attack, Celaya hears from her mother that Candelaria, the daughter of the woman who worked for Soledad, was her half sister. Such a reveal forces the reader to work backward with the knowledge that Candelaria could or should have been in the photo also; we readers belatedly can now understand Celaya's cryptic comments about the photo. Moreover, by the close of the novel readers must contend with the realization that like the family *recuerdo*, this portrait that the novel draws is also incomplete. We have been offered only fleeting glimpses of Candelaria.

Moreover, the big reveal at the novel's end undermines the entire story, undoing the portrait of a generous, close-knit family; it is as if Celaya admits defeat, "What more is there to say?"[24] With this question the narrator introduces a series of speculations:

> I want to ask Father questions about the girl Candelaria, my sister. About his other daughter, the one he made before we were all born, when we were dirt. I want to know about Amparo, about her child. . . . *Why would you tell a lie? And was it a healthy lie? . . . And why didn't the Little Grandfather remind you of your responsibility if he was so feo, fuerte, y formal?* . . . I think crazy things. How maybe I can hire a detective. How maybe I can place an ad in the paper.[25]

The revelation of Candelaria's parentage emerges twice: the first time opaquely, the second explicitly. In both cases, two angry women try to take another woman down a peg—they seek a belated recognition. For the reader this revelation breaks apart the intimacies and endearments scattered across the text. The revelation demands readers rethink the whole narrative, reinterpret it. Not only must we face the glaring gap between how Soledad was treated and how she treated Candelaria, we must also acknowledge the family's easy acquiescence to the treatment of Candelaria and her mother, the apparent lack of any real sense of responsibility. After such a big reveal, readers must belatedly dwell on the figure of Candelaria; readers must remember how badly she was treated by the children, the way that she was cast away, put on a bus without ceremony or adequate care. The harshness of this action tears a hole in the tender portrait of Narciso. So instead of being left with the warm sense that all is right in the world of the book, we are left at the close with Candelaria's vulnerability and Celaya's confusion.[26]

Candelaria's story disrupts the novel's pretense as a double bildungsroman (telling the story of Mexico's and Celaya's coming-of-age). Or, it suggests the real costs of coming of age, of the uneven treatment of people that enables some to flourish and forces others to disappear. The absence of Candelaria's story is introduced as *Caramelo*'s closure, and with this absence the novel signals the gaps, the refusals that scalar logic requires and that the bildungsroman stages. Candelaria's story is unfinished, just as the *caramelo* rebozo has been left undone. It is worth noting that the novel form, especially the bildungsroman, sustains the scalar imaginary by tying stories together into coherent, intricately related pieces of a whole, locating relations within comparative frameworks, containing them as types. The novel form also moves toward closure, typically providing the sense that all is well in its world at the moment we say goodbye. Novels often impart delight by building suspense toward such a satisfactory ending; we endure the suspense for the satisfactory conclusion. *Caramelo* resists such a straightforward plot. Its convoluted movements and dense descriptions don't depend on suspense. And even the revelation of Candelaria's parentage emerges almost as an afterthought during a crisis, rather than as something the plot moves toward.

The revelation about Candelaria undermines the truthiness of the family history. It signals the labor that romantic sayings embroidered on pillows perform to cover up the costs of shunting aside others, of maintaining accounts of rectitude, of justifying the casting out and abandoning of children who don't fit the frame. Candelaria has been cast out of the family record, abandoned to the embarrassment and shame of propriety's demands. Her story cannot be told; it is refused as too risky, too unknown, too lodged outside of the normativity of family logics. Candelaria is the cast-out child that is the marker of the coloniality of power, serving as the remainder within the castagorical management of kin structures enabling ongoing raciality. This conclusion leaves us with loss.

If, on the one hand, the novel seeks to explain the treatment of Candelaria by providing abundant details of the breadth and depth of Mexico's racializing imaginary, the ongoing coloniality of raciality, it also, on the other hand, thrusts readers into the position of having to acknowledge this history of complicity and from there to question whether they themselves are not somehow incriminated as well. The reader cannot remain a lurker, as Susan Koshy puts it.[27] The reader must confront the gap between Candelaria's abandonment and Celaya's rescue; the gap forces the reader to question the dynamics of identification and disidentification set in motion by the *casta* system, modernized by costumbrismo, and alternately romanticized and satirized by *Caramelo*. The novel thereby creates the possibility that a reader will linger not only with the family's complicity, its silence and acquiescence, but also with the larger question of a social system built to feed on such complicity.

Put differently: the *casta* system produced and costumbrismo elaborated a grid of social intelligibility that pivots on recognition, on identification and disidentification. Cisneros, like Arrieta's painting, plays with the importance of framing and curating, of the utility margins and edges provide by setting the stage for expected recognition. But unlike Arrieta, Cisneros insists that readers dwell with what these edges occlude, with the built-in ironies and hypocrisies that shore up such edges and occlusions. Candelaria is at the center of the plot yet left out of the frame. This contradiction forces open what may finally be a tricky decolonial move on Cisneros's part. In leaving readers with the disappearance of Candelaria, and by refusing to offer a tidy ending in which Celaya locates her and cares for her, Cisneros offers the reader the opportunity to condemn the racial management system so carefully nurtured first by the Spanish and then by a Mexican state.

Caramelo illustrates how romance and rectitude provide the alibis for the racial state—just as it explores in its portrayal of Soledad how corrosive loyalty to castagories, to the logic of raciality, can be. Soledad is trapped in her own narratives, and narrator Celaya, by the close of her story, realizes the power of such narrative traps and the costs of them. If the novel consistently critiques Soledad's racism, even as it evokes as natural the Mexican habit of denigrating Indigenous peoples but celebrating Indigenismo as a cultural feat that makes Mexico unique, *Caramelo* insists that we travel toward a contrapuntal legacy, toward an acknowledgment of the costs such systems extract, of the way aesthetics and forms of pleasure may be complicit in this structuring logic, which finally messes everyone up.

NOTES

I am grateful to Sonia Saldívar-Hull for her transformative scholarship and mentorship and for the way she introduced me to the work of Sandra Cisneros. I am also grateful to Geneva M. Gano for her wonderful editorial insight and patience and for the opportunity to work on this exciting project. Finally, I am grateful to Richard T. Rodríguez, Ariana Vigil, Esmeralda Arrizón-Palomera, and Armando García for patiently discussing these ideas with me over several years.

1. For a helpful discussion of the evolution of paintings celebrating quotidian practices, see Mey-Yen Moriuchi, *Mexican Costumbrismo: Race, Society, and Identity in Nineteenth-Century Art* (University Park: Pennsylvania State University Press, 2018). For definitive discussions of *casta* systems and art, see Ben Vinson, *Before Mestizaje: The Frontiers of Race and Caste in Colonial Mexico* (Cambridge: Cambridge University Press, 2018); Danielle Terrazas Williams, *The Capital of Free Women: Race, Legitimacy, and Liberty in Colonial Mexico* (New Haven, CT: Yale University Press, 2022); María Elena Martínez, *Genealogical Fictions: Limpieza de Sangre, Religion, and Gender in Colonial Mexico* (Stanford, CA: Stanford University Press, 2007); Edward J. Sullivan, *The Language of Objects in the Art of the Americas* (New Haven, CT: Yale University Press, 2007); Ilona Katzew, *Casta Painting* (New Haven, CT: Yale University Press, 2004).

2. Sandra Cisneros, *Caramelo or Puro Cuento* (New York: Vintage Books, 2002).

3. Francisco López de Gómara, *Historia general de las Indias* (Madrid: Calpe, 1922), 2.

4. Moriuchi, *Mexican Costumbrismo*, 2–29.

5. Cisneros, *Caramelo*, n.p.

6. Maria Lugones, "The Coloniality of Gender," *Worlds & Knowledges Otherwise* 2, dossier 2 (2008).

7. For a splendid discussion of the novel and the rebozo, see Gabriella Gutiérrez y Muhs, "Sandra Cisneros and Her Trade of the Free Word," *Rocky Mountain Review* 23 (Fall 2006): 23–36.

8. Cisneros, *Caramelo*, 7.

9. Vinson, *Before Mestizaje*, 52.

10. Cisneros, *Caramelo*, 85.

11. Cisneros, *Caramelo*, 113.

12. See Arturo Escobar, *Encountering Development: The Making and Unmaking of the Third World* (Princeton, NJ: Princeton University Press, 2011).

13. Cisneros, *Caramelo*, 36, 267.

14. Cisneros, *Caramelo*, 96, 117.

15. Cisneros, *Caramelo*, 163, 211.

16. Cisneros, *Caramelo*, 353.

17. Vinson, *Before Mestizaje*, 29.

18. Vinson, *Before Mestizaje*, 31, 34.

19. Cisneros, *Caramelo*, 17.

20. Cisneros, *Caramelo*, 348.

21. Cisneros, *Caramelo*, 388.

22. Cisneros, *Caramelo*, 3, 4.

23. Cisneros, *Caramelo*, 4.

24. Cisneros, *Caramelo*, 427.

25. Cisneros, *Caramelo*, 427.

26. While there have been several excellent essays published on *Caramelo*, few scholars have paid much attention to Candelaria. For an exception, see Olga L. Herrera, who draws us toward thinking about Candelaria in terms of liminality in her essay "Finding Mexican Chicago on Mango Street: A Transnational Production of Space and Place in Sandra Cisneros's *The House on Mango Street* and *Caramelo*," in *Bridges, Borders, and Breaks: History, Narrative, and Nation in Twenty-First-Century Chicana/o Literary Criticism*, ed. William Orchard and Yolanda Padilla (Pittsburgh, PA: University of Pittsburgh Press, 2016), 103–120.

27. Susan Koshy, "Manifest Diversity and the Empire of Finance," *Post45*, September 20, 2022, 37.

CHAPTER 2

THE RACIAL CITY
Navigating Chicago's Racialized Space in *The House on Mango Street*
Olga L. Herrera

The House on Mango Street's origin story is well known: in the mid-1970s Sandra Cisneros was a young MFA student at the Iowa Writers' Workshop and found herself at odds with the class privilege inherent in a seminar discussion of the metaphor of a house in Gaston Bachelard's 1957 *The Poetics of Space*. She thought, "What did I know except third-floor flats? Surely my classmates knew nothing about that," and went on to craft a series of vignettes in which women and girls navigate the constrained domestic and urban spaces of their neighborhood.[1] In the book that grew out of these vignettes the young narrator, Esperanza, fervently wishes for her own house far away from Mango Street. Scholars have recognized the significance of space in this text, especially for Esperanza's coming-of-age story as she conceives of her maturity in terms of the neighborhood space she traverses and the private space of which she dreams. Little attention has been paid, however, to how race and ethnicity configure city space in this text and how Esperanza learns to define insider and outsider status based on the logic of de facto segregation. I propose that key to developing her sense of self is Esperanza's awareness of her racial and ethnic identity in contrast to that of others. This sense of difference is amplified through segregated city space, in which Mango Street appears pluri-ethnic, with a mix of white and Latinx neighbors, but in fact excludes African Americans and Asian Americans. Esperanza navigates the city with a persistent awareness of race, and in key moments where she feels discomfort in a space, she associates that space with a racial Other. I suggest that an examination of the author's early experience of Chicago's segregated space, informed by Cisneros's childhood diaries, can help us better understand how she imagined Esperanza's own critical consciousness coming into being. In particular, the diary entries recording Martin Luther King Jr.'s assassination and the uprisings on the West and South Sides express anxiety about violence and fear for her neighborhood's safety. Contextualizing Cisneros's diary within Chicago's longer history of race relations allows us to see her anxiety as part of a collective understanding about segregated space stretching at least as far back as the race riots of 1919. Ultimately, as Cisneros learned to navigate Chicago's racialized boundaries, so does Esperanza narrate with a deeply informed awareness of racial and ethnic belonging within a neighborhood at least partially defined by segregated boundaries.

In the body of critical scholarship that has amassed around this slim text, scholars have generalized the setting as a Latino neighborhood, often calling it the barrio. It is important to recall, however, that Mango Street is based on a specific Chicago place, as in writing the vignettes Cisneros drew on memories of growing up in Humboldt Park, where her parents bought their first house at 1525 North Campbell Street. When we bring this context to bear on our reading, the text reveals nuances of midwestern urban community formation influenced by Chicago's distinctive histories of migration and immigration from Latin America and the South. *The House on Mango Street* eschews a homogeneous Latinidad to represent Puerto Rican and Mexican characters.

Humboldt Park, however, is not exclusively Latinx, and neither is Mango Street. In fact, her neighborhood's racial and ethnic diversity plays a significant role in Esperanza's critical understanding of community and belonging in a segregated city. While at times she demonstrates a critical awareness of the racism inherent in segregated space and white flight, at other times she uncritically reproduces its logic. In a text that yields rich conversations about the significance of community, we must consider equally Esperanza's critical insights and her blind spots when it comes to race and ethnicity in her neighborhood. Discerning her own position as a young woman of color allows Esperanza to recognize the intersectional, systemic lack of power among the women on Mango Street and inspires her toward solidarity. Moments in which she identifies race in a way that further alienates a character demonstrate how exclusion is perpetuated within a community by members that are themselves minorities. Both types of responses illustrate the complex dynamics of interracial relations in a city with a painful history of racial violence and segregation. Esperanza's coming-of-age as a young Mexican American girl in Chicago thus includes a perceptive recognition of how her own racial, ethnic, and gender identity is constituted by her location within a racially and ethnically diverse city. By looking at Sandra Cisneros's childhood diaries, we can glimpse the author's own emerging understanding of ethnic and racial identity and appreciate the influence of these early experiences on the creation of Esperanza's character.

SANDRA CISNEROS'S LITERARY CONSTRUCTION OF SPACE

In the rich body of scholarship on *The House on Mango Street*, several essays have explored the representation of space and place in the book. Julian Olivares's "Sandra Cisneros' *The House on Mango Street* and the Poetics of Space" considers the production of space of the titular house as a response to Cisneros's now-familiar experience of studying Bachelard's *The Poetics of Space* at the Iowa Writers' Workshop.[2] Scholars have followed in examining the significance of the novel's gendered domestic and public spaces, as Marci McMahon does in *Domestic Negotiations: Gender, Nation, and Self-Fashioning in US Mexicana and Chicana Literature and Art*.[3] Monika Kaup in "The Architecture of Ethnicity in Chicano Literature" explores Mango Street as a spatial extension of home and argues that Esperanza's hatred for her small house transforms into a love for the street and its community.[4] Esperanza's coming-of-age narrative has been considered via spatial and geographic terms, including Elisabetta Careri's "Home, Streets, Nature: Esperanza's Itineraries in Sandra Cisneros' *The House on Mango Street*," Juanita Heredia's "Down These City Streets: Exploring Urban Space in *El Bronx Remembered* and *The House on Mango Street*," Ana María Manzanas Calvo's "*The House on Mango Street* and Chicano Space," and Tomoko Kuribayashi's "The Chicana Girl Writes Her Way In and Out: Space and Bilingualism in Sandra Cisneros's *The House on Mango Street*."[5]

However, rarely have scholars discussed the book's production of space with specific attention to the city of Chicago or recognized the Mango Street neighborhood as a pluri-ethnic one. Cristina Rodriguez recognizes this limitation when she notes that Kaup writes of Mango Street as populated by Latino neighbors; Rodriguez observes that "it matters that the neighborhood is a Puerto Rican one" and that the community, although it includes Chicanos, is not a majority Chicano neighborhood but is transnational in nature.[6] To name the Puerto Rican, Mexican, and Chicana/o characters is the right move away from generalizing Latinidad and toward recognizing distinctions, but here Rodriguez's critical focus is on the transnationality of *Mango Street* and *Caramelo*, not the presence of white, African American, and Asian characters in the text.

In my own efforts to write about the representation of Chicago's racialized space in Cisneros's work, I build my readings on the body of scholarship theorizing the social production of space, which includes work by Henri Lefebvre, Edward W. Soja, and Doreen Massey.[7] I rely on this work to understand the operation of power in the urban landscape, particularly when dominant state and capitalistic forces have reshaped working-class and ethnic neighborhoods through redevelopment and expressway construction projects. While Mary Pat

Brady's landmark essay "The Contrapuntal Geographies of *Woman Hollering Creek and Other Stories*" does not address *The House on Mango Street* directly, I find valuable her reading of Cisneros's fiction for making explicit the terms of spatial production. Brady writes, "Power accrues to those who exercise control over the environment; similarly, power adheres to those who produce narratives that sustain and naturalize places as opaque, natural, or fixed—and thus beyond contestation or negotiation."[8] We might assume that the state holds power through city planning and federal and state development projects, for which official narratives naturalize conditions of poverty and neglect in minority and immigrant neighborhoods. However, Brady also notes that "conceptualizing place as process draws attention to ongoing contests over the production of space and the struggle to control its representation—to determine how social existence will be 'spatially inscribed'"—and suggests that any dominant claim to public space will encounter repeated challenges.[9] While this statement points to the ability of a community to make claims to space against state control, I also see a field in which racial and ethnic minority groups compete with one another over spatial production and control, particularly within the terms of Chicago's racialized and segregated space. In some neighborhoods defined by their racial or ethnic identity, this competition may be especially intense for newcomers, as the community itself surveys and polices those crossing a boundary. In Humboldt Park, the neighborhood Mango Street is based on, these contests over space are perhaps not battles but negotiations, as diverse residents and businesses stake out their places and form relationships that allow them some distance but nevertheless bind them as community. On Mango Street, Esperanza narrates this delicate dance between neighbors, recognizing their differences and understanding her own racial, ethnic, and cultural identity in relation to others. To understand Esperanza's spatial negotiations, it is instructive to contextualize them against Chicago's longer history of race relations and one young African American man's inability to negotiate racialized space in the waters of Lake Michigan.

RACE AND ETHNIC SPATIALIZATION IN CHICAGO

De facto segregation in Chicago results from a combination of factors, including redlining, housing covenants, and city urban development projects. In the early twentieth century, housing for African Americans was limited by racist rental practices to a neighborhood on the South Side that came to be known as the Black Belt, which was bounded by 12th and 79th Streets, and Wentworth and Cottage Grove Avenues. In the summer of 1919, the Chicago race riots demonstrated clearly the way that urban space is identified with race, segregated, and policed by its own citizens. While today the riots are mostly absent from the city's popular consciousness, their legacy remains embedded in the way residents navigate space as racial insiders or outsiders. Notably, this legacy is marked with a distinct anti-Blackness that ascribes danger and violence in the city to African American neighborhoods, even though the violence in the 1919 riots was largely directed against African American residents. On July 27, 1919, an African American teen named Eugene Williams was swimming in Lake Michigan and drifted across the imagined boundary of 29th Street, the line separating a Black neighborhood and a white neighborhood on the city's South Side. The notion that segregated boundaries should extend into the lake seems to violate the fluid nature of water, but in Chicago that summer, white residents policed that line vigilantly. A group of white men on the beach spotted Eugene and started throwing rocks at him. Some accounts say that he was hit and then drowned; others say that in trying to avoid the stones and not being a strong swimmer, he drowned. African Americans on the beach tried to get the attention of the police nearby, who did nothing. A riot began, which soon spread into the city and lasted until August 3. When it was over, fifteen white people and twenty-three African Americans were dead, and more than five hundred people were injured. An additional one thousand Black families were left homeless after white rioters torched their residences. After the riots, Illinois governor Frank Lowden formed the Chicago Commission on Race Relations, which published a report titled *The Negro in Chicago: A Study of Race Relations and a Race Riot.* Valuable as a historical account of the 1919 events, the report is also significant in its careful documentation of the spatial dimensions of the riot, naming the streets, intersections, and addresses at which violence took place. In the report, descriptive language suggests that neighborhoods were "hostile territories" or were places "invaded" by violence and "raided" by opportunistic gangs.[10]

By midcentury, newer demographic trends had shifted the racial and ethnic landscape, with growing populations of Mexican, Puerto Rican, and Cuban residents. Humboldt Park, closely abutted by Ukrainian Village to its east and African American communities to its south, emerged as a predominantly Puerto Rican neighborhood with a mix of other races, ethnicities, and nationalities. Lilia Fernández describes the changes taking place in Humboldt Park and neighboring West Town as Puerto Ricans arrived in large numbers due to labor recruitment in industry and domestic service. She notes that in 1960, 99 percent of the population in Humboldt Park was classified as white; a decade later, 15.6 percent of the population was Spanish speaking, and 20 percent of its residents were African American. Fernández writes that remaining white residents policed the boundaries of their imagined and physical community, and she quotes one Italian resident in West Town as saying that the Puerto

Ricans are "making a circle around us."[11] Cisneros and her family moved to Humboldt Park in 1965, during this decade of swift neighborhood change.

By the 1980s, these neighborhoods had few white residents left. Gina M. Pérez writes that "although these neighborhoods are popularly imagined as 'the Puerto Rican community,' they are actually quite mixed. Small Polish bakeries and restaurants, established decades ago . . . can still be found, now adjacent to Mexican taquerias and Puerto Rican cafeterias along Western Avenue and Division Street." She affirms, as Fernández does, that although Puerto Ricans do not make up the majority in Humboldt Park, it and West Town "continue to be an important symbolic and material space for Chicago Puerto Ricans."[12] Ana Y. Ramos-Zayas also writes of the neighborhood's Puerto Rican identity, recognizing "spatially constructed views of authenticity" in the deployment of class identities and solidarities, and observing that these claims to authenticity often depend on connections to places "considered the real Puerto Rican Chicago: namely, landmarks like Clemente High School and, more generally, the greater Humboldt Park area."[13] In *The House on Mango Street*, Cisneros constructs a diverse neighborhood as Esperanza identifies Marin and her family as Puerto Rican and her own family as Mexican, but also references other races and ethnicities. While preserving these distinctions, Esperanza also creates a brown identity for the neighborhood in "Those Who Don't," drawing lines between inside and outside space and marking it as safe or dangerous. As we will see, Cisneros's childhood diary does not register a fear of encountering danger when she leaves Humboldt Park; rather, she is afraid that danger, tinged by racial anxiety, will find its way into her neighborhood. This belief that her own neighborhood might be threatened by the riots in 1968 harks back to the 1919 riots and accounts of race-based violence. The young Cisneros's anxieties recall the city's history of racialized space and tap into a collective understanding of how de facto segregation governs spatial mobility and sets the stage for conflict.

SANDRA CISNEROS'S DIARIES AND CHICAGO SPACE

Sandra Cisneros's archives at the Wittliff Collections at Texas State University hold three diaries, one for each year from 1967 to 1969. Examining the diaries for their evocation of urban space in conjunction with our reading of *Mango Street* reveals a young girl comfortable with navigating the city. Through school-arranged field trips, she knew the wider expanse of the city and visited Lincoln Park Zoo to the east and the Museum of Science and Industry on the South Side. For the most part, however, the diaries show that she was intimately familiar with the local geography of her neighborhood, detailing trips to the local Boys' Club for summer craft activities, the nearby high school for swimming, and Milwaukee Avenue for shopping excursions with her mother. Tellingly, the diary entry from May 14, 1968, demonstrates an acute spatial awareness of her neighborhood, as she describes a nearby house fire. She writes, "More excitement when we got home [from the museum]. There was a fire on the next street. Large and huge. Firemen and everything!"[14] At the bottom of the lined page, she maps out the geography, drawing her street and house separated by an alley and the next street from the burning house, and indicating the backs of the houses with jagged lines representing rooftops. She labels a tiny square with a peaked roof "our house," and carefully draws the burning house on the next street and one house over, with another alley bisecting the space diagonally and offering additional distance and a sense of safety (see figure 2.1). This map demonstrates the nuances of her street, as each house is drawn a little differently, with less detail appearing on the houses across the alley. It employs alleys and streets to define the space and to show how close the fire was, but at the same time to locate the space that a house fire could not presumably cross to spread to her own home. In *The House on Mango Street*, Esperanza persistently maps familiar city space, from the first page, when she names the various streets she has lived on, to "Our Good Day," in which she and Rachel and Lucy ride "past my house, sad and red and crumbly in places, past Mr. Benny's grocery on the corner, and down the avenue which is dangerous. Laundromat, junk store, drugstore, windows and cars and more cars, and around the block back to Mango."[15] The avenue, bustling with people and cars, is dangerous, but the alley is a protected space in "Louie, His Cousin & His Other Cousin," where Louie's cousin takes them for a joyride in a presumably stolen Cadillac.[16] Sites farther afield are mentioned but not detailed, much like in the diaries: "downtown" in "Marin" and "A Smart Cookie" is a distant and mysterious place, and real North Side places like the Embassy and the Aragon Ballrooms are mentioned in one breath in "Geraldo No Last Name," familiar to Marin but not to Esperanza.[17]

In April 1968, Cisneros writes of the South Side when she records the day on which Martin Luther King Jr. was assassinated in Memphis, and the days immediately afterward. Nationally, grief-fueled violence broke out soon after his death, most notably in major cities such as Washington, DC, Baltimore, and Chicago. In Chicago, the communities most affected by the violence were African American residential areas on the city's West Side and South Side. Rioting lasted for forty-eight hours, until Mayor Richard J. Daley established a curfew on April 6 and the National Guard was called in to restore order. In the end, eleven Chicago citizens were killed and forty-eight were injured; there were 125 fires and 210 buildings damaged, totaling more than $10 million in damage. The damages left devastating effects on these neighborhoods, as the

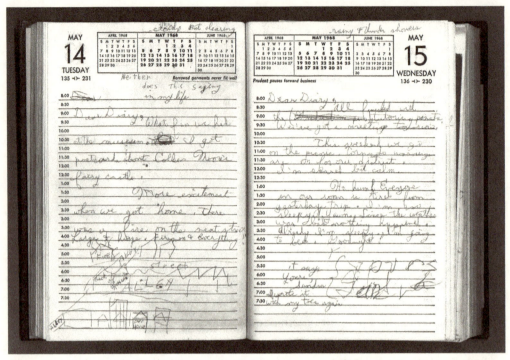

Figure 2.1. Diary pages, May 14 and 15, 1968. Image courtesy of the Sandra Cisneros Papers, Wittliff Collections, Texas State University. Copyright © 1968 by Sandra Cisneros. By permission of Stuart Bernstein Representation for Artists, New York, NY, and protected by the Copyright Laws of the United States. All rights reserved. The printing, copying, redistribution, or retransmission of this content without express permission is prohibited.

city's cleanup involved bulldozing damaged buildings and leaving vacant lots in their wake.

Cisneros's diary records these events, noting the assassination itself, the mayor's curfew, and the National Guard helicopters surveilling the city, even as she narrates the personal concerns typical of a middle schooler's diary. On April 4, she starts by describing the weather, grousing about getting snow flurries in the spring and hoping that they stop soon. Then she writes, "Martin Luther King died today! It's so unbelievable."[18] She doesn't remark further, going on to mention the present that she has bought for a friend, and concluding that Easter is two weeks away, but none of the family has new clothes. More concerned at this moment with that particular shame, Cisneros does not take much note of King's death—it has not yet affected her personally. On April 5, however, she begins, "There were riots in Chicago today! The negroes were rioting, and it broke out because King died yesterday!" Her brothers Kiki and Junior had been let out of school early, but she wasn't let out until ten minutes to three, after which she ran home, having never been "so scared in my entire life." Cisneros notes that nothing had happened on their neighborhood block, but in exacting detail she describes the riot's effects in the city and in her surrounding area: "down in the south of the city were fires, vandalism, and theft. Tuley, a high school a block away from our school, was burned and there was rioting, even as close to division street which is about five blocks away." She concludes by writing that her father was scheduled to come home the next day from Mexico, and signs off with "Yours, still scared, Sandra."[19] The hand-drawn map from May 14 is useful to recall in this context, showing how the thirteen-year-old Cisneros perceived a threat in her neighborhood and mapped her house in relation to that danger. In this entry, however, she correlates race with space, distinguishes the South Side, and narrates the incursion of violence into her own neighborhood. She says that "the negroes were rioting," defining the violence in racial terms, and when she writes that "down in the south side of the city were fires, vandalism, and theft," it is to orient Humboldt Park spatially and to show the distance of the South Side from her neighborhood.[20] But, unlike the house fire, which was safely distanced by the alleys from her house, this destruction does leap across the city into Cisneros's neighborhood space, and she marks where it occurs in relation to her own safe spaces—as close as a block away from her school, and five blocks away on Division Street (see figure 2.2).

The next entry, on April 6, is the most comprehensive and the most reflective of the events in Chicago after King's death. She remarks that there is still rioting in Chicago, and that "King was shot and caused a uproar among the negroes. Both black and white lamented because of the death of this peacemaker who died pass yesterday or Thursday. Now that he is dead, there is no one to calm the negroes."[21] The formal diction and tone here suggest that the thirteen-year-old author writes with a sense of the significance of this event and an awareness of contemporary civil rights discourse, noting that the national grief has crossed racial divides. The last sentence in that passage, however, distances her from Black anger, even as it recognizes this anger and foretells more violence. More immediately, it confirms and magnifies her fear about violence from the riots spilling into her neighborhood. She returns to describe the violence in spatial terms, writing that "fires and looting are still in progress in the south side of the city!" and that "everyone is like a frightened puppy." Cisneros's use of the word *everyone* does not imply the rioters but represents fear as the popular reaction. She notes the enforcement of Mayor Daley's curfew and remarks that the National Guard helicopters are "being constantly seen in our park," referring surely to Humboldt Park, half a mile from her house. She concludes by exclaiming, "Rioting all over the nation! Even Wash. D.C."[22] Her incredulous last comment connects the events in her immediate neighborhood—the fires burning at the nearby high school and the military surveillance in her very own park—to the national stage. But the

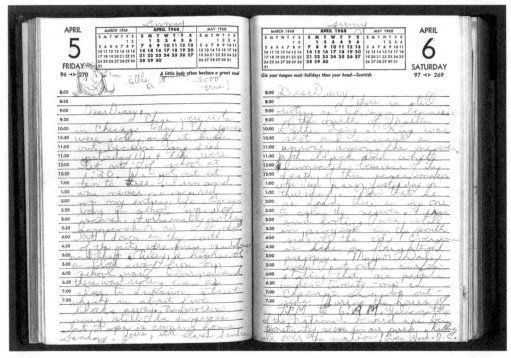

Figure 2.2. Diary pages, April 5 and 6, 1968. Image courtesy of the Sandra Cisneros Papers, Wittliff Collections, Texas State University. Copyright © 1968 by Sandra Cisneros. By permission of Stuart Bernstein Representation for Artists, New York, NY, and protected by the Copyright Laws of the United States. All rights reserved. The printing, copying, redistribution, or retransmission of this content without express permission is prohibited.

next day's entry says nothing about the riots, and on Monday, April 8, Cisneros's daily routine and preoccupations reassert themselves, as she expresses joy over her father's return from Mexico and notes only that school has been cancelled in honor of Martin Luther King Jr.

These pages evoke a young girl's growing consciousness about race as it is shaped in the crucial year of 1968 in Chicago. The city's racial segregation provides the context for young children to learn that they are located in a network of racially and ethnically defined relationships that govern the way they occupy city space and their ability to move through that space. Here, we see Cisneros's awareness that the African American–dominated South Side is burning, and while it is more concerning to her than the events in Washington, DC, it is still distant. She registers serious alarm when the destruction spreads into neighborhood streets and places that she is familiar with in intimate detail. In writing about her childhood diaries, I offer context for the way that Esperanza in *The House on Mango Street* navigates city space and understands that space as defined by race, ethnicity, and segregation practices. My purpose is not to show that Mango Street is autobiographical, but rather to propose that

Cisneros drew on early experiences in order to imagine this fictional world. Her youthful understanding of race relations, city space, and her own position as a person of color within that matrix is useful for examining the emergence of Esperanza's own critical racial consciousness.

WHO BELONGS TO MANGO STREET? RACIAL EXCLUSION IN THE NEIGHBORHOOD

I now turn to *The House on Mango Street* to consider Esperanza's narrative expression of racially and ethnically informed spatial knowledge. From the book's first vignettes, we can see that she is astute about matters of neighborhood identity, white flight, and segregation. Her wry comment about neighbor Cathy's impending move away from Mango Street—"Then as if she forgot I just moved in, she says the neighborhood is getting bad"—reveals a perceptive understanding of her own location in this racially and ethnically defined social matrix.[23] Esperanza knows the score when she remarks that Cathy and her family will just have to keep moving "a little farther away every time people like us keep moving in."[24] Her critical awareness carries over into "Those Who Don't," which recalls the category "people like us" and fully elaborates the dynamics of an insider-outsider gaze in spatial terms. Here she also specifies the racially identified nature of this space; while it was only suggested before, she defines it as "all brown all around, we are safe." Coming after her sharp critique of people who "come into our neighborhood scared," she acknowledges her and her neighbors' fear of other neighborhoods as "our knees go shakity-shake and our car windows get rolled up tight and our eyes look straight."[25] This is the power of segregation to limit her gaze and feelings of safety and trust in other city neighborhoods. These feelings of powerlessness are magnified within the context of the city's longer history of racial segregation, including the 1919 riots.

These examples, however, are the clear moments in the text in which Esperanza demonstrates an explicit understanding of racially constructed space and her position within it. Other moments in the text more implicitly suggest the influence of race and ethnicity on Esperanza's interactions with others. Two characters that receive little scholarly discussion are Gil (the African American furniture store owner) and the unnamed older Asian American man at Peter Pan Photo Finishers; they are just outside of our critical gaze because they lie outside of Esperanza's. They occupy space either on the margins of Mango Street or entirely outside; Gil's Furniture Store ("a junk store") is presumably the same "junk store" that is on the avenue in "Our Good Day," and if Peter Pan Photo Finishers is on North Broadway as she says, then it is northeast of Humboldt Park.[26] These men are also racial outsiders to Esperanza, as there are no other African American or Asian American characters in *The House on Mango Street*.

In "The First Job," Esperanza lands a job at the place where her Aunt Lala works. On her first day at work, far from home and the youngest person there, she feels acutely lonely. She takes refuge on her break in the coat closet, where she meets "an older Oriental man" coming in for the next shift. Esperanza feels herself put at ease by his offer to have lunch with her next time and by his "nice eyes."[27] Then the man tells her that it is his birthday and asks for a kiss, in a moment that recalls the "bum man" promising Rachel a dollar in exchange for a kiss in "The Family of Little Feet."[28] As the older man grabs her face, kisses her, and doesn't let go, why is it important that readers know that he is "Oriental"? We may argue that Cisneros relies on Orientalist tropes of untrustworthiness and sexual deviance to amplify the sense of Esperanza's betrayal. In fact, the only other reference to Asianness in the text is about deceit: in "My Name," when Esperanza tells us that she and her great-grandmother were born in the year of the horse, unlucky if you are a woman, she intones that "this is a Chinese lie because the Chinese, like the Mexicans, don't like their women strong."[29] Diverse as Mango Street may seem, it does not include Asian American residents, so in "The First Job," the character's Asian identity locates him racially outside of the neighborhood, physically distant in the photo shop on North Broadway. Historically in Chicago, while Japanese Americans and Chinese Americans settled throughout the city, the Chinese community was established in Chinatown, far from Humboldt Park on the South Side. In this instance, Esperanza foregrounds otherness constituted by racial difference and spatial distance from Mango Street in her experience of physical and sexual violation.

In "Gil's Furniture Bought & Sold," otherness is represented by a Black store owner who is located within the world of Mango Street but whose difference is marked by race. Gil's store is within neighborhood boundaries, because in "Our Good Day," the girls ride down the "avenue which is dangerous," past a junk store, and at the start of this vignette, Esperanza identifies it again: "there is a junk store."[30] The store is close enough to Mango Street to walk there, and her family has done business there before. However, the vignette hums with a current of tension as Esperanza evinces suspicion toward Gil and he tempts them with merchandise that is not actually for sale. This tension may be better understood when placed into historical context. In the city's labor history, when Mexicans and African Americans were positioned as the least desirable workers, some employers demonstrated a clear preference for Mexicans. As historian Gabriela F. Arredondo writes, "when Clyde Brading of Wisconsin Steel hired light-skinned Mexicans, not only was he favoring a degree of whiteness, he also was actively not hiring Blacks."[31]

THE RACIAL CITY

This kind of workplace racism, which set groups against one another, surely generated resentment that spilled over into other matters of daily life.

In "Gil's Furniture Bought & Sold," Gil's curt attitude toward the girls may be read in the context of preexisting tensions between Black and Mexican residents in Chicago.[32] Esperanza's feelings of vulnerability are expressed in spatial terms in the text, as Gil keeps the lights off "unless you got money to buy things with," and she and Nenny try to find their way in the dark through the store, disoriented even though it is clear that they visit regularly.[33] In a city where African Americans have been historically vulnerable outside of their racially defined neighborhoods, this small shop demarcates a space of power for Gil. The store is piled high with tables and couches and refrigerators, and Esperanza observes that "everything is on top of everything so the whole store has skinny aisles to walk through. You can get lost easy."[34] Esperanza says that Gil is "a black man who doesn't talk much and sometimes if you didn't know better you could be in there a long time before your eyes notice a pair of gold glasses floating in the dark," a reminder that although Gil is invisible to the girls, he is watching them.[35] It is in this expression of unease and distrust that she identifies Gil as Black. Esperanza's discomfort is further emphasized when she says that while Nenny talks to "any old man" and asks Gil a lot of questions, Esperanza herself "never said nothing to him," except when buying a trinket.[36] In fact, he is not named in the story, unlike the other shopkeeper, Mr. Benny in "Our Good Day" and "The Family of Little Feet"; the only reason we know his name is because his store's name is the title of the vignette.

Thus, Esperanza and Gil are counterpoised in mutual suspicion. Then Nenny asks about the music box. It is an old wooden music box, and when Gil winds it, "it's like all of a sudden he let go a million moths all over the dusty furniture and swan-neck shadows and in our bones. It's like drops of water. Or like marimbas only with a funny little plucked sound to it like if you were running your fingers across the teeth of a metal comb."[37] In this shared moment of beauty, Esperanza thinks of marimbas, which are found in Latin America but are said to have been brought from Africa, and thus this moment represents a cultural connection between the characters. But when Nenny expresses interest, Gil abruptly snatches away the object. "This, the old man says shutting the lid, this ain't for sale." Somehow Esperanza anticipates the snub, because she says, "And then I don't know why, but I have to turn around and pretend I don't care about the box so Nenny won't see how stupid I am. But Nenny, who is stupider, already is asking how much."[38] In being caught off guard in their desire, they are made more vulnerable in a space in which they already feel uneasy. This feeling of displacement in the store recalls feelings of displacement in the city. Esperanza's remarks that "you can get lost easy" and "if you didn't know better you could be in there a long time" recall her appraisal of people who stumble into her neighborhood in "Those Who Don't": "those who don't know any better come into our neighborhood scared ... they are stupid people who are lost and got here by mistake."[39] In the store, however, it is Esperanza who feels lost and "stupid." For Esperanza, being "stupid" entails being unable to master knowledge of space and, in "Those Who Don't," forgetting the consequences of crossing lines of segregation. However, in Chicago for a person of color, losing one's bearings in a space directly identified with another ethnicity or race means more than simply getting lost—it has historically meant becoming vulnerable. If we read this exchange in the store not in isolation but in connection to this wider, complex web of interracial relationships, segregation, and the city's protection of white property, we understand why Gil carefully maintains his spatial advantage in the store and keeps his precious objects off the market. For Esperanza, it is a Black-identified space that she cannot navigate comfortably and will not name except as a "junk store"; in a text preoccupied with mapping neighborhood geography, Gil's store remains barely legible on the margins of the knowable and familiar Mango Street neighborhood.

CONCLUSION

These close readings of *The House on Mango Street*, paired with an examination of Cisneros's diary entries, cleave open a space for Latinx participation in the discourse of race relations in the city, which has been typically expressed in terms of white and African American experiences. In keeping with David Roediger's concept of a racial "in-betweenness" as certain groups of immigrants have historically worked toward whiteness, Esperanza's brownness reflects some in-between privilege inflected by gender and class status that allows her to navigate neighborhood space with a constrained mobility.[40] As a young girl with more education than her parents had, Esperanza will not inherit the domestic "place by the window" that so many of the Latina characters occupy, and as she traverses the neighborhood her in-between privilege lets her go into Gil's store, while he does not come into Mango Street. Ultimately, we see that Esperanza walks a complicated path through the segregated city, a city that she understands her complicity in creating.

One of Esperanza's preoccupations in *The House on Mango Street* is with belonging, as she learns more about who she is by understanding where she doesn't belong. Her narrative recognizes the patriarchal, oppressive spaces that she will not belong to, while associating safety with the "all brown all around" character of Mango Street. Negotiating her sense of self, then, includes coming into her gender, racial, and ethnic identity and seeking those spaces where

THE RACIAL CITY

she belongs and feels safe. How does one feel safe when living in a city organized by racial and ethnic division? Esperanza follows the logic of segregation and identifies danger and ambivalence in spaces of racial otherness, even as she critiques it in "Those Who Don't." In Chicago, as racial segregation has historically fostered fear and distrust of difference, *The House on Mango Street* offers a nuanced look at the role of race and ethnicity in Esperanza's sense of community and belonging.

NOTES

Thanks to editors Geneva M. Gano and Sonia Saldívar-Hull, and especially to Geneva, who directed me to the archives; to the Wittliff Collections at Texas State University for generous travel support; and to James Kyung Lee for asking provocatively about the "older Oriental man" in *The House on Mango Street*.

1. Sandra Cisneros, "Ghosts and Voices: Writing from Obsession," *Americas Review* 15, no. 1 (1987): 74.

2. Julian Olivares, "Sandra Cisneros' *The House on Mango Street*, and the Poetics of Space," in *Chicana Creativity and Criticism: Charting New Frontiers in American Literature*, ed. María Herrera-Sobek and Helena María Viramontes (Houston, TX: Arte Público, 1988), 160–169.

3. Marci McMahon, *Domestic Negotiations: Gender, Nation, and Self-Fashioning in US Mexicana and Chicana Literature and Art* (New Brunswick, NJ: Rutgers University Press, 2013).

4. Monika Kaup, "The Architecture of Ethnicity in Chicano Literature," *American Literature* 69, no. 2 (1997): 361–397.

5. Elisabetta Careri, "Home, Streets, Nature: Esperanza's Itineraries in Sandra Cisneros' *The House on Mango Street*," in *Landscapes of Writing in Chicano Literature*, ed. Imelda Martín-Junquera (London: Palgrave Macmillan, 2013), 13–22; Juanita Heredia, "Down These City Streets: Exploring Urban Space in *El Bronx Remembered* and *The House on Mango Street*," *Mester* 22, no. 2 (1993): 93–105; Ana María Manzanas Calvo, "*The House on Mango Street* and Chicano Space," *Revista de Estudios Norteamericanos* 7 (2000): 17–26; Tomoko Kuribayashi, "The Chicana Girl Writes Her Way In and Out: Space and Bilingualism in Sandra Cisneros' *The House on Mango Street*," in *Creating Safe Space: Violence and Women's Writing*, ed. Tomoko Kuribayashi and Julie Tharp (Albany: State University of New York Press, 1997), 165–177.

6. Cristina Rodriguez, "Find Yourself Here: Neighborhood Logics in Twenty-First Century Chicano and Latino Literature" (PhD diss., University of California, Irvine, 2015), 222.

7. Henri Lefebvre, *The Production of Space* (Cambridge: Wiley-Blackwell, 1991); Edward W. Soja, *Postmetropolis: Critical Studies of Cities and Regions* (Cambridge, MA: Wiley-Blackwell, 2000); Doreen Massey, *Space, Place, and Gender* (Minneapolis: University of Minnesota Press, 2000).

8. Mary Pat Brady, "The Contrapuntal Geographies of *Woman Hollering Creek and Other Stories*," *American Literature* 71, no. 1 (1999): 118.

9. Brady, "The Contrapuntal Geographies," 118.

10. Chicago Commission on Race Relations, *The Negro in Chicago: A Study of Race Relations and a Race Riot* (Chicago: University of Chicago Press, 1922), 6–7.

11. Lilia Fernández, *Brown in the Windy City: Mexicans and Puerto Ricans in Postwar Chicago* (Chicago: University of Chicago Press, 2012), 152.

12. Gina M. Pérez, *The Near Northwest Side Story: Migration, Displacement, and Puerto Rican Families* (Berkeley: University of California Press, 2004), 131.

13. Ana Y. Ramos-Zaya, *National Performances: The Politics of Class, Race, and Space in Puerto Rican Chicago* (Chicago: University of Chicago Press, 2003), 116.

14. Sandra Cisneros, diary, May 14, 1968, box 12, folder 2, Sandra Cisneros Papers, Wittliff Collections, Texas State University. All subsequent citations to the diary refer to this same archival folder.

15. Sandra Cisneros, *The House on Mango Street* (1984; New York: Vintage Books, 1991), 16.

16. Cisneros, *The House on Mango Street*, 23–25.

17. Cisneros, *The House on Mango Street*, 26–27, 65–66, 90–91.

18. Cisneros, diary, April 4, 1968.

19. Cisneros, diary, April 5, 1968.

20. Cisneros, diary, April 5, 1968.

21. Cisneros, diary, April 6, 1968.

22. Cisneros, diary, April 6, 1968.

23. Cisneros, *The House on Mango Street*, 13.

24. Cisneros, *The House on Mango Street*, 13.

25. Cisneros, *The House on Mango Street*, 28.

26. Cisneros, *The House on Mango Street*, 16, 19, 54.

27. Cisneros, *The House on Mango Street*, 55.

28. Cisneros, *The House on Mango Street*, 41–42.

29. Cisneros, *The House on Mango Street*, 10.

30. Cisneros, *The House on Mango Street*, 16, 19.

31. Gabriela F. Arredondo, *Mexican Chicago: Race, Identity, and Nation, 1916–39* (Urbana: University of Illinois Press, 2008), 63.

32. Despite tensions exacerbated by labor practices, Black and brown communities also worked in solidarity during the civil rights era. A political coalition formed in the 1980s led to the election of Harold Washington, Chicago's first African American mayor, in 1983.

33. Cisneros, *The House on Mango Street*, 19.

34. Cisneros, *The House on Mango Street*, 19.

35. Cisneros, *The House on Mango Street*, 20.

36. Cisneros, *The House on Mango Street*, 20.

37. Cisneros, *The House on Mango Street*, 20.

38. Cisneros, *The House on Mango Street*, 20.

39. Cisneros, *The House on Mango Street*, 28.

40. David Roediger, *Working toward Whiteness: How America's Immigrants Became White* (New York: Basic Books, 2005).

CHAPTER 3

TELENOVELA FEELING IN SANDRA CISNEROS'S *LOOSE WOMAN*
"I Think of Me to Gluttony"
Adriana Estill

Sandra Cisneros's fiction has long been recognized for its attention to telenovelas as a powerful site of cultural meaning for Mexican and Chicana women. Belkys Torres contends that her narratives reveal "the deception and frustration inherent in living vicariously through telenovelas," while Amara Graf argues that *Caramelo* (2002) compels "the reader to interpret her fiction through the lens of the telenovela and recognize it as Mexicanized melodrama."[1] *Caramelo* features such key moments as the paratextual footnote that revels in the techniques of melodrama:

>—¿Qué intentas ocultar?
>—¿Por qué eres tan cruel conmigo?
>—Te encanta hacerme sufrir.
>—¿Por qué me mortificas?
>*Say any of the above, or say anything twice, slower and more dramatic the second time 'round, and it will sound like the dialogue of any telenovela.*[2]

In other words, the telenovela appears within Cisneros's work not just as a symbol of border culture or as a mass media text destined to produce oppressive hegemonic discourse, but as a generative, affective genre that, in prioritizing the self's excessive feeling, makes possible new forms of self-knowledge and relationality.

While Cisneros's narratives gesture at telenovelas overtly, her *Loose Woman* embraces this aesthetics of excess too.[3] The collection's poems boast big, unproductive feelings and, in so doing, embrace an abundance that emerges through and in relationship to Mexicanness. In her recent study on Black and

Latina embodiment and style, Jillian Hernandez states that "to exceed is to trespass." She goes on to argue for an "aesthetics of excess" that "embrace[s] abundance where the political order would impose austerity about the racialized poor and working class, viewed as excessive as in unnecessary, unproductive."[4] Hernandez highlights the way excess is a politicized mode, a framing that echoes Jesús Martín-Barbero and Sonia Muñoz's assessment of the telenovela as a genre that affirms the individual life and its vital sociality against and through the larger forces of modernity, which "makes it possible for the popular classes to recognize themselves."[5] Accordingly, in the title poem, the speaker exclaims, "Rowdy. Indulgent to excess. / My sin and success— / I think of me to gluttony."[6]

My reading of *Loose Woman* emphasizes that its aesthetics of excess can be understood as an extension of Cisneros's interest and investment in the telenovela as a potentially subversive genre that reconfigures self and others through its "affective grammar" of telenovela feelings. These telenovela feelings work to own emotion's potential to refuse social norms and challenge patriarchal demands on women's bodies. Telenovela feelings trespass, they refuse containment, and they emerge victoriously over various social repressions.

Loose Woman's sustained pleasure in telenovela feeling as a key to powerful and abundant excess contrasts with how trespass and transgression appear in *My Wicked Wicked Ways*, Cisneros's second book of poetry. *My Wicked Wicked Ways* traces the Chicana speaker from childhood up to adulthood, playfully positioning the speaker's wickedness as a transgression of various boundaries particular to Chicanas' history, culture, and family structure: "To be wicked, then, is to know you have sinned—against your parents, against the norms of society."[7] The poems "illustrate the progression of wickedness" as the speaker becomes a sexual adult who travels far beyond her home of Chicago, but, as I have claimed elsewhere, "although the speaker flaunts her 'wickedness,' her own body and the 'wicked' sexual act are invisible."[8] Whatever transgressions there are in *My Wicked Wicked Ways* operate in the background, made invisible and inaudible within the poems as those acts of transgression get tamed through a language that remains beholden to the norms of society. In contrast, *Loose Woman*, published in 1994, seven years after *My Wicked Wicked Ways*, makes the transgression louder through the disruptive affective grammar of telenovelas: repetition, emphasis, and exaggeration.[9] But this doesn't mean that the transgression—these excessive, unproductive feelings—comes easily.

While *Loose Woman* centers the power of telenovela feeling, it also worries about this feeling's aftermath: What will happen to me and to others if I let my inner terrorist speak, feel, do? If I fail to stifle my mariachi howl? This is because telenovela feeling—its excessiveness, its refusal to be contained, its invocation of the edge of chaos—necessarily undoes the modern, disciplined body (particularly the female one). Nora Mazziotti, speaking of the melodrama of telenovelas, proclaims, "hay una pasión que te arrebata y que tenés que dar rienda suelta a esa emoción" (there is a passion that bowls you over and then you must let that emotion loose).[10] In the poems, these emotional whirlwinds find concretization in violent figures: terror, anarchy, natural and historical disasters, and more. This telenovela feeling often remains hanging in the air, unresolved and big, leaving the self *arrebatada* (undone), thus emphasizing the body's role as the key generator of desire and emotion and as the key site of meaning-making.

Loose Woman's affective grammar emphasizes the power that telenovela feeling wields. Expansion (of sound and image) acts as a form of transgression; repetition creates emphasis and excess; and the invocation of violence done and violence possible, attention to the unruly body and the insufficiency of language, and the metonymic accumulation of metaphors all add up to a reconfiguration of the speaker's understanding of body, self, and her relationship to the world. For example, the title poem, "Loose Woman," unspools through a series of declamations that build power through a repetitive structure and shifted nouns: "They say I'm a beast"; "They say I'm a bitch"; "They say I'm a *macha*."[11] Repetition develops the metonymic chain of positions that the speaker refuses (even as others try to impose them on her), demonstrating their weight on her. The turning point comes when "Diamonds and pearls / tumble from [her] tongue. / Or toads and serpents. / Depending on the mood [she's] in," confirming that language and wordsmithing give her power to defy the "they."[12] The speaker acknowledges that language and stories are messy ("myth and bullshit") and proclaims boldly, "I live like so," with "heart as sail, ballast, rudder, bow." The metaphor of the heart reveals the centrality of feeling to figuring out direction and movement, even as the speaker recognizes that this decision-making is a kind of sinfulness ("I think of me to gluttony") in its refusal of Christian morality. This stanza also emphasizes the "rowdiness" of this heart—it steers, but into indulgence and excess. The following stanzas reveal that this transgressive heart makes the speaker a "danger to society," someone who "upset[s] the natural order," who "strike[s] terror among the men," who announces that "I'm Pancha Villa" and "I break things."[13] The invocation of violence in the feminized body of the hero of the Mexican Revolution emphasizes the speaker's self-understanding as revolutionary, "upset[ting] the natural order," until finally, in the last stanza, she reclaims the terms she rejected: "I'm Bitch. Beast. *Macha*. / ¡*Wáchale!*"[14]

The speaker's understanding of revolution suggests that Chicana writing—and, more specifically, Chicana feeling—has the potential to explode into our sexist, racist society with the power to make change. In her analysis of *The*

House on Mango Street, Geneva M. Gano argues that "domestic tales become revolutionary ones" when we understand that the home has been rewritten "as a war zone: a public, political space."[15] In "Loose Woman," when the speaker takes on the mantel of the "supermasculine hero" Pancho Villa, it reveals the power of a code-switching Chicana armed with telenovela feeling to interrupt the traditions and institutional structures (law, religion, patriarchy) that have contained her.[16]

Loose Woman provides multiple stagings of what it means for the Chicana speaker to experience and fight back against patriarchal norms with the tool of telenovela feeling. Telenovela feelings provide such power principally through the rescripting of emotions—desire, anger, disappointment, joy—from matters of the private heart and the domestic sphere into concerns that require airing in the public domain. The eruption of private feeling into the public shows that the personal is always and already political as an interruption of patriarchal language, histories, norms, and spaces. The telenovela feelings that suffuse this speaker allow her to reconceptualize and remake her body, the very site that has been repressed and contained in the patriarchal and European imaginaries of her. Poetry accentuates these voicings and transformations by highlighting the way boundaries of bodies and texts get established and undone, and by emphasizing the extraordinariness of telenovela feeling through modes of excess particularly visible and audible in poetry: expansion, accumulation, repetition, and emphasis.

Ultimately, *Loose Woman* emphasizes the power of telenovela feeling to explode the personal and contained tradition of the Western lyric by interrupting and invading the public sphere with sound, fury, and intensity, demanding that Chicana meaning (and meaning-making) has a place in a world that tends to see it as "unnecessary, unproductive," and, ultimately, as Hernandez points out, as something on which "the political order would impose austerity."[17]

BROWN MELODRAMA: CONCEPTUALIZING TELENOVELA FEELING

In "You Bring Out the Mexican in Me," one of the best-known poems from this collection, telenovela feeling provides the affective grammar of the text (through the metonymic chains of desire and the indulgently excessive proclamations of elicited emotion) and also the subject matter: "You bring out the Mexican in me. / The hunkered thick dark spiral. / The core of a heart howl. / The bitter bile. / The tequila *lágrimas*."[18] The speaker makes explicit the reactive and yet generative nature of this emotion—the lover elicits this welling of desire, but the desire for the lover also produces an unearthing of the self, particularly its Mexicanness—which had been "hunkered," presumably hidden, suppressed, or kept at bay. Previous scholars have read the excess in this and other poems through frames that stress the conformability of this excess to dominant structures. For example, Suzanne Chávez-Silverman argues that the excess relies on a series of essentialisms—whether about Mexicanness or about gender—that belie the collection's titular goal to let loose and refuse societal demands on women's bodies. She further suggests that the trope of the "hot fiery Latina" lives on in this collection: "Chicanas *are* 'good girls and more,' in the dominant as well as traditional Chicano discourse, which always already allow the 'hot tamale' or 'luscious Latina' alongside the good mother/virgin."[19] Consequently she reads "You Bring Out the Mexican in Me" as functioning through a series of paradigmatic substitutions, an analysis that centers the notion that the "I" commands a discursive (and sequential) construction of identity. Dislodging the idea of control, Xochitl Estrada Shuru places *Loose Woman* in conversation with theories of hysteria and the relationship between sexuality and power to emphasize how many of the poems suggest a fragmentation of self and the way tropes of hysteria and unpredictable behavior create powerful responses to patriarchal modes of control.[20]

The lens of telenovela feeling underlines an understanding of *Loose Woman* as both essentialist (succumbing to dominant structures) and "hysteric" (chaotically refusing those structures), because it stresses the temporal present—the precise moment of excess and exclamation. In other words, it emphasizes how the speaker's body can no longer contain the speaker's voice and self. In this climactic moment, the speaker experiences what José Esteban Muñoz calls disidentificatory reception and performance: "the enacting of self at precisely the point where the discourses of essentialism and constructivism short-circuit."[21] "You bring out the Uled-Nayl in me. / The stand-back-white-bitch in me" proclaims the speaker of "You Bring Out the Mexican in Me" as she lodges meaning in concrete, essentialist tropes of otherness that "work on and against dominant ideology."[22] In these poems, telenovela feeling erupts from the body in response to the dominant ideologies of gender and white affect and provides nascent language and feeling that cannot always fully interrupt or remake the dominant.

In other words, telenovelas and telenovela feelings are not inherently radical and do not inevitably upend racial, gendered, or class norms and hierarchies. As Catherine L. Benamou emphasizes, "There is a stress [in telenovelas] on the ability of national societies to absorb the crises that accompany modern change . . . the ability of patriarchal structure to restore order while accommodating feminine ambition and desire and the possibility of cultural authenticity."[23] Similarly, Sonia Saldívar-Hull emphasizes how Cisneros's narratives often recognize that telenovelas teem with conservative cultural scripts that reify traditional gender roles and stress the importance of heterosexual romance. The last stanza of "You Bring Out the Mexican in Me" illuminates a conservative feature of telenovela feelings in its submission to romance: "Let / me show you. Love the only way I know how."[24] Even as the fragmented grammar of these last two lines hints at the reorganization of the self through telenovela feelings, the enjambment highlights the dominant power of the lover as the speaker pleads to demonstrate her love.

To acknowledge this particular conservatism of telenovelas and telenovela feelings should not obscure the radical work that they do, unraveling and remaking the gendered body and, even if momentarily, performing powerful disidentification with dominant ideologies of race, gender, and class. The scant scholarship and few reviews written on *Loose Woman* in the late 1990s understood the effervescent, playful, emotive, and excessive voice as a participant in a larger-scale revision of the masculinist Chicano canon, tackling patriarchal mythologies of gender.[25] The revision of patriarchal mythologies of gender parallels the interruption that Martín-Barbero and Muñoz insist that telenovelas do in Latin America: countering the daily dull routines of life and refusing "the mark of bourgeois education [which] is manifested in everything which is the opposite of melodrama."[26] "Bourgeois education" gestures to the ways that becoming part of the middle class entails a careful self-fashioning that curtails and channels affective lifeways (including through acquiescence to gender norms) in order to gain access to the privileges of capitalism.

From its title onward, "You Bring Out the Mexican in Me" reveals the speaker's sense of herself as exceeding her earlier self-fashioning, "the Mexican" positioned as a textual and corporeal excess that emerges in response to the lover. This transgressive excess linked to Mexicanness suggests that telenovela feelings are a sort of "feeling brown" in Muñoz's terms. Brown feeling, he argues, emerges in relationship to an "official national affect, a mode of being in the world primarily associated with white middle-class subjectivity [that] reads most ethnic affect as inappropriate."[27] "The Mexican in me," unspooled throughout the three pages of the poem, defies the norms of whiteness *and* middle-class sensibilities of gender propriety through an emphasis on the unassimilability of this now-released Mexicanness. The speaker's body is a Pandora's box ("the Pandora's curiosity in me"): what it has released will not get recaptured.[28]

In addition, what has been released defies easy summary or categorization; the disparate things named accumulate in metonymic chains that together lead not to narrative or metaphoric substitutions but to attitude, verve, and brownness. Stanzas three, four, six, and seven (out of nine total) are primarily composed of lists of things that "you" bring out "in me." Thus we get constructions like the following, in the third stanza:

> You bring out the Dolores del Río in me.
> The Mexican spitfire in me.
> The *raw navajas*, glint and passion in me.
> The raise Cain and dance with the rooster-footed devil in me.
> The spangled sequin in me.
> The eagle and serpent in me.
> The *mariachi* trumpets of the blood in me.
> The Aztec love of war in me.
> The fierce obsidian of the tongue in me.
> The *berrinchuda, bien-cabrona* in me.[29]

What does it mean to "bring out the Mexican" in the speaker? This partial stanza suggests a broad, in some ways incoherent, sense of Mexicanness—that is, brownness. Mexicanness isn't operative here as a nationality or a heritage; rather, the speaker identifies her desire as the thing that is Mexican. Indeed, the sheer quantity of allusions and the metonymic way in which they move—not progressively, not leading up to an "answer" or an Ur-Mexicanness—but sideways and expansively, through association and lateral connections, disrupts any attempt to pin down Mexicanness except as a feeling, a telenovela feeling. The speaker's desires reel out of her by power of association, a potentially never-ending list that concretizes her feelings.

While her feelings are concretized, the precise nature of this Mexicanness never can be; the brownness that telenovela feelings produce is always and only an affective response. As such, the brownness/Mexicanness produced is elusive, a range of sensations. For example, as cited earlier, the sixth stanza invokes the Uled-Nayl (a tribe in Algeria known for a dance exoticized and seen through colonial eyes in the nineteenth century) right before the "stand-back-white-bitch in me" and then segues to the switchblade, the Acapulco cliff diver, the Flecha Roja mountain disaster, the dengue fever, and the "*¡Alarma!* murderess in me."[30] Ranging over geographies and time periods, these concretions of what the lover has "brought out" in the speaker accumulate so that time, space, and history collapse, coalescing around the relatively grounded "you bring out the Mexican in me."

Loose Woman's telenovela feeling emerges and becomes useful both as a sort of affective "home" for transnational, diasporic communities—naming an affective Mexicanness that explicitly and deliberately contains multitudes—and also as a contestation of the normative national affect, much like actual telenovelas do.[31] Muñoz describes the normative national affect as "minimalist to the point of emotional impoverishment. Whiteness claims affective normativity and neutrality, but for that fantasy to remain in place one must only view it from the vantage point of US cultural and political hegemony."[32] Telenovela feeling refuses that fantasy, instead "indulging" in excess and effusion.

The normative and minimalist affect is not just a condition of whiteness in *Loose Woman*, but also and perhaps above all, a structuring of gender norms through and with Mexicanness in the United States. In "You Bring Out the Mexican in Me," references jostle between incredibly specific intimacies like "*barbacoa taquitos* on Sunday in me" and sweeping mythologies like "Popocatepetl/Ixtaccíhuatl in me." Phrases like "*berrinchuda, bien-cabrona*" and "*Quiero amarte. Atarte. Amarrarte*" reveal playful poetic code-switching as a sign of this speaker's travels between cultures and languages and geographies. Of course, Spanish also emphasizes the gendered nature of this complicated, layered Mexicanness "brought out" by the addressee: "*Me sacas lo mexicana en mi*, / like it or not, honey." The Spanish here is ungrammatical: Mexicano has been rescripted to Mexican*a*, emphasizing that the telenovela feelings that have been elicited must, indeed, push back against grammatical structures, even as those structures remain intact. So many lines hint at the latent violence of telenovela feelings: "the hunkered thick dark spiral," the "hopeless romantic," the "glint and passion," the "nasty obsession in me."[33]

In fact, telenovela feeling carries with it a consistent underbed of violence and the threat of violence. "You Bring Out the Mexican in Me" emphasizes the "raw" *navajas* (pocket knives) that are connected to raising "Cain and danc[ing] with the rooster-footed devil"—that is, a violence that is about refusing social norms, including religious mandates about pleasure. Later the poem turns to "rainforest disaster" and "nuclear threat," both examples of global disasters produced by the state. The possibility of violence looms larger than the speaker, and while she teases her interlocutors with it, she is not fully in control. Excess violence signals impossibly huge feeling by collapsing the very public histories and power relationships into the private, feeling body of the speaker. The speaker of "You Bring Out the Mexican in Me" first contains the disparate multitudes of Mexicanness and then recognizes herself in this expansive Mexicanness.

Beyond processes of recognition, telenovelas also offer, according to Martín-Barbero and Muñoz, a focus on relationality, kinship, and revelation (the unraveling of secrets, the recognition of truths) that personalizes and makes concrete the abstract political and cultural conflicts that surround us. Melodrama is thus an explicit and amplified personalization of the impossible-to-understand large forces that lie beyond individuals. For Martín-Barbero and Muñoz, the excess of the telenovela "represents a victory over repression, a form of resistance against a particular 'economy' of order, saving and polite restraint."[34] "You Bring Out the Mexican in Me" moves through recognition to relationality and revelation as the speaker's litany accumulates. Ultimately, the accumulation expands and explodes her private, feeling body and self into the public sphere. The final stanzas of the poem demonstrate this transformation, the phrase *you bring out the X in me* shifting as she becomes and now embodies the telenovela feelings: "I am evil. I am the filth goddess Tlazoltéotl / I am the swallower of sins."[35] "You Bring Out the Mexican in Me" thus traces—through the concatenation of places, events, and violence that the addressee brings out in her—the undoing of the speaker as a tame, contained self. The culmination (becoming goddess, becoming sin) allows for the ritual and declaration of the final stanzas: "*Quiero ser tuya* . . . Let / me show you. Love the only way I know how."[36] While the rest of the poem lays the responsibility for the storm of emotion—for its enormity and its danger and its uncontrollability—on the addressee's shoulders, for bringing out "the Mexican" in her, this last stanza owns her feeling and her desire. Telenovela feeling allows her to reconfigure her relationship to her own desire, to name it and to act on it. And most importantly, it makes urgent claims to the public sphere for her voice, her gender, and her Mexicanness.

TELENOVELA FEELINGS AND AFFECTIVE PEDAGOGIES

Telenovela feelings provide an affective pedagogy that encourages the movement of "private" feeling into the public sphere as a way to reconfigure relationships and societal mores. Poems like "Old Maids" and "Original Sin" recognize how structures of religion, family, patriarchy, and whiteness contain and control the speaker: the "armpits clean / as a newborn's soul" of "Original Sin" mirror the "lessons that served us well" of "Old Maids," both poems demonstrating the speaker's circumstantial willingness to flatten affect and conform to the expectations of her family, as well as the way she chafes at these constraints.[37]

Repressive social structures weigh heavily; the speaker recognizes that the telenovela feelings that could resist them will themselves be painful and violent. "I Don't Like Being in Love" emphasizes this tension: "I don't care for this fruit. This / Mexican love hidden in the boot," ending with, "Oh, not like this. / Not this."[38] The naming of the love as "Mexican" and the sense of foreboding that comes with the alliterative punch of a "birthcord buried beneath the knuckle of the heart" combine to reveal that telenovela feelings are latently available, even as the speaker buries them deep, the poem ending before they emerge. Note, however, that the elision that happens in those final lines—from "not *like* this" to "not this"—eliminates the simile, thus emphasizing the dangling deictic and, in doing so, suggesting that a burst of telenovela feeling is imminent.[39]

Throughout much of the collection, telenovela feeling erupts into figures of terror and terrorism, suggesting the high stakes around gender roles and traditional norms. As argued earlier, "You Bring Out the Mexican in Me" highlights the possibility of disruptive and even terroristic violence: "I could . . . brandish a fork and terrorize rivals."[40] Telenovela feelings wield a chaotic power that lies in wait inside the speaker, ready to emerge into the public eye. Other poems, like "Pumpkin Eater," depict the speaker struggling to understand this violent potential, attempting to both control it and distance herself from it: "I'm no hysteric, / terrorist, / emotional anarchist."[41] By the last poem of the collection, "Loose Woman," the speaker uses the figure of the terrorist to name the way she is seen by patriarchal society: "I strike terror among the men."[42] To the extent that the use of terrorism/ist reveals a progression, this last example suggests that the speaker no longer struggles to contain this power, in part because she recognizes that the terror she exerts reflects the necessary and world-reordering power of her feelings.

Mariachi music, in particular the *grito* (shout), serves as another symbol that traces the speaker's struggles to adapt or conform to social norms while recognizing and learning how to develop her big feelings and their generative power. Writing about "Woman Hollering Creek" and Felice's "yell as loud as any mariachi," Saldívar-Hull states that the *grito* "opens up a radical political trajectory for the text."[43] Mary-Lee Mulholland's study of women mariachis in Jalisco suggests that the range of emotion and embodiment allowed them is circumscribed by notions of femininity.[44] Thus the *grito* operates as a perfect instantiation of telenovela feelings because of how it exceeds narrative and societal expectations for women's self-expression. The repeated invocation of mariachi and *gritos* in *Loose Woman* evokes the emotional force of mariachi music—a genre understood to be "extroverted, expressive, exciting"—opening up that range of expressive power to women. The *gritos* express big feelings that defy words—emerging in songs, they are sorrow and laughter, screams and calls to arms. They "mark emotion-packed moments in mariachi music" with big, seemingly spontaneous, boundless voicings.[45]

"You Bring Out the Mexican in Me" explicitly connects the power of mariachi music to terrorism through sequences like "*mariachi* trumpets of the blood in me," which leads into the "Aztec love of war in me."[46] The mariachi—and in particular the bright sounds of the trumpet, with its association to battle—stands ready as a potential in the speaker that must emerge. That the trumpets are of "the blood" connects to the next image of war, emphasizing violence, but also alludes to the self, blood standing in as a metaphor for her lineage, kinship, and roots. In this way, the emergence of the mariachi trumpets reflects telenovela feeling, which is essential to both self-making and self-understanding, and which always contains some amount of violence and undoing.

Thus, like the figure of terrorism, the mariachi and its *grito* serve as concrete symbols that gesture at boundless, sometimes frighteningly excessive, emotion. In "Small Madness," this *grito* must be suppressed: "I press my mouth to yours, / my faithful wife-beater, / and stifle this *mariachi* / howl."[47] Stifling the howl requires submission to "my faithful wife-beater," an image that emphasizes the misogynistic violence embedded in the term, revealing how telenovela feeling gets tamed and cowed within heteronormative structures.

The mariachi howl links metonymically to the "dial tone howling like my heart" in the poem "After Everything." This line follows a stanza in which the speaker details what her lovers say as they leave her: "You're nuts, / Go screw yourself, / Stop yelling and speak English please!"[48] The "dial tone howling like my heart" thus emphasizes the fruitlessness of emotions in a void. The ex-lover gets the last word, while the direction of the simile codes the speaker's agony as loud, monotonous, and inarticulate, like a dial tone. It also emphasizes that her heart (like her dial tone) is loud only to herself: no one is on the other end of the line. Telenovela feelings in solitude produce no response, thus the importance of making them public. In this poem, though, the emphasis is on the constraints that society places on women, a disciplining of femininity that is enforced through the concomitant suppression of feeling and containment of sexuality, even as the *grito* gestures at the possibility of contestation.

TELENOVELA FEELING TRANSFORMING THE GENDERED BODY

The power of telenovela feelings, ultimately, is the way they refuse containment and, through their aesthetics of excess, unsettle the gendered body. That transformation begins at the core, with a number of poems invoking the heart, imagining what is possible when the "heart [acts] as sail, ballast, rudder, bow," in other words, when the heart does *everything*.[49] But the speaker doesn't start with that full embrace of her heart as engine, GPS, and stabilizer. Both "Little Clown, My Heart" and "Heart, My Lovely Hobo" use initial apostrophes—"little clown" and "my lovely hobo"—that position the speaker outside or beyond her body and emotion, a move that suggests the speaker wants to control and clarify the unruliness of love by making it her object of study.[50] In the context of the collection, this self-disciplining has clear connections to the structural disciplining of gender and race, the way the speaker's world renders telenovela feelings undesirable.

Telenovela feeling refuses disciplining, however, and each of these poems traces the results of that refusal. For example, the second stanza of "Little Clown, My Heart" features a set of paradoxes: the heart is a "gimp-footed hooray" and a "paper parasol of pleasures" that conjoins joy/celebration with fragility or a state of injury. But by the third stanza, the personification of the heart shifts to an Acapulco cliff diver, emphasizing the increasing lack of control that the speaker has over her heart as well as the sense of risk and volatility attributed to the speaker's desire/emotion: "alley-oop and here we go / Into the froth, my life / Into the flames!"[51] As the first poem in the collection, "Little Clown, My Heart" establishes how telenovela feelings inevitably overpower and power the speaker through the unruly self and its violent immolation.

In "Heart, My Lovely Hobo," the heart and its telenovela feelings are not just understood to be irrational and wayward; rather, these big, uncontainable feelings reveal the limitations of the speaker's body. With the heart removed from humanness through similes invoking oysters and plums, the speaker points to the heart's "dumbness"—a descriptor that gets at both its "irrationality" and its inability to speak. The enjambment of "As if love / could be" stresses the impossibility of controlling love, this excessive, mind-of-its-own emotion: it sits at a precipice and *will* fall, will fall prey to "daily beatings." The third stanza's attempt to establish a peaceful future—"Not this throbbing. / This."—instead, through the use of the deictic, emphasizes language's insufficiency in the face of telenovela feeling.[52] Ending with this apostrophic cry reveals the ways language is incommensurate with (and cannot contain/translate) feeling. In the end, corporeal throbbing stands in metaphorically for all the feeling that pulses through the heart with rhythm and force.

The metonymic accumulation of metaphors, expansive repetition, and violence that fuel telenovela feeling fully remake the body in "I Am So in Love I Grow a New Hymen."[53] The title and premise of the poem serve as an extended homage to Madonna's song "Like a Virgin." Madonna's lover makes her feel "shiny and new. / Like a virgin / touched for the very first time."[54] In embodied contrast, "I Am So in Love" highlights the materiality of this new virginity—the hymen—and then, instead of focusing on the "shiny and new," moves into a stanza that overflows with historical allusions that accumulate as a sign of the "old," that is, past relationships and lovers. Collapsing personal and public, the speaker rescripts her past through histories of violence against the state: "Terrorists of the last / decade. Anarchists who fled / with my heart." This dual image stresses not only the abrupt and violent interruption of the "normal" but also the dispersed nature of it—there is no core organization/governing force that does this to the speaker. Her heart and personhood have been under unpredictable and devastating attack. The stanza escalates through historical specificity ("Nelson Algren impersonators") and broad-stroke character "tropes" ("politically-correct-Marxists-tourists-voyeurs"), climaxing into the speaker's claim that this whole messy heap of entangled personal and political histories is "Forgot, forgotten, forget. / Past tense and no regrets."[55]

If the first stanza, in collapsing the public and the personal, suggests the melodramatically high stakes of the speaker's past loves, the second stanza emphasizes the relational nature of her current love: the way that her telenovela feeling is elicited or provoked in her in the encounter with the current lover. The speaker articulates the importance and vitality of relationality with a series of combative, historically grounded metaphors. These metaphors mark a telenovela feeling that can only understand the self and her needs and desires through comparison to public, big-scale events; whether the lover is Pancho Villa (and the speaker John Pershing's dizzy troops) or eucalyptus (and the speaker a California fire), the metaphors emphasize the lover's power to overwhelm (as with Villa's evasion of Pershing) and defy (as with eucalyptus's resilience after burning) the speaker. Both metaphors suggest that her pursuit of her lover ultimately ends in defeat. These already-drastic metaphors escalate to the lover being "eucharist, Euclidean geometry," metaphors suggesting absoluteness and, thus, divinity or purity. In the face of the lover's perfection, whether spiritual or mathematical, the speaker removes herself from the picture, with a series of ultraspecific historical metaphors that name and define the lover: "Chinese traders of Guangzhou, / Zapatistas breakfasting at Sanborn's, / Sassoferrato's cobalt blue, / Museo Poldi Pezzoli's insurance rate, / Gaudi's hammer against porcelain plates." These metaphors situate images of the aesthetically and ideologically incomparable in relation to structures of capitalism and imperialism.[56] The metaphors don't easily coalesce around a common feeling or idea, even as the speaker emphasizes the lover's rarity and value to her. In this way, the metaphors are all surface, acting as a metonymic chain of meaning: the more the speaker lists, the more "meaning" accrues to the lover, but it fails to add up to something that can easily be grasped. The meaning exceeds these parts; it is beyond the grasp of language.

Finally, the poem exposes how desire and feeling override and restructure the body and reorganize its social context, as its metonymic escalation of love for the speaker culminates with orgasmic delight. Because no reference in all of world history can provide the words/concepts that this speaker needs, all she has left is repetition and exclamation:

Ay daddy, daddy, I
don't give a good goddamn. I
don't give
a good
god damn.[57]

This outburst exhibits the height of telenovela feeling, both in form and in the way it materializes the metaphor of the title: her feelings of love generate a new hymen. The emotions that exceed the body rebuild and remake it in this moment of pure pleasure.

Poetic form emphasizes both the telenovela feeling and the corporeal remaking. The expansion of "don't give a good goddamn. I" gives way to short, staccato lines—out of breath? And after a poem that features only a few playful enjambments, the last stanza provides a full set of enjambments that reveal the speaker's lack of control. As the speaker claims, twice, to not give "a good goddamn," the enjambments and spacing emphasize "good," "god," and "damn" to reveal that she does indeed feel this pleasure; she does indeed care, deeply. This last stanza asserts feeling that can be neither logically absorbed nor asserted by the text.

Telenovela feeling takes the desiring, feeling signs of otherness (of brownness) and, in their trespass into the public sphere, makes them unavoidable and excessive against the white norms and expectations of those spaces. Telenovela feelings disrupt the white norms of affect that police emotion, that restrict their expression; *Loose Woman*, alive with the needs and demands of telenovela feelings, argues that the Chicana speaker feeling deeply is not a marginal subject but, rather, that her outcries are necessarily public and potentially world shattering. Her desires are not just directed at her interlocutors, they serve, too, as a claim to space, to freedom, to her overfullness: "I think of me to gluttony."[58] *Loose Woman*'s telenovela feelings remind us that feeling expansively can unsettle our worlds and recenter us as the meaning-makers.

NOTES

A huge thank you to Geneva M. Gano for her encouragement and suggestions, to Bianet Castellanos, Lourdes Gutiérrez Nájera, Desirée Martín, Yolanda Padilla for all their comments on my earliest, messiest drafts, and to Audrey Goodman and Ricky Rodríguez for their incisive insight.

1. Belkys Torres, "Hybridity in Popular Culture: The Influence of Telenovelas on Chicana Literature," in *Soap Operas and Telenovelas in the Digital Age: Global Industries and New Audiences*, ed. Diana Isabel Arredondo Ríos and Mari Castañeda (New York: Peter Lang, 2011), 204; Amara Graf, "Mexicanized Melodrama: Sandra Cisneros's Literary Translation of the Telenovela in *Caramelo*," *Label Me Latina/o* 4 (2014): 1. Sonia Saldívar-Hull, *Feminism on the Border: Chicana Gender Politics and Literature* (Berkeley: University of California Press, 2000), started the conversation.

2. Sandra Cisneros, *Caramelo or Puro Cuento* (New York: Vintage Books, 2002), 15.

3. Thanks to Graf for her endnote about the glimmers of telenovela influence in Cisneros's poetry titles. Graf, "Mexicanized Melodrama," 17n3.

4. Jillian Hernandez, *Aesthetics of Excess: The Art and Politics of Black and Latina Embodiment* (Durham, NC: Duke University Press, 2020), 11.

5. Jesús Martín-Barbero and Sonia Muñoz, *Televisión y melodrama: géneros y lecturas de la telenovela en Colombia* (Bogotá: Tercer Mundo Editores, 1992), 227. The telenovela—often compared to the US soap opera—shares the soap opera's melodramatic DNA.

6. Sandra Cisneros, *Loose Woman* (New York: Alfred A. Knopf, 1994), 113.

7. Tey Diana Rebolledo, *Women Singing in the Snow: A Cultural Analysis of Chicana Literature* (Tucson: University of Arizona Press, 1995), 193. See also Sandra Cisneros, *My Wicked Wicked Ways* (Bloomington, IN: Third Woman Press, 1987).

8. Rebolledo, *Women Singing in the Snow*, 192; Adriana Estill, "Building the Chicana Body in Sandra Cisneros' *My Wicked Wicked Ways*," *Rocky Mountain Review of Language and Literature* 56, no. 2 (2002): 35.

9. As Ricky Rodríguez pointed out to me in conversation, *Loose Woman* was published after Cisneros's move to San Antonio; perhaps the move allowed a reinvention of self.

10. "El melodrama y la telenovela, por Nora Mazziotti," YouTube video, uploaded December 22, 2014, by DIGO - Televisión Hecha por Televidentes, 3:24.

11. Cisneros, *Loose Woman*, 112.

12. Cisneros, *Loose Woman*, 112–113. While both images (diamonds and pearls or toads and serpents) evoke fairy-tale motifs, the magic (and control) comes from within the speaker rather than from an external, magical being.

13. Cisneros, *Loose Woman*, 113–114.

14. Cisneros, *Loose Woman*, 115.

15. Geneva M. Gano, "Campobello's Cartuchos and Cisneros's Molotovs: Transborder Revolutionary Feminist Narratives," *Journal of Transnational American Studies* 6, no. 1 (2015): 16, 17.

16. Gano, "Campobello's Cartuchos and Cisneros's Molotovs," 5.

17. Hernandez, *Aesthetics of Excess*, 11.

18. Cisneros, *Loose Woman*, 4.

19. Suzanne Chávez-Silverman, "Chicanas in Love: Sandra Cisneros Talking Back and Alicia Gaspar de Alba 'Giving Back the Wor(l)d,'" *Chasqui* 27, no. 1 (1998): 35.

20. Xochitl Estrada Shuru, "The Poetics of Hysteria in Chicana Writing: Sandra Cisneros, Margarita Cota-Cárdenas, Pat Mora, and Bernice Zamora" (PhD diss., University of New Mexico, 2000).

21. José Esteban Muñoz, *Disidentifications: Queers of Color and the Performance of Politics* (Minneapolis: University of Minnesota Press, 1999), 6.

22. Cisneros, *Loose Woman*, 5; Muñoz, *Disidentifications*, 11.

23. Catherine L. Benamou, "Televisual Melodrama in an Era of Transnational Migration: Exporting the Folkloric Nation, Harvesting the Melancholic-Sublime," in *Latin American Melodrama*, ed. Darlene J. Sadlier (Champaign: University of Illinois Press, 2009), 150.

24. Cisneros, *Loose Woman*, 6.

25. For example, see Leigh Johnson for a reading of *Loose Woman* as a response to Rodolfo "Corky" Gonzales's epic poem *I Am Joaquín*: "Unsexing *I Am Joaquín* through Chicana Feminist Revisions," in *A Sense of Regard: Essays on Poetry and Race*, ed. Laura McCullough (Athens: University of Georgia Press, 2015), 72–78.

26. Martín-Barbero and Muñoz, *Televisión y melodrama*, 113.

27. José Esteban Muñoz, *The Sense of Brown*, ed. Joshua Chambers-Letson and Tavia Nyong'o (Durham, NC: Duke University Press, 2020), 10.

28. Cisneros, *Loose Woman*, 4.

29. Cisneros, *Loose Woman*, 4.

30. Cisneros, *Loose Woman*, 5–6.

31. Notably, "You Bring Out the Mexican in Me" has inspired a number of poets to follow with their own "you bring out" litanies. See, e.g., Bao Phi's poem "You Bring Out the Vietnamese in Me": "_You Bring Out the Vietnamese in Me_ Bao Phi (Def Poetry)," YouTube video, uploaded May 10, 2010, by neaatotube, 1:52.

32. Muñoz, *The Sense of Brown*, 11.

33. Cisneros, *Loose Woman*, 4–6.

34. Martín-Barbero and Muñoz, *Televisión y melodrama*, 119.

35. Cisneros, *Loose Woman*, 6.

36. Cisneros, *Loose Woman*, 6.

37. Cisneros, *Loose Woman*, 7, 9.

38. Cisneros, *Loose Woman*, 51.

39. Cisneros, *Loose Woman*, 51 (emphasis added).

40. Cisneros, *Loose Woman*, 6.

41. Cisneros, *Loose Woman*, 37.

42. Cisneros, *Loose Woman*, 114.

43. Sandra Cisneros, "Woman Hollering Creek," in *Woman Hollering Creek and Other Stories* (New York: Random House, 1991), 55; Saldívar-Hull, *Feminism on the Border*, 122.

44. Mary-Lee Mulholland, "*Mariachi*, Myths and *Mestizaje*: Popular Culture and Mexican National Identity," *National Identities* 9, no. 3 (2007): 247–264.

45. Daniel Sheehy, *Mariachi Music in America: Experiencing Music, Expressing Culture* (Oxford: Oxford University Press, 2006), 2, 95.

46. Cisneros, *Loose Woman*, 4.

47. Cisneros, *Loose Woman*, 66.

48. Cisneros, *Loose Woman*, 41.

49. Cisneros, *Loose Woman*, 113.

50. Cisneros, *Loose Woman*, 3, 69.

51. Cisneros, *Loose Woman*, 3.

52. Cisneros, *Loose Woman*, 69.

53. Cisneros, *Loose Woman*, 16–17.

54. Madonna, "Like a Virgin," track 3 on *Like a Virgin*, Sire/Warner Records, 1984.

55. Cisneros, *Loose Woman*, 16.

56. Cisneros, *Loose Woman*, 17.

57. Cisneros, *Loose Woman*, 17.

58. Cisneros, *Loose Woman*, 113.

CHAPTER 4

"YOU WERE TELLING *COCHINADAS*"
Performative Metaphors for Storytelling in
Sandra Cisneros's *Caramelo*

Shanna M. Salinas

Stories, specifically Celaya "Lala" Reyes's stories about her family's personal and familial histories, as told by various family members, are the primary subject matter as well as the narrative mechanism that propels the plot of Sandra Cisneros's *Caramelo or Puro Cuento*. The central conceit of the text is an ongoing, protracted battle between Lala and the imagined voice of Soledad Reyes, her deceased paternal grandmother, whom she refers to as the Awful Grandmother. Throughout the novel, as Soledad and Lala fight for narrative control over Lala's depiction of her family, Cisneros highlights the complicated motivations and questionable veracities embedded within the stories we tell. Lala and Soledad's repeated disagreements over the Reyes family history likewise represent a weightier authorial intervention by Cisneros: an interrogation of cultural norms that determine allowable and appropriate storytelling. By using storyness itself as a site of negotiation, Cisneros not only provides a rationale for how and why such stories must be told, but supplies a model for a type of narrative performativity within Chicana/o/x literature that speaks to and for a racialized gendered positionality within storytelling.[1] In this essay, I analyze Cisneros's utilization of the rebozo as an extended performative metaphor for Chicana storytelling. Tracing Lala's discovery of both the limitations and capacities of stories, Cisneros showcases Lala's attempts to mine the sources and sites of willfully repressed shame, specifically in relation to race and gender within the multigenerational stories and cultural structures that inform her identity and sense of self. At the novel's conclusion, Cisneros, via Lala, succeeds in constructing an expansive familial and national project that reincorporates the omitted or repressed stories of and *by* dark-skinned and Indigenous women. In centering repressed and so-deemed inappropriate, filthy, or shameful stories—what Soledad calls "telling *cochinadas*"—Cisneros willfully confronts and instantiates the inherited narratives that circumscribe Lala, and Chicanas more broadly.

The following exchange between Lala and her grandmother highlights the novel's investment in storytelling as a central plot focus while also illustrating the way Cisneros literalizes the processes through which stories are constructed, told, and heard:

Celaya, why are you so cruel with me? You love to make me suffer. You enjoy mortifying me, isn't that so? Is that why you insist on showing everyone this . . . dirt, but refuse me one little love scene?
For crying out loud, Grandmother. If you can't let me do my job and tell this story without your constant interruptions . . .
All I wanted was a little understanding, but I see I was asking for too much.
Just trust me, will you? Let me go on with the story without your comments. Please! Now, where was I?
You were telling *cochinadas*.
I was not being filthy. And to tell the truth, you're getting in the way of my story.
Your story? I thought you were telling *my* story?
Your story *is* my story. Now please be quiet, Grandmother, or I'll have to ask you to leave.[2]

Soledad's interjections, noted in the text in bold, frequently interrupt the narrative flow of Lala's storytelling attempts. She repeatedly contests the accuracy of Lala's narration, in an attempt to dictate what stories Lala tells and to influence the manner in which she tells them. In return, Lala critiques her grandmother for her lack of honesty, and for her investment in details Lala deems unimportant to the story she wants to tell. Through Lala's negotiation with the looming, always dissenting figure of the Awful Grandmother, Cisneros emphasizes the legacy of inherited familial narratives and makes the stakes of telling such stories irrefutably immediate and tangible. Ultimately, Lala's interjection that "your story *is* my story" not only asserts that Soledad's "story" is the intended content of Lala's own story, but suggests that grandmother and granddaughter share a common story and, therefore, an equal claim to and stake in what is told. Moreover, Cisneros's storytelling mechanisms in *Caramelo* move beyond mere representative metaphor to performative metaphor, allowing her to manifest the processes that silence Lala and thereby create a material structure in which Lala's stories can be told and fully understood. This technique is crucial to the novel's representations of racialized gender subjectivity, underscoring the need for stories written by, and *for*, racialized, gendered bodies. As Cisneros transforms narrative into a type of textual body that can account for Lala's perspectives, knowledges, and experiences, she makes the stakes of storytelling for raced and gendered Chicana bodies in the United States materially tangible.

This approach contests the view that formal and stylistic attributes in narratives are mere abstractions; rather, these formal concerns can be conversant with, or operate as an extension of, the sociocultural and sociohistorical contexts of Chicana literature. Christopher González addresses conventional trespasses in formal and stylistic approaches in Latina/o/x/e literature and positions the ways in which narrative theory, or narratology, and critical race theory can inform each other.[3] He argues that "some formalist considerations are very much relevant to larger societal concerns," responding to cultural critics who would argue that narrative form and narratology are not relevant to, or a substantive means with which to analyze, subject matter like racism or sexism.[4] His analysis of *Caramelo*'s "paratextual playfulness" and the overriding importance of Cisneros's rebozo footnote inform my analysis of Cisneros's performative metaphor.[5] However, I distinguish my intervention from González's through an analysis of Cisneros's enactment of her metaphor, an analysis informed by N. Katherine Hayles's theorization of "material metaphors," or the "traffic between words and a physical object."[6] Through material metaphor, Hayles emphasizes the importance of the textual medium for meaning, argues for the inextricability of content and medium, and showcases the manner in which subject and object coalesce as a result. By making her metaphor material, and deploying it to perform accordingly, Cisneros forces readers to participate in the novel's metaphoric network and material structure. This process makes legible the way that stories and bodies are regulated by cultural traditions and structures that actively work to silence them.

Since Cisneros's novel is, in effect, a story about storytelling, the rebozo's physicality becomes the means to extend a similar tactile composition to writing and storytelling. As such, critical race narratology, a theoretical field that emerged in the 2010s, gives us a method for understanding how and why *Caramelo* is constructed in this manner. Crystallized by Sue J. Kim's work on "decolonizing narrative theory" and advanced by James J. Donahue, Jennifer Ann Ho, and Shaun Morgan in *Narrative, Race, and Ethnicity in the United States* (2017), critical race narratology considers race and racial constructs to be central to narratives by and about BIPOC communities. Drawn in part from feminist narratology, critical race narratology is indebted to what Kim describes as Susan Lanser and Robyn Warhol's "demonstrat[ion] that gender and sexuality are constitutive considerations of texts, rather than simply extra-textual considerations."[7] Informed by this framework, critical race narratology demands that race and ethnicity in literature function as more than ethnographic subject matter. Moreover, as Donahue contends, "race and ethnicity might force us to reconsider what we know about the *nature* of narrative."[8] This type of reading can be further understood through literary materialist Espen J. Aarseth's theorization of "ergodic" literature, in which the reader becomes an active participant in meaning-making through the "nontrivial effort . . . required for the reader to traverse the text."[9] Meaning, according to Aarseth, emerges through the interplay between text, the text's medium, and the reader, or a participatory network of interpretation produced by embedded textual mechanisms that demand readers account for both the text's content (e.g., the content of the vignette) and its materiality (e.g., the footnote threads that perform the weave in the caramelo rebozo) simultaneously. The performative metaphor of the rebozo gives a multidimensional capacity to the process of storytelling that would be foreclosed without the physicality of the objects themselves. Cisneros's mechanism for narration via the weaving of story with the rebozo effectively uses, and thus *performs*, the very apparatus it deploys. The literary form is not extratextual, but intrinsic to narration and meaning.

WOVEN TEXTUALITY: THE REBOZO AS PERFORMATIVE METAPHOR FOR STORYTELLING

Caramelo, an expansive, multigenerational, transnational history, traces approximately one hundred years of the Reyes family's experiences in Mexico and the United States. Lala—the youngest of seven children, and only daughter—navigates both countries, as she and her immediate family travel from Chicago to Mexico City every summer. In the same fashion, she explores her family's told and untold stories. Throughout, the novel upholds the primacy of storytelling, deftly deploying Lala as the interlocutor and disseminator of the family archive. Intertwining her own experiences and memories with those of individual family members, Lala draws attention to flawed or inaccurate details, exposes willfully distorted facts, and chronicles hidden motivations behind faulty representation. She exposes her family's most shameful secrets, those that family members labor to keep unexposed: affairs, out-of-wedlock children, family discord, fractured relationships, bad behavior, insults, arguments, and the like. Through Lala, Cisneros weaves layers of stories, all of which are shaped by varying influences: competing memories; constructed fantasies that become truth only because they have been repeated with such frequency; the cyclical nature of tradition and cultural and familial expectations; the legacy of sociohistorical constructs. In doing so, Cisneros emphasizes what the members of the Reyes family cling to, romanticize, and reject. By focusing on what is absented, elided, or denied, Cisneros shows how Lala seeks to make sense of her family and herself, within and through such stories.

Cisneros clearly situates and announces her expansive narrative project during an exchange between Lala and Soledad, the Awful Grandmother, that uses a complicated footnote structure to reinforce meaning:

> **Ah, but that story is another story, inside another story, inside a story.**
> Soon we shall see.[10]

This exchange, which closes the vignette, is followed by a footnote that connects to a statement from Soledad a few pages earlier: "**I remember Narciso had a box of his father's papers with many waltzes composed in his own hand. I have some of them, but who knows where they all are now.***"[11] The footnote that links to this statement reinforces the recurring tension in the novel, particularly as it occurs between Lala and Soledad, between verifiable truth and memory, while also linking to a new footnote of its own: "*'*A Waltz Without a Name*' *because I lost that paper but I remember it went* . . . †"[12] The exchange thus serves as the anchor for a series of footnotes within footnotes, including one that details the waltz's lyrics and a corrective interjection that contests the validity of the initial footnote. The interplay exhibited by this sequence enacts the overarching apparatus of storytelling at work in the novel: a highly complex textual interplay achieved via Cisneros's stylistic and formal techniques, which weave together the numerous voices and contested perspectives, the stories within stories that will soon be revealed to readers. While critics have analyzed the recurring image of the rebozo as a guiding metaphor for storytelling, and also accounted for Cisneros's paratextual and intertextual elements, I combine these critical interventions in order to analyze how the novel's *intratextuality* constructs the rebozo as a performative metaphor. In contrast with approaches that privilege the circuits of information and knowledge that occur outside the text, intratextuality insists on the text's internal relations. By emphasizing the transit and interrelation between what would otherwise be considered external components of the text, thereby making the external internal, *Caramelo*'s intratextuality intertwines the intertextual and paratextual apparatuses as an internal mechanism of and *for* storytelling itself. As such, the narrative threads of Cisneros's novel aren't simply woven together in a manner akin to the rebozo; they *actively perform* that weaving and, thus, forecast its importance in the novel.

The footnote within a footnote that historicizes and contextualizes the importance of the rebozo doesn't appear until the first vignette in part 2, notably the section in which Soledad's narrative interjections are introduced. As González astutely observes, the inclusion of this footnote is unusual because it defies the conventional systematization of academic footnotes: "if the history of the rebozo is footnote-worthy, why not deploy the footnote when the rebozo is first mentioned on page 26?"[13] Cisneros's use of footnotes has been polarizing among scholars and critics of Chicana/o/x and Latina/o/x/e literature. Ellen McCracken lauds its usage as an "innovative technique" that enables Cisneros to contend with the "multiple, complicated layers of the story" and to account for "counternarratives" to colonial discourses.[14] Ilan Stavans, however, refutes the claims of structural innovation, dismissing the footnotes as "postmodern play" that overcomplicates the novel.[15] Unlike critics that claim Cisneros's footnotes are unruly, poorly or illogically placed, intrusive, and nonessential, González resists the suggestion that the footnotes could be "excised without disruption to the storyworld proper."[16] In fact, the atypical placement of the rebozo footnote, almost one hundred pages into the novel, should immediately signal the need to consider its function in the novel differently. The immediate context of the footnote is crucial to understanding why it would appear at this stage of the novel: Lala has begun to narrate Soledad's history, including the long-established tradition of rebozo weaving, passed down from mother to daughter. Lala relays this inherited tradition through Soledad's mother, Guillermina, who learns how to weave from her own mother. Here, the rebozo's metaphoric capacities for storytelling are established, as seen through Guillermina's mother's chastisement of her daughter: "*¡Puro cuento!* What a *mitotera* you are, Guillermina! You know I did that myself. You like weaving stories just to make trouble."[17] The fact that the exclamation *puro cuento*, or pure story, serves as the novel's subtitle, adds another level of significance to this utterance.

Moreover, the footnote's appearance in this vignette emphasizes information that is both known and unknown by respective parties, including Soledad, Lala, and the reader. Soledad does not have access to this tradition, or the skills to weave in the same manner, because Guillermina died before teaching Soledad. Lala is doubly removed, and the reader even further distanced, from this tradition. As a result, the footnote directly announces what Lala has access to and what she doesn't know at the precise moment she undertakes the task of telling Soledad's history. This footnote performs the act of textual weaving during Lala's own "puro cuento" weaving, thereby reinforcing the construct of the novel overall: Cisneros's crafting of a plot about a young girl who tells a story based on the stories told to her by others, all of which have been influenced by personal and historical biases that are interrogated and destabilized by Lala and frequently supported by Cisneros's own outside historical research. In turn, readers are required to sift through these multiple layers of story and meaning and negotiate them all simultaneously in order to see the various threads as part of a cumulative whole.

McCracken refers to *Caramelo*'s rebozo as the "reconfigured central motif" and a "metaphor of narrative, family history, and ethnic identity."[18] McCracken is not the only scholar to center the rebozo as a crucial cultural object in and for the novel; however, her contextualization of its visual symbology, the way it functions as part of the cultural discourse and also for racialized signification, provides an analogue for my analysis of Cisneros's performative formal and stylistic technique. McCracken's use of the phrase "performative ethnicity," as derived from her analysis of Cisneros's fashion and aesthetic adornments, adds to Cisneros's racialized body to signal the way in which "visual displays of ethnicity are a part of a larger constellation of semiotic performance." By contending that these visual displays can "function as second-degree signifiers of ethnicity," McCracken codes the rebozo and the racialized body as visually imagistic and performative texts.[19] For *Caramelo*, the visual—in this case the formal and stylistic accoutrement that enables the text to perform—provides a mode of storytelling reflective of Lala's stories. Further, *Caramelo*'s performativity is also noted by Tereza M. Szeghi, who considers the "disruption and revising of narrative" by Lala and Soledad as "*performing* the view of story the Reyeses have articulated and bequeathed for generations."[20] Such visual performativity of storyness relies on the manner in which the text codes its narrative processes. While Soledad and Lala's voices and perspectives are distinguished by font, they operate within and across a generational continuum of familial similitude and distinction. These moments of narrative insistence, contestation, or consolidation construct stories as tactile and living entities: they are embodied texts that operate as an extension of the storyteller.

Cisneros's footnotes are implemented as a technique in order to instantiate exactly how much mediation Lala and the reader must undertake in their consideration of inherited narratives. My consideration of the significance of Cisneros's footnote structure is reinforced by Adriana Estill's assessment of *Caramelo*'s Maxwell Street as a "fictional and extra-fictional" space that effectively mimics the "marginal nature" of the gentrified location, enabled by Cisneros's utilization of a "footnote within a footnote" that renders the information "twice removed from the primary story."[21] Notably, Cisneros's footnotes are denoted by asterisks rather than the contemporary conventions of Arabic or Roman numerals, and occur after a word instead of at the end of the sentence. Since these footnotes aren't sequentially arranged, readers must labor to relocate themselves in the sentence so as to reestablish the necessary context and continue reading.[22] As such, Cisneros's footnotes do not operate as loose threads or tangents; rather, they compel readers to participate, to trace the threads, in the narrative process, which in turn creates a literary form that aligns literary content and narrative technique with textile and weaving mechanics. By making the woven narrative threads more difficult to discern—readers can't see the pattern or where the addition meets the primary text unless every word in the vignette is scrutinized again—Cisneros demands that each narrative thread be considered attentively. The "messiness" of Lala's story content is reflected in the narrative itself, something Estill describes as derived from "odds and ends found here and there."[23] In this way, we see the narrative structure of Lala's story reflect its conditionality: it performs Lala's status as a purveyor of multiple stories and perspectives. Cisneros thus utilizes a literary technique to reinforce Lala's positionality as a young Chicana who moves back and forth between Chicago and Mexico in the present, but who likewise must traverse temporal gaps and generational divides within her family in order to capture properly the various personal perspectives and national histories that inform the stories they tell.

RECUPERATIVE REMEDIATIONS: THE MATERIAL INCORPORATION OF FAMILIAL SHAME

While Cisneros deploys the rebozo as a means to represent and contextualize storytelling, specifically inherited familial stories, she uses performative metaphors to disrupt the way in which those familial stories trap Lala within restrictive or shameful narratives of racialized gender. In order to showcase how metaphoric performativity allows Cisneros to amplify the impact and effect of storytelling for Lala, I dwell here on the rebozo footnote. The performative metaphor enacts rebozo weaving in order to reveal the multiple layers of embedded stories and racial systems Lala must mine, including Mexico's and the Reyes family's relationship with and to Indigeneity, as constructed and regulated historically:

> The *rebozo* was born in Mexico, but like all mestizos, it came from everywhere. It evolved from the cloths Indian women used to carry their babies, borrowed its knotted fringe from Spanish shawls, and was influenced by the silk embroideries from the imperial court of China exported to Manila, then Acapulco, via the Spanish galleons. During the colonial period, mestizo women were prohibited by statutes dictated by the Spanish Crown to dress like Indians, and since they had no means to buy clothing like the Spaniards', they began to weave cloth on the indigenous looms creating a long and narrow shawl that slowly was shaped by foreign influences. The quintessential Mexican *rebozo*

is the *rebozo de bolita*, whose spotted design imitates a snakeskin, an animal venerated by the Indians in pre-Columbian times.[24]

The rebozo, in this context, possesses numerous complicated racial and ethnic imbrications that are internalized by the nation and the Reyes family. The colonial origin story of the rebozo as an artifact produced by and from Indigenous looms, artistic heritage, and state disavowal circumscribes the rebozo as simultaneously coded by Indigenous reliance and denial. With that consideration, the inheritance of rebozo weaving, both as a system of knowledge and as a cultural practice, is analogous to intergenerational stories in *Caramelo*. Since Soledad is never taught rebozo weaving from her own mother, she learns to disavow Indigeneity from a replacement mother figure, her future mother-in-law, Regina Reyes.

Regina is initially described by Lala as "a woman dark and feral, with eyes that seemed to burn," someone "dark as a cat" but who "held herself like a queen," and someone who possessed "the same face you see in the Mayan glyphs," a series of descriptions that celebrate her Indigenous features.[25] Regina feels "obligated" to take in Soledad because she is family, but Lala underscores the distinction between these two women and their positionalities within the Reyes family: "It must be remembered that Soledad was a Reyes too, although of that backward, Indian variety that reminded Regina too much of her own humble roots.*"[26] The word *roots* is followed by an asterisk, which leads to a footnote a few pages later: "*Because a life contains a multitude of stories and not a single strand explains precisely the who of who one is, we have to examine the complicated loops that allowed Regina to become la Señora Reyes."[27] The remainder of the two-page footnote emphasizes a familial history of internalized racism and tactical social maneuvering that enabled the Reyes family to deny Indigeneity: "she had only risen in social standing by riding on the back of her husband, the Spaniard."[28] The weaving of these narrative strands, the "complicated loops," highlights the active, ongoing construct of Indigenous disavowal in the Reyes family, as modeled by and through Regina.[29]

As Soledad's replacement mother figure, Regina imparts these lessons to her daughter-in-law; in turn, Soledad has learned to associate Indigeneity with shame, according to Heather Alumbaugh: "Regina essentially transfers her embarrassment regarding her own background onto Soledad as a means to distance herself from it and, in the process, she teaches Soledad to be ashamed of her own ethnic, racial, and class identity."[30] Soledad, consequently, projects her own shame onto Zoila, her own daughter-in-law, by weaponizing anti-Indigeneity. She seeks to shame Zoila publicly during an argument, not only by accusing her of not speaking "proper Spanish" and of being "dark as a slave," but by telling Zoila that her husband, Inocencio, fathered a child before Zoila and Inocencio were married.[31] This shame is doubly imbued because that daughter, Candelaria, the dark-skinned offspring of another Indigenous woman, has been working for the Reyes family. Soledad's tactics are an attempt to deny her own connection with Indigeneity and dislodge it—as well as her dark-skinned daughter-in-law and out-of-wedlock granddaughter—from inclusion in the Reyes family. Paul Wickelson argues that Candelaria functions as the "rejected Indian sister," a spectral "residue" of racialized trauma within the "continuing logic of patriarchy and colonial power."[32] More broadly, Candelaria's rejection is the Reyes family's disavowal of Indigeneity writ large, and, by extension, Indigenous disavowal is the shameful familial story Lala inherits, one "caught in the uncanny repetition of poverty, patriarchy, and national exclusion."[33] These repetitions are, in effect, generational "loops" in the Reyes family's woven story that Lala must unravel and reweave in order to recover and reincorporate Indigenous women into the Reyes family without shame. By showcasing the repetition in weaving, these historical loops that get passed down generationally, Cisneros represents Lala's story as a recuperative remediation of the Reyes family's tradition of rebozo weaving. Lala mines the source of Soledad's racial and gendered trauma in order to help heal the family wounds that have marginalized Zoila, omitted Candelaria, and disavowed Indigeneity in the Reyes familial line.

The parallels between family and nation regarding Indigenous erasure are established through Lala's chastisement of her grandmother, after Soledad "forgot" to narrate how her "arrival to the Reyes household" coincided with the "centennial of Mexican independence [and] 'the era of order and progress,'" wherein the government constructed Mexico as "'civilized,'" a descriptor Lala signals as a euphemism for "European."[34] She confronts Soledad for leaving out crucial historical details that implicate the Reyes family home as a valuable site of colonial acquisition, a former "Aztec temple" that was converted to a monastery by conquistadores responsible for leading the Santa Inquisición.[35] Lala reprimands Soledad about these omitted details and seeks to recover and reinstantiate willfully removed Indigeneity:

> Grandmother, you always want to tell stories and then when you should tell them, you don't tell. What about the 16th of September, the day of the Centennial celebrations? . . . Indians and beggars were routed from the downtown streets where you lived so as not to spoil the view . . . while the little girls of the well-to-do were recruited to toss rose petals in the Centennial parade before a phalanx of Indians dressed as "Indians."[36]

Lala's excavation of this history identifies a performative ethnic cleansing, wherein the image of the "Indian" is highlighted at the expense of actual Indigenous people living in Mexico. Cisneros's intervention underscores the importance of a narrative reconstruction that takes account of erasure. Indigeneity cannot be fully reincorporated without including the history of disavowal, both personally and nationally. In this way, Lala's reconfigured rebozo is not simply a composite that weaves together the "Reyes family history with national and transnational histories," but a recuperative text(ile), a textual body capable of reinstantiating Indigenous disavowal.[37] She inherits a cultural product that, in its current form, cannot be continued or completed: "When Guillermina departed from this world ... she left behind an unfinished rebozo, the design so complex no other woman was able to finish it without undoing the threads and starting over."[38] Lala's stories and the footnotes are, in effect, recuperative loops in the narrative. She keeps Soledad's design, in all its complexity, in place, supplying the sutures necessary to complete the project, without unraveling the integrity or substances of what had been created before. Lala seeks to recover the lost multigenerational, matrilineal legacy of rebozo weaving by learning from her mother's and Soledad's stories; she likewise understands that she must at once disrupt this legacy of shame and reincorporate what has been disavowed: "Maybe it's my job to separate the strands and knot the words together for everyone who can't say them, and make it all right in the end."[39] Lala becomes the nexus of narrative connections and Indigenous recovery. She effectively weaves her mother and Candelaria into the fabric of the rebozo, thereby recording shame and disavowal as fundamental components of these intertwined national and family histories, all of which have informed her present understanding of her racialized and gendered identity.

INTERWOVEN COCHINADAS: THE INCORPORATION OF CHICANA EMBODIMENT IN STORYTELLING

Performative metaphor enables Cisneros to instantiate familial shame in both a physical and formal way. The rebozo, as a cultural object and a textuality that actively replicates its form, functions accordingly to reveal the processes that undergird the Reyes family's narrative construction and Lala's reconstruction. Lala's stories—specifically, the revisitation of her family's past and present stories and her direct contestations—allow her to reincorporate inaccurate or absent details central to the narratives she inherits. As such, the recovery of Lala's erased sister, Candelaria, becomes a crucial intervention on multiple levels: a direct indictment of discursive power, be it cultural or historical; an interrogation of mediums that perpetuate and disseminate racialized and gendered cultural norms; the ongoing repercussions of silenced or absented voices and perspectives; and, ultimately, the need for responsive personal, interpersonal, and familial healing through recuperative stories.

Toward the end of the novel, Lala's father attempts to secure the familial function of the rebozo as an object of disavowal and shame when he attempts to control Lala and prevent her from sharing family stories that may bring further shame:

> —But Lala, Father whispers in my ear, —these things I've told you tonight, my heaven, I tell them only to you, Father says, adjusting the *caramelo rebozo* on my shoulders properly. —Only you have heard these stories, daughter, understand? *Sólo tú*. Be dignified, Lala. *Digna*. Don't be talking such things like the barbarians, *mi vida*. To mention them makes our family look like *sinvergüenzas*, understand? You don't want people to think we're shameless, do you? Promise your papa you won't talk these things, Lalita. Ever. Promise.[40]

Her father gently cajoles her silence while "adjusting" the rebozo so that it "properly" encases Lala's shoulders, thereby reinforcing and compounding the message of propriety as a cover for shame. Importantly, the caramelo rebozo not only wraps Lala within this family tradition, it also implicates her body as shrouded by this inherited history of shame and disavowal. While Lala initially promises her father that she will not reveal these stories, her direct incorporation of her father's pleas about her responsibility to the family further heightens the stakes of her story. In doing so, Lala situates her storytelling as an outright refusal to cooperate with a tradition of silent shame and indicts her family, including her father, whom she loves more than anyone, for encouraging her to participate in its continuation. More than that, Lala has imbued Candelaria—and Indigeneity more broadly—with the same reverence the rebozo holds within the family, a reverence that allows them to valorize the status of the artifact over its *and their* Indigenous history. Thus, it is important that the first mention of caramelo in the novel is aligned with Candelaria—or, more specifically, Candelaria's skin color—rather than the rebozo:

> The girl Candelaria has skin bright as a copper *veinte centavos* coin after you've sucked it. Not transparent as an ear like Aunty Light-Skin's. Not shark-belly pale like Father and Grandmother. Not the red river-clay color of Mother and her family. Not the coffee-with-too-much-milk color like me, nor the fried-*tortilla* color of the washerwoman Amparo, her mother. Not like anybody. Smooth as peanut butter, deep as burnt-milk candy.[41]

Almost instinctively, in tracing the varied skin colors in her family, Lala incorporates Candelaria into the family tree, even before they are revealed to be siblings. Her rumination subtly outlines the colorist hierarchies indebted to a racialized colonial framework, further reinforced by Cisneros's descriptions, which intertwine the flesh of bodies with money, animals, land, agribusiness food products, and delectable sweets, thereby noting their range of commodifiable worth culturally and historically. Lala's comparisons delineate a generational and racialized divide that reveals the manner in which the members of the Reyes family have leveraged their lightness and distanced themselves from any kind of Indigenous association.

Lala, however, views Candelaria in a way only a child unlearned in social expectations can: possessing the same status and allure as candy. Candelaria forces Lala to unsettle her understanding of beauty: "Until I meet Candelaria I think beautiful is Aunty Light-Skin, or the dolls with lavender hair I get at Christmas, or the women on the beauty contests we watch on television."[42] In this moment, Lala illustrates her capacity to conceive beyond both cultural standards and familial expectations. Notably, a few pages later, Candelaria's beauty becomes aligned with the more revered, conventional beauty of the caramelo rebozo, when it is described exactly like Candelaria's skin: "And in that instant I can't think of anything I want more than this cloth the golden color of burnt-milk candy."[43] Lala's desire to "have" the rebozo is denied by the grandfather, and her first attempt at physical contact with it is interrupted by Soledad, whose "shriek" of Lala's name from the courtyard causes Lala to "jump back as if the *rebozo* is made of fire."[44] While Soledad interrupts not because Lala is about to touch her beloved rebozo but because she wants Lala to sing for her and the others who congregate in the courtyard, this scene is paired with a refrain that recurs throughout the novel: "the body always remembers."[45] This response, provided by Soledad when Lala claims she doesn't remember the song Soledad wants her to perform, not only connects the body to memory, but suggests that the forgotten is always recoverable. Moreover, given Soledad's relationship to the rebozo—a *recuerdo*, as Lala's grandfather calls it, both a memory and a memento at once—memory becomes an embodied, tactile symbol of love lost and withheld, as seen in young Soledad's transference of grief over her losing both her father and mother to the rebozo itself: "She would never know what it was like to have a father hold her again. . . . No one would touch her again with a mother's love. No soft hair across her cheek, only the soft fringe of the unfinished shawl, and now Soledad's fingers took to combing this, plaiting, unplaiting, plaiting, over and over."[46] Candelaria's body, as aligned with the rebozo and memory, becomes the willfully forgotten, but she is also someone wholly necessary for the completion of the Reyes family caramelo rebozo, a task Lala is only able to finish fully after Soledad's death.

At its core, Lala's recovery of Candelaria is a loving act, one in which she willfully labors to reinstate her intentionally absented sister into a family structure and narrative textile that denied her. Cisneros reinforces Lala's effort as such via the construct of her novel, the ending of which asks readers to contest the very ending of stories themselves. *Caramelo* has an opening disclaimer, three distinct parts (labeled accordingly), and a coda that appears after the "Fin" and that suggests the novel has concluded. This coda, "Pilón," what the novel refers to as "something extra thrown in," is, in fact, a rejoinder to what appears to be the conclusion: Lala's promise to her father not to share their stories.[47] Notably, "Pilon" and the anchoring memory of the family portrait that begins part 1 are the only unnumbered chapters in *Caramelo*, and they are, essentially, interlocking representations of both family memory and Lala's role in and with the story: the "incomplete" family portrait without Lala that frames the novel and the emotional and sensory perspective Lala adds to the portrait with "Pilon."[48] This structure, the final act of performativity in the novel, compels readers to revisit the family portrait with a clearer understanding of the tensions between and within representative discourses, in particular the gaps and fissures that frequently separate storytelling forms and delineate rigid categories that demand strict adherence. Cisneros makes readers acutely aware of a continuum of past, present, and future, one that requires renegotiation and reconstitution without erasure to make room for the stories and bodies of storytellers and the people about whom stories are told.

Reading the novel's opening scene and "Pilon" together enables readers to see Lala's additions to the family portrait with acute clarity. In "Pilon," Lala revisits the familial rupture that occurs with Zoila's public shaming; however, in her version, Lala recodes the aftermath of Candelaria's parentage reveal and presents an image of familial reconciliation alongside the reassociation of caramelo:

> The taste of a *caramelo* called Glorias on my tongue. At la Caleta beach, a girl with skin like *cajeta*, like goat-milk candy. The *caramelo* color of your skin after rising out of the Acapulco foam, salt water running down your hair and stinging the eyes, the raw ocean smell, and the ocean running out of your mouth and nose. My mother watering her dahlias with a hose and running a stream of water over her feet as well, Indian feet, thick and square, *como de barro*, like the red clay of Mexican pottery.[49]

The second-person address is resonant and implicative: the "your" belongs at once to all the women in her family, Lala herself, and the reader. Caramelo, under Lala's gaze and with Lala's words, becomes a Mexicanness that can be both beautiful *and* Indigenous. Lala reconstructs the "dirt," all the cochinadas Soledad never wanted revealed, including the variegated colors of disavowed Indigeneity—from Candelaria's candied skin to her mother's red-clayed feet—as part and parcel of her own Indigenous lineage. This scene simultaneously functions as a recollection of Lala watching Candelaria at the beach, a memory from before her family's shame turned Candelaria's body into something to reject, and a reclamation of the past and Lala's reconstituted relationship to her own body as racialized and gendered. By concluding the novel in this manner, Cisneros replaces shame and disavowal with acceptance and joy.

Through Lala's recovery and reincorporation of previous sites and subjects, Cisneros provides a final reminder of the power of storyness and storytelling, leaving readers acutely aware of the precarity of racialized gendered stories, as well as of the absenting of those who would tell their stories without shame or reproach. Performative metaphor, in this way, asks us to question the narratives we inherit and to interrogate our obligation to them. It models a way to tell stories about racialized gender identity, and the respective positionalitie and embodiments within, that are indebted to familial, cultural, and historical narratives that shape and inform subjectivities. Such influences cannot possibly be separated because they are so intimately intertwined in both bodies and stories. *Caramelo* showcases the complicated processes involved in telling such stories and enables readers to see and understand that, while the narratives and forms Lala inherits have the potential to inflict and perpetuate trauma, particularly in the way they encode racialized and gendered norms for young Chicanas, they likewise are the narratives we must return to in order to heal and self-create.

NOTES

My infinite gratitude to the three fierce and fabulous women at the heart of this edited collection: Sandra Cisneros, for her beautiful, honest texts that replenish my spirit; Sonia Saldívar-Hull, for her steadfast belief in me; and Geneva M. Gano, for her unceasing generosity and support.

1. While the *Chicana/o/x* designation is clunky, I use it to signal the need for inclusivity in the field of literary and cultural studies more broadly. However, since my analysis centers a cisgender adolescent girl written by an author who self-identifies as Chicana, I have elected to use *Chicana* in reference to identity and identification rather than maintain the more inclusive terminology throughout. Additionally, I have elected not to italicize Spanish words in order to normalize their usage throughout my analysis, though I have maintained the authors' original italicization in all direct quotations.

2. Sandra Cisneros, *Caramelo or Puro Cuento* (New York: Vintage Books, 2002), 172.

3. As with my previous usage of *Chicana/o/x*, I acknowledge the existing discursive tensions around inclusive terminology through the designation *Latina/o/x/e* in order to present the continuing evolution of these discussions. My use differs from González's *Latino/a*.

4. Christopher González, *Permissible Narratives: The Promise of Latino/a Literature* (Columbus: Ohio State University Press, 2017), 2.

5. González, *Permissible Narratives*, 4, 17.

6. N. Katherine Hayles, *Writing Machines* (Cambridge, MA: MIT Press, 2002), 22.

7. Sue J. Kim, "Decolonizing Narrative Theory," *Journal of Narrative Theory* 42, no. 3 (Fall 2012): 236.

8. James J. Donahue, introduction to *Narrative, Race, and Ethnicity in the United States*, ed. James J. Donahue, Jennifer Ann Ho, and Shaun Morgan (Columbus: Ohio State University Press, 2017), 3.

9. Espen J. Aarseth, *Cybertext: Perspectives on Ergodic Literature* (Baltimore: Johns Hopkins University Press, 1997), 1.

10. Cisneros, *Caramelo*, 122.

11. Cisneros, *Caramelo*, 120–121.

12. Cisneros, *Caramelo*, 122.

13. González, *Permissible Narratives*, 161.

14. Ellen McCracken, "The Postmodern Continuum of Canon and Kitsch: Narrative and Semiotic Strategies of Chicana High Culture and Chica Lit," in *Analyzing World Fiction: New Horizons in Narrative Theory*, ed. Frederick Luis Aldama (Austin: University of Texas Press, 2011), 177, 178.

15. Ilan Stavans, "Familia Faces: Genealogy Rules Latino Literature Tyrannically," *Nation*, February 10, 2003.

16. González, *Permissible Narratives*, 161.

17. Cisneros, *Caramelo*, 93.

18. McCracken, "The Postmodern Continuum," 167–168.

19. McCracken, "The Postmodern Continuum," 167.

20. Tereza M. Szeghi, "Weaving Transnational Cultural Identity through Travel and Diaspora in Sandra Cisneros's *Caramelo*," *MELUS* 39, no. 4 (Winter 2014): 179 (emphasis added).

21. Adriana Estill, "Mexican Chicago in Sandra Cisneros's *Caramelo*: Gendered Geographies," *MELUS* 41, no. 2 (Summer 2016): 113.

22. For a more detailed overview and analysis of Cisneros's "paratextual network" in the footnote structure, see Ellen McCracken, *Paratexts and Performance in the Novels of Junot Díaz and Sandra Cisneros* (New York: Palgrave Macmillan, 2016), 117. McCracken offers inexhaustible coverage and intricate detailing of Cisneros's footnotes as an apparatus, including a breakdown of the categories and functions within. While she notes that these footnotes "carry on the performative strategies of the main text" and how "difficult [it is] to locate and return to the place of departure in the text after engaging with the notes," she doesn't account for the intentionality of this technique as a kind of performativity in and of itself, one that compels the reader to participate in the processes of dislocation and relocation (118).

23. Estill, "Mexican Chicago in Sandra Cisneros's *Caramelo*," 110.

24. Cisneros, *Caramelo*, 96.

25. Cisneros, *Caramelo*, 112–113.

26. Cisneros, *Caramelo*, 113.
27. Cisneros, *Caramelo*, 115.
28. Cisneros, *Caramelo*, 116.
29. Szeghi, "Weaving Transnational Cultural Identity," 173.
30. Heather Alumbaugh, "Narrative Coyotes: Migration and Narrative Voice in Sandra Cisneros's *Caramelo*," *MELUS* 35, no. 1 (Spring 2010): 67.
31. Cisneros, *Caramelo*, 85.
32. Paul Wickelson, "Shaking Awake the Memory: The Gothic Quest for Place in Sandra Cisneros's *Caramelo*," *Western American Literature* 48, no. 1–2 (Spring–Summer 2013): 110.
33. Wickelson, "Shaking Awake the Memory," 94.
34. Cisneros, *Caramelo*, 124.
35. Cisneros, *Caramelo*, 111.
36. Cisneros, *Caramelo*, 110–111.
37. Nassim Balestrini, "Transnational and Transethnic Textures, or 'Intricate Interdependencies' in Sandra Cisneros's *Caramelo*," *Amerikastudien/American Studies* 57, no. 1 (2012): 75.
38. Cisneros, *Caramelo*, 94.
39. Cisneros, *Caramelo*, 428.
40. Cisneros, *Caramelo*, 429–430.
41. Cisneros, *Caramelo*, 34.
42. Cisneros, *Caramelo*, 34.
43. Cisneros, *Caramelo*, 58.
44. Cisneros, *Caramelo*, 58.
45. Cisneros, *Caramelo*, 59.
46. Cisneros, *Caramelo*, 95.
47. Cisneros, *Caramelo*, 433.
48. Cisneros, *Caramelo*, 4.
49. Cisneros, *Caramelo*, 434.

CHAPTER 5

MAPPING THE DECOLONIAL
Community Cartography in Sandra Cisneros's *Woman Hollering Creek*

Teresa Hernández

Readers of Sandra Cisneros's work are familiar with the fluidity and dynamism of the literary geographies she crafts from memory and *puro cuento*.[1] Cisneros seamlessly transports readers within and across the United States and Mexico, while also often rupturing those national boundaries, making her writing distinctly diasporic among American letters. Cisneros's work has become, consequently, essential to our understanding of Latinx and Chicanx feminisms through her contributions to the (re)imagining of space in relation to questions of gender, class, language, and community. Her work also complicates these categories with characters that defy and disorient, but also guide and orient, our understanding of intimate community relationships. This essay brings us to view her various forms of social mappings as new beginnings for rereading her work. In this way, Cisneros expands our understanding of the geospatial—layering of streets, space, and narrative—by creating a new social orientation that makes material a critical relationship between community and geography.

While we have previously categorized our examinations of her work under various capacious categories like Latinx literary studies, border feminisms, and border studies, we have also continually looked at her work through a US-centric lens, which brings us to the limits of such nationalistic categories. I consider here the possibilities of opening her body of work, more specifically her celebrated 1991 volume *Woman Hollering Creek and Other Stories*, to a new spatialized imaginary that does not rearticulate a language of conquest, territorialization, or belonging. While Cisneros's texts place, locate, and position both characters and readers in a specific geographic, they also displace, dislocate, and unsettle these precise geographies. I utilize terms such as *geographic*, *literary geography*, and *cultural geographies* to further complicate how nationalism, citizenship, subjectivity, and belonging are layered within the making of territory even in literary contexts. We may liken Cisneros's use of space to the decolonial imaginary, where we can begin to deconstruct a patriarchal nationalist trapping, as Emma Pérez states in her landmark text *The Decolonial Imaginary*.[2] I draw from Pérez's decolonial imaginary to further consider how Cisneros's social geographies deconstruct the limits of space, of geography, of memory, and of time. Her work illuminates the communal possibilities that materialize from those very limits by giving us what I call a community cartography. In this culturally geographic reading practice, social orientations reveal the layered and dialogic communities and spaces within border feminist narratives. Furthermore, Cisneros's community cartography illustrates that the decolonial is neither inside nor outside of any temporality or geography, but already at work within the diasporic narratives across both Mexico and the United States.

Unlike authors who might utilize literary geography merely to station a story in a tangible place, Cisneros's texts use literary geography to make story out of place. As such, her *cuentos* (stories) begin in mappable locations and then move to reorient the reader's focus onto the social networks and relationships at work in that location. Spatial theorist Doreen Massey states that we must "recognize space as always under construction."[3] That is, we must first recognize how space is always active and reactive, not passive or dormant: how it is always in a constant negotiation with multiple emergent subject formations through a response, conversation, and negotiation with the space in which these narratives take place. As such, Cisneros's literary geographies materialize a decolonial, transnational, and social politic of space that conceives of space as communal and interdependent. Her collection *Woman Hollering Creek* utilizes space to reflect that constellated relationship between the borderlands and the border heroines emerging from and through their positioning in distinct geographics.

In this essay, I focus on *Woman Hollering Creek* to access the making of a community cartography. In particular, I examine the short stories "Tepeyac" and "Woman Hollering Creek" to better understand how Cisneros's writing opposes a conception of space and geography as things to possess or rule. Cisneros's narrators and mappings show us the limits and thresholds of nationalisms and the risks they pose to the decolonial. Furthermore, Cisneros's work illustrates a shared responsibility between numerous colliding communities across Mexico and the United States. As Pérez writes of the "diasporic configuration" in spaces like Texas, where "populations dispersed through a land named, renamed, bordered, measured, mapped, and fenced," Cisneros's *cuentos* show us that to practice the decolonial we must first renegotiate what it means to enter border narratives as both colonized and settler.[4]

I use despatialization here as a theoretical and geopolitical reading practice to both articulate decoloniality within Cisneros's collection and critique the (im)material definitions of decoloniality. As Eve Tuck and K. Wayne Yang note, decolonization is not a metaphor.[5] Critical Indigenous studies scholars call on non-Indigenous scholars and readers to not forget that decoloniality is ultimately a demand for land repatriation and acknowledgment of their sovereignty. This essay considers how Cisneros's *cuentos* facilitate novel discourse between geography and community, made possible through metaphors, invention, and defamiliarization. As I have argued elsewhere, Cisneros utilizes language to disorient space and demarcate time within her texts.[6] Such disorientation is not meant to posit herself or her texts as being outside of Western time or space. In fact, claims to that effect only recenter and reify Western thought, time, and geography as the origin to which communities of color must always defer when making meaning of our lives, communities, and histories. When we consider Cisneros's *cuentos* as neither synchronous nor asynchronous, neither Western nor Third World, her work also begins to engage other modalities of being, expression, and meaning that cannot be articulated through a language of territorialization.

By addressing how Cisneros's narrators orient the relationship between themselves and their communities, against and through the geographic spaces they occupy, we can also derive what space is producing and how it is being produced for her narrators. As Gayatri Spivak reminds us, reading is always an "active transaction between past and future."[7] Cisneros's texts similarly engage readers to consider space through multiple lenses that ask us to grapple both with what we know and with what we cannot know about a community. In this way, Cisneros's geographies show us that the decolonial must remain responsible and accountable to multiple subject formations that exist across any given geography. As such, I begin with "Tepeyac" as it most explicitly opens with what we may call, perhaps mistakenly, the laying down of a setting. I say "mistakenly" here to highlight how settings and locales remain fluidly ambiguous throughout Cisneros's body of work. Unlike the neat urban mapping Cisneros does of inner-city Chicago via Mango Street in *The House on Mango Street* or of San Antonio in *Have You Seen Marie?*, "Tepeyac" cannot be easily spatialized or territorialized. When the narrator names the city of Tepeyac, she also brings into focus the dense dialogic, social, and cultural spatializations of the geographic site where Our Lady of Guadalupe first appeared to Juan Diego, in 1531.

As Raúl Homero Villa argues in *Barrio-Logos*, the barrio as a social space primarily takes shape through "the experience of being displaced in multiple ways from a perceived homeland . . . in this country."[8] Villa adds that Chicanidad has always contended with questions of belonging as they relate to space in the United States. However, Cisneros's geographies and spatializations in *Woman Hollering Creek* are not so easily confinable to or delineated by the United States as a nation-state. Rather, her narrators always seem to be speaking at a distance from any single nation or nationalism. In "Tepeyac," we might assume that the narrator grew up in the eponymous locale because of her intimate orientation to certain places on the plaza, but there is also a defamiliarization at work as she later feels almost like a foreigner herself— now only able to conjure up Tepeyac through a distant, but vivid, memory. In moving away from spatializing Tepeyac as nation or state, we move toward a new vantage point where Tepeyac can be read as a site of community, which, as Villa argues of the city, can be a "meeting ground" and not simply a terrain.[9]

"Tepeyac," moreover, does not utilize one primary geopoint, a mappable geographic location, to spatialize the story. While we may be initially drawn to consider La Basílica de Nuestra Señora as the primary geopoint, the narrator does not begin with the church, but instead moves our gaze upward, looking first at the "ink of Japanese blue" and those "first thin stars" in Tepeyac's sky.[10] For some readers of "Tepeyac," this initial illustration and rich description of the sky, its colors, and its stars may conjure a direct image of La Virgen de Guadalupe's mantle.[11] In fact, the narrator relies on what Mary Pat Brady identifies as the reader's "local knowledge" and a cultural familiarity with these signs to convey the signification of the space as a dialogic discursive system within Mexico.[12] For readers familiar with Guadalupe's momentous role in Mexican and Mexican American cultural studies, that familiarity transforms Tepeyac from physical site within the text into one whose geography is inseparable from La Virgen's presence, history, genealogy, and signification. The descriptive narration in this opening sentence demands, as Brady states, a "fluency in several discursive systems."[13] The narrator utilizes these initial links of title, geopoint of Tepeyac, and figurative description of the sky to situate La Virgen de Guadalupe as a cultural, national, religious, spiritual, and political symbol, without even having to name her. As Cisneros's readers know, her narratives always make legible specific geographies, and "Tepeyac," in this sense, appears not unlike her other *cuentos*. The meaning of Tepeyac's geography asks readers to first begin to "know" the physical site of Tepeyac.

The reader must be able to "read" the literary and social map that Cisneros's narrator has begun to draw for us and recognize that the church also appears as more of a social and conceptual referent than a static geopoint in the narrative. Cisneros's story moves us outside of the familiar urban spaces of Mexico City by naming Tepeyac as a geopoint that can initiate both pre-

Columbian and post-Columbian discourse. As Octavio Paz writes of México-Tenochtitlán, Tepeyac as an imagined cultural geography is also a space where multiple historical, genealogical, and political traditions collide.[14] While Brady has already attended rigorously to the overlapping discursive systems of geography at work in "Tepeyac" through the signaling of Tepeyac, Tonantzín, Guadalupe, and the basilica, I wish to extend her reading of how (un)familiarity in this *cuento* points us to the limits of a literary geography and further illustrates a new despatialized and social imaginary. For unlike the decolonial imaginary of Tuck and Yang, still tethered to concepts of nationhood, sovereignty, and territoriality, Cisneros's narrator does not seek to reterritorialize or reoccupy Tepeyac as a pre-conquest/Indigenous space, or to affirm a Spanish or Catholic mapping as the only way to "read" Tepeyac as a site. Rather, "Tepeyac" offers us a community cartography that does not rely on material structures or colonial forms of mapping.

Cisneros's narrator asks us to shift our gaze beyond the colonial structures of the church to the repeated intonations of the word *above*. The opening lines, thus, shift readers away from a vertical, horizontal, linear, or even symmetrical view of the literary geography within the story and toward a multifaceted community spatialization:

> *above* the bell towers of La Basílica de Nuestra Señora, *above* the plaza photographers and their souvenir backdrops of La Virgen de Guadalupe, *above* the balloon vendors and their balloons wearing paper hats, *above* the red-canopied thrones of the shoeshine stands, *above* the wooden booths of the women frying lunch in vats of oil, *above* the *tlapalería* on the corner of Misterios and Cinco de Mayo . . .[15]

By asking us to gaze first not on the church but toward that green-blue sky that drapes itself over Tepeyac and its community, the narrator establishes a spatial politic that orients Tepeyac not around the church but around a social and cultural geography. Unlike Indigenous scholar Mishuana Goeman's *Mark My Words*, which articulates the act of literary "(re)mapping" as a way of "unsettling [an] imperial and colonial [geography]," Cisneros's text here does not wish to respond to these geographies by simply remapping or reterritorializing this space.[16] Instead, the narrative and narrator complicate the relationship between the numerous extant discursive systems by asking the reader to look above to the unmappable sky of Tepeyac while simultaneously calling us to look at the plaza, the church, and the exchanges at work in a single site. Thus, even as the narrator demands that we look above the church and above the plaza, the text also recognizes that looking above is already dependent on what is below, which further articulates Tepeyac as a dialogic space that is dependent on multiple interdependent material and immaterial spatial and social relationships. Thus, even as La Basílica has been largely understood as a sign within a specific sixteenth-century Catholic system that is then positioned within other discourses related to power, coloniality, and genocide, the text's shift away from merely remapping or reorienting Tepeyac shows the ontological distinction the text also facilitates between La Basílica and La Virgen de Guadalupe. Cisneros's narrator demands that we negotiate the history of colonial violence that predates the text while also asking us to mark spiritualism and religion as wholly different signs and systems being accessed within the narrative.

This dialogic and layered view of Tepeyac further illustrates how Cisneros's *cuentos* always narrate through multiplicity: no single perspective, narrative, history, or vantage point is privileged over another. This multiplicity is evidenced through the long, paratactic phrasing of the sentence, which runs from the first page into the top of the next page. The commas fuse and constellate multiple vantage points that both give us access to new ways of seeing Tepeyac and show us the ways in which complete knowledge of and access to this geopoint is not possible. This parataxis allows us to consider how space beyond and between the merchants, the plaza, the church, and the sky is all interconnected, in a single sentence and through a panoramic view of Tepeyac. The social exchange at work here is also multifaceted; we understand the competing ways in which Tepeyac becomes a single terrain on which culture, capital, religion, spirituality, and history must make space for one another.[17]

By reading Cisneros's *cuentos* as a community cartography, we can then read the tensions formed between often opposing systems such as religious institutions and communities, spirituality and religion, and materiality and immateriality, as well as the other fragmented social systems that are elided in a topical or strictly geographic reading of "Tepeyac." When Cisneros's narrator redirects our gaze to the multiple merchants on the plaza, the text's orientation rejects our impulse to hold the space to any fixed point. The narrative geography demands fluidity from the reader by shifting our focus away from a colonial reading of space as merely geopoints defined in relation to a nation-state. La Basílica remains a historically, culturally, and spiritually rich geopoint, but it does not take precedence over the social geography at work in Cisneros's *cuento*. Instead, the narrator illustrates Tepeyac's social geography by showing us the plaza in a state of fluidity and action:

> *when* the photographers have toted up their tripods and big box cameras, have rolled away the wooden ponies *I don't know where, when* the balloon men have sold all but the ugliest balloons and herded these last

few home, *when* the shoeshine men have grown tired of squatting on their little wooden boxes, and the women frying lunch have finished packing dishes, tablecloth, pots, in the big straw basket in which they came, *then* . . .[18]

Cisneros's narrator creates a tension between overlapping temporalities of "when" and "then," over the common space of the plaza. The social geography here presents a contradictory coupling of distance/intimacy and unfamiliarity/familiarity. Even as we may initially think that the narrator has an intimate and familiar connection to this community and space, there is also a clear admission of unfamiliarity and distance from the social networks that span the plaza.

"I don't know *where*," the narrator states, which further puts her in that borderland space of insider/outsider all too familiar to the Latinx and Chicanx reader. The narrator here seems to both belong and not belong, to be both familiar and foreign to the space, at the cusp of two intersecting "citizenships." At this brink of "then"—at this admission that she cannot access the totality of Tepeyac's social geography—is when the narrator feels she can begin to access and remember this geography as it once was for her. As the narrator navigates her spatialization of Tepeyac from territory to community geography, she similarly calls on readers to sit in the dislocation of "I don't know where." And yet the narrator has observed this geography and the movements and expert tasks of its social pillars—those that a tourist or visitor would consider as merely adjacent to this landmark and public sphere. The narrator orients setting through a community cartography that reveals space as its own dynamic, fluid, and layered social discourse in this literary geography.

Brady identifies the literary mapping of "Tepeyac" as "loiterature," or "loiterly writing," which brings into focus how the plaza is illustrated through a communal, interactive, and intimate spatialization.[19] As she notes, Cisneros's geographies do not merely work as locations or settings, but rather always transform space through literary techniques like historical allusions and collaborative storytelling. Notably, for the first part of this *cuento*, the narrator does not privilege herself or her story. Instead, the narrator gives legibility and intelligibility to other subjects, even though such designations of other subjects are already fragmented. We, as readers, are then placed at these thresholds of reading a fragmented Other: we can "see" the merchants, vendors, and women through the visual geography the narrator lays before us, but we are also unable to truly see, know, and define them in specific terms.

Time, too, is intimately linked to the ways in which space is rendered within "Tepeyac," which takes a type of geopoetical snapshot of the moment "when" and before everything changes through the narrator's social mapping.

Following the shift from a community cartography of the plaza, the rest of the narrative is orientated by some initially relational "I" statements: "*I* take Abuelito's hand . . . past the candy store where *I* buy my milk-and-raisin gelatins, past La Providencia tortillería where every afternoon Luz María and *I* are sent."[20] Again, Cisneros utilizes a community cartography to take us through the familiar space of Tepeyac as it relates to memory and community members. Alongside a mappable geographic location are the unmappable relationships between family, kin, and neighbors. In her work *Mapping Memory*, Kaitlin M. Murphy, too, suggests that maps are often "defined by time, because they enable viewers to perceive how events happen in succession."[21] However, Cisneros's works are not beholden to mapping either the nation-state or a single temporality. Instead, "Tepeyac" develops and expands our understanding of time by weaving together two temporalities, past and present.

Memory, too, shapes the community cartography at work in "Tepeyac" when the narrator writes of her relationship to this space. However, the *cuento* should not be read merely as a nostalgic rendering of the narrator's past: the narrator does not long for a return to Tepeyac as it once was. Rather, the narrator's textual mapping turns inward toward the community and family relationships that have been most affected by time, those that remain enmeshed between a material and immaterial rendering of Tepeyac:

> to the house on La Fortuna, number 12, that *has always* been our house. Green iron gates that arabesque and scroll like the initials of my name, familiar whine and clang, familiar lacework of ivy growing over and between . . . years later *when* the house on La Fortuna, number 12, is sold, *when* the tlapalería, corner of Misterios and Cinco de Mayo, changes owners, *when* the courtyard gate of arabesques and scrolls is taken off its hinges and replaced . . . years afterward when I return to the shop on the corner of Misterios and Cinco de Mayo . . . to the plaza photographers, the balloon vendors and shoeshine thrones, the women whose faces *I do not recognize* . . . to the house on La Fortuna . . . smaller and darker than *when* we lived there . . .[22]

Instead of remapping Tepeyac as she remembers it, the narrator sets forth a social geography that attends to an intimate and relational representation of space that cannot be located on any map outside of this narrative. Even when the narrator states that the house on La Fortuna had "always" been their house, we understand that "always" is attached to a single temporality of her past. New residents have moved in, and physical changes have taken place that have transformed the familiar space of "home" to something unfamiliar and distant. She can only now see it once again from the outside, as the house stands as a material representation of what remains central to Cisneros's spatial imaginary: community. The house, La Fortuna, and Tepeyac hold meaning only as they relate to the social geographies that she once knew: "the mad parrot voice of the Abuela . . . the Abuelito snoring," all leading up to "when Abuelito falls asleep one last time." It is then that the counting trails off and new faces are rendered unrecognizable and unfamiliar. And yet, the narrator is the only one that can remember "when everything else is forgotten."[23] Her memory and her recollection of Tepeyac emerge as sites through which she narrates her sacred, intimate, and layered relationship to space. She understands that in mapping her memory of Tepeyac as it once was, she can create a community cartography that centers those intimate relationships that give meaning to the spaces in the past, present, and future.

While my reading thus far has been limited to narrative spatialization within the *cuento* "Tepeyac," here I shift to the title story of her collection. "Woman Hollering Creek" has been broadly read through the lenses of border feminisms and queer studies, but here I consider how Cisneros utilizes a similar community cartography to dislocate both reader and narrator in the indeterminate "el otro lado" (the other side). A precise geography within this border narrative is withheld from the reader until much later in the *cuento*, which, like in my reading of "Tepeyac," further disrupts our narrative orientations away from land as terrain/territory or from nation-state belonging. All that is initially known to the reader are the "several miles of dirt road and several miles of paved, over one border and beyond to a town," that stand between Cleófilas in Texas and her father, Don Serafín, who remains in Mexico. The narrative quickly discloses that Cleófilas marries and crosses into the United States and this further strains her relationship to Don Serafín, who imagines his daughter looking "south" toward home with regret for leaving him behind.[24] The unpaved and paved road here presents a tension between the "premodern" state of Mexico and the "modernity" of this unnamed US town. As such, the naming of either town is initially inconsequential to the development of Cleófilas's narrative. As we come to understand from the rest of the *cuento*, Cleófilas eventually loses the early optimism that she placed on her new home and the region that once seemed so "far away and lovely."[25] The name of the US town, Seguin, is initially withheld from readers, which emphasizes that what matters most to Cleófilas in those few moments is the reality that she will no longer be in Monclova, Coahuila. Rather, what lies across the border is a spatialized promise of modernity, urbanity, and social fluidity in which her new American life can unfold. Such ideas, of course, are subject to their own class critiques; however, this should not distract us from the call to bear witness to a story of immigration that unfolds in and through a spatial displacement between Mexico and Texas.

In our consideration of how Cleófilas orients our reading of space back toward the social relationships in Seguin, the geographic emerges as another part of Cisneros's border feminist practice in *Woman Hollering Creek*. For Cleófilas, Seguin initially holds tremendous potential for her to access success through a figuring of America as a utopic geography. For her, this is materialized through the very naming of Seguin early in the narrative:

> *Seguín, Tejas.* A nice sterling ring to it. The tinkle of money. She would get to wear outfits like the women on the *tele*, like Lucía Mendez. And have a lovely house, and wouldn't Chela be jealous.
>
> And yes, they will drive all the way to Laredo to get her wedding dress. That's what they say.[26]

Even as Cleófilas longs for a social and class-based mobility and fluidity, she is faced with multiple exclusions that make this longing for the American dream inaccessible: she is a woman, an immigrant, and a Mexican. The Tejanas in "Woman Hollering Creek," too, are unable to access the promises of class mobility because of their racialized positioning as Mexican American women, but this is not something that is explained to Cleófilas, who has limited visibility as "another one of those brides from across the border."[27] Thus, the idyllic rendering of Seguin and the United States is quickly ruptured as Cleófilas learns the ways in which women are sexualized and violently treated as disposable subjects north of the border. She recalls the newspaper stories that narrate the murders of women "found on the side of the interstate. This one pushed from a moving car. This one's cadaver, this one unconscious, this one beaten blue. Her ex-husband, her husband, her lover, her father, her brother, her uncle, her friend, her co-worker. Always."[28] Any intimacy or familiarity with men is weighted with a risk to her body, her mental health, and her livelihood. Even in Seguin, the men at the icehouse and her own husband are direct threats to her safety, which further emphasizes an engendered border politic. That is, the immigrant border body, the engendered body, is always at risk of violence and erasure in the Americas.

Seguin, however, is not the primary geopoint of this *cuento*. Much like in "Tepeyac," we are called to rethink space and geography in Cisneros's text. Cleófilas is most drawn to Woman Hollering Creek, initially for its curious name of "La Gritona," which is spatialized geographically around its proximity to the small Texas town of Seguin. For Cleófilas, Seguin is spatialized around the creek, which draws her to it and its history. However, much like how she fails in her efforts to connect with the women in the town, she arrives at no clearer understanding of the creek's namesake:

Though no one could say whether the woman had hollered from anger or pain. The natives only knew the *arroyo* one crossed on the way back to San Antonio, and then once again on the way back, was called Woman Hollering, a name no one from these parts questioned, little less understood. *Pues, allá de los indios, quién sabe*—who knows, the townspeople shrugged, because it was of no concern to their lives how this trickle of water received its curious name.[29]

For the townspeople, Woman Hollering Creek holds no intrinsic or immediate value in their everyday lives. Instead, the creek functions primarily as setting and landscape for their social lives. This reveals the tensions at play within this Texas space by illustrating how violence and erasure are inherently attached to spaces within a racial and colonial US geographic context. For Cleófilas or the townspeople of Seguin to "know" where the name Woman Hollering Creek or La Gritona comes from, first there must be an admission of settler violence and Indigenous erasure. There must be acknowledgment of the Texas-Indian Wars, which show how as early as 1820 this Texas region became a contentious terrain for "resolving" disputes around land, culture, tradition, and language. Seguin, too, must be recognized as a dynamic discursive space for the competing sovereignties of Indigenous, Mexican, and Spanish peoples during the Comanche Wars, further illustrating how territorialization remains enmeshed in the townspeople's imagining of Tejas.[30]

The Texans and Tejanxs in "Woman Hollering Creek" distance themselves, at least momentarily, from the history of this geography and the unspoken history of colonial and settler violence under six distinct flags and numerous other territorial delineations that remain contested and unknowable within Texas's long settlement history. They neither know this history nor seem to want to contend with it, but rather suggest that it is *allá de los indios*—an Indigenous history outside and beyond their own inherited histories in Texas.[31] "Allá" connotes not just time but also space and geographic framework, which further limits their ability to understand Cleófilas's interest in the creek, its name, and its origins. In this way, Cisneros's community cartography asks us to renegotiate with a settler colonial history. As readers, we also become implicated in that history. We see the Tejanx characters, speaking from their inheritance as both colonized subject and settler subject. "Woman Hollering Creek" thus critically spatializes Seguin by narrating its dialogic and layered history between Mexican, Mexican American, and Indigenous communities, which situates a decolonial border feminist practice.

Certainly, "Woman Hollering Creek" is as much a border feminist narrative as it is an immigrant narrative. While Cleófilas is not necessarily in exile from Mexico, she is not solely a Mexican national. To identify her as Tejana would also be to further obfuscate her positioning as a recently immigrated Mexicana, an identity that problematizes the categories of citizenship and nationalism. Thus, even as we may want to consider her relationship to Seguin through a US spatial imaginary, we must also consider the ways in which Cleófilas remains outside of US social orders in this Texas narrative geography. While Brady notes that multiple contrapuntal spatial points map and orient the relationships between locations and individuals, Cleófilas is always outside of these social and nationalistic orders and border geographies.[32]

Notably, Cleófilas is made to feel like an outsider primarily by the Tejanas. For example, it is Trini, the laundromat attendant, who first tells Cleófilas that her customs and ways of being do not align with the conventions of this region, on this *otro lado* (other side):

> "What do you want to know for?" Trini the laundromat attendant asked in the same gruff Spanish she always used whenever she gave Cleófilas change or yelled at her for something. First for putting too much soap in the machines. Later, for sitting on a washer. And still later, after Juan Pedrito was born, for not understanding that in this country you cannot let your baby walk around with no diaper and his pee-pee hanging out, it wasn't nice, ¿entiendes? Pues.[33]

Cleófilas finds herself in a "new country" without the alliances and community that are essential to her self-preservation and safety. In an abusive relationship with Juan Pedro, and estranged and distanced from her father and brothers back home in Monclova, Cleófilas is also negotiating motherhood alone at the same time that she is navigating a new culture, community, and social system that do not legitimate her existence. Trini simply tells her that this is not how it is done "in this country"—do you understand? "In this country" delineates the ways in which Cleófilas stands outside of the orientations and formations of both Seguin and Texas, which further complicates her subjectivity as a Mexican immigrant.

Later, when Cleófilas does ask for help, Felice and Graciela, the ultrasound technician and her friend who resolve to help Cleófilas after she discloses her domestic violence situation to them, struggle to understand her cultural identity or personal narrative. In their exchange, they minimize Cleófilas's life story and render her only legible as "[another] one of those brides from across the border" who "doesn't even speak English."[34] Even as Felice and Graciela are responsible for getting Cleófilas, Juan Pedrito, and Cleófilas's unborn child to safety, they also initiate a type of mimicry of her situation. At the end of their phone call, Graciela likens the situation to "a regular soap opera" and says "qué vida" (what a life), which further emphasizes the incommensurability of their positioning as Tejanas and Cleófilas's positioning as a Mexican immigrant.[35] As such, Cisneros layers the physical geography of Tejas alongside the social geography of Seguin to show how Cleófilas faces rejection because she cannot be read as either American or Tejana.

As Debra A. Castillo and María Socorro Tabuenca Córdoba note, such readings of Cleófilas, within Latinx feminisms, have thus far been largely drawn from our perspectives as feminists within the United States.[36] We can begin, however, to understand her positionality as an immigrant in Texas by reading how she remains only a partially intelligible citizen in Seguin and in the community cartography rendered through the Tejanxs in the *cuento*. Because the bulk of Latina and Chicana feminist analysis of border feminist literature has assessed its subjects from a US positioning, we have also become limited in our understanding of *cuentos* that cross and traverse these distinctions. Instead, as Castillo and Tabuenca Córdoba state, we must work from a "politics of location by which partiality and fragmentation rather than universality or coherence delimit the conditions of possibility for claims to knowledge, whether dominant culture-based or border-inflicted."[37] That is, literary critics and scholars must first understand how these *cuentos* narrate partiality and ask us to be critical of community cartographies that also reject women like Cleófilas.

If, as Emma Pérez proposes, "the colonial imaginary hides something, [and] the decolonial imaginary in a third space recognizes what is left out," then Cisneros's community cartographies, in narratives like "Tepeyac" and "Woman Hollering Creek," bring us to the threshold of recognizing these spatialized, classed, and gendered social mappings.[38] As such, Cisneros's community cartographies trace how aspects of our collective histories, communities, and relationships can never be recovered or fully articulable through an imagining of space as something to own, conquer, or possess again. Moreover, such a reading practice makes visible how singular geographies, like Tepeyac or Seguin, hold multiple contested and competing genealogies that illustrate the intimacy and complexity of social orientations. Like Cisneros's narrators show us, these genealogies and social orientations are often fragmented, partial, or no longer accessible due to time, erasure, forced displacement, or coerced assimilation. Unlike the social mappings narrated in "Tepeyac," "Woman Hollering Creek" begins by narrating space through Cleófilas's alienation and isolation from Seguin's community.

"Woman Hollering Creek" thus shows us the tensions, violences, and erasures of and by Tejanx communities. Cleófilas makes her keen awareness of space in Texas legible through her isolation and exclusion. Cleófilas remains attuned to the ways in which she both does and does not belong in either geographic or social context, and the ways in which such connections "map" her social world in the United States and Mexico quite differently. For even as she feels that there is little to do in Monclova, she is also not socially isolated there. The mundane activities of accompanying aunts and godmothers on visits and socializing with her friend Chela stand in stark contrast to the social ostracism that she faces in Seguin.[39] There is a communal rejection of Cleófilas by the women of Seguin, whom the narrator likens to a "town of gossips." She notes the distancing between houses—albeit a distancing that offers "no more privacy because of it"—and this itself marks the greatest strain on Cleófilas.[40] She says:

> Because the towns here are built so that you have to depend on husbands. Or you stay home. Or you drive. If you're rich enough to own, allowed to drive, your own car.
> There is no place to go. Unless one counts the neighbor ladies. Soledad on one side, Dolores on the other. Or the creek.[41]

Cleófilas offers a critique that not only makes legible the ways in which these spatial constraints reinforce a patriarchal and misogynistic order in Seguin, but also places the United States in tension with Mexico. As we can remember from her social mappings of Monclova, Seguin does not have the same fluidity, openness, and social emphasis that her town once had. "Here," Cleófilas feels restrained, confined, and ostracized from the general population and social space of this Texas and US town, and from "here" there is nowhere else to go. In the place of an elsewhere, Cleófilas's attention comes back to the creek, which initially draws her in with its strange naming and fluid orientation, but later becomes an "alive thing, a thing with a voice all its own . . . calling in its high, silver voice."[42] The active, personified, agential description of the creek stands in contrast to the rigidity and seclusion she feels in Seguin, surrounded by shops with "nothing, nothing, nothing of interest."[43]

What Cisneros's community cartography makes possible, then, is a decolonial futurity that responsibly engages with communities and individuals beyond national borders and state-centered discourses of citizenship and nation. As Cisneros's collection speaks to us from multiple geopoints along and within both the United States and Mexico, she never asks us to remain static in these spaces. The narrative mappings that are rendered in these two stories do not articulate space and geography as simply terrain or territory; they do not call on us to consider border spaces as spaces to be repossessed or reconquered. Rather, they show how deterritorialized literary geographies can help reorient our focus onto the social relationships that actually exist and coexist in these contested spaces. By making clear the limitations of racial, ethnic, and state nationalisms and citizenships that obscure immigrant positionalities and destroy possibilities for coalition between border subjects, Cisneros calls on her critics and readers alike to spatialize in new ways that serve and show care for all communities. Furthermore, Cisneros's community cartographies mark fractured chronologies and fragmented orientations across numerous geographics, revealing a new spatial possibility within Latinx and Chicanx feminist literatures that gives wholeness to our communities. By shifting the reader to a social mapping and community-specific cartography, Cisneros's *cuentos* emerge as geocriticism that defines space, time, and memory as not tethered to a recapitulation of nationalism and citizenship. Ultimately, Cisneros's *cuentos* expand our understanding of narrative space as dialogic and conversant with multiple border subjectivities that show us how mapping the decolonial is beholden to a community cartography.

NOTES

I would like to thank Geneva M. Gano, Kirby Brown, Olga L. Herrera, and Georgina Guzmán for their generous feedback and support in the writing of this essay, as well as to the Center for the Study of Women in Society (University of Oregon) for its financial support in seeing this project through. Gracias, finally, to Michael and Auden—my love always.

1. *Puro cuento* roughly translates into English as "all story" or "pure fiction." It suggests an act of invention and crafting when (re)telling a written or oral story.

2. Emma Pérez, *The Decolonial Imaginary: Writing Chicanas into History* (Bloomington: Indiana University Press, 1999), 73–74.

3. Doreen Massey, *For Space* (London: Sage, 2005), 9.

4. Pérez, *The Decolonial Imaginary*, 77. As Pérez notes, diasporic narratives can lend readers the scope with which to encounter the making of space and the colonial process through which geography is often configured in both literary and nonliterary mappings.

5. Eve Tuck and K. Wayne Yang, "Decolonization Is Not a Metaphor," *Decolonization: Indigeneity, Education, and Society* 1, no. 1 (2012): 1–40.

6. Teresa Hernández, "Invented Geographies: The Material and Immaterial Geopoetics of Sandra Cisneros's 'Pilón,'" *MELUS* 45, no. 2 (2020): 154–172.

7. Gayatri Spivak, *In Other Worlds: Essays in Cultural Politics* (New York: Routledge, 1985), 270–304.

8. Raúl Homero Villa, *Barrio-Logos: Space and Place in Urban Chicano Literature and Culture* (Austin: University of Texas Press, 2000), 1.

9. Villa, *Barrio-Logos*, 241.

10. Sandra Cisneros, "Tepeyac," in *Woman Hollering Creek and Other Stories* (New York: Random House, 1991), 20.

11. La Virgen's *tilma*, which carries numerous symbolic interpretations that defy

any single meaning or tradition, is manifested through the reference to that green-blue sky stamped with thin stars from the heavens.

12. Mary Pat Brady, "The Contrapuntal Geographies of *Woman Hollering Creek and Other Stories*," *American Literature* 71, no. 1 (1999): 117–150.

13. Brady, "The Contrapuntal Geographies," 134.

14. See Octavio Paz, *The Other Mexico: Critique of the Pyramid*, trans. Lysander Kemp (New York: Grove Press, 1972), for Paz's discussion of the constellated positioning and overwriting of histories (Aztec, Mexican, and Spanish) through a single material structure.

15. Cisneros, "Tepeyac," 21 (emphasis added for the word *above*).

16. Mishuana Goeman, *Mark My Words: Native Women Mapping Our Nations* (Minneapolis: University of Minnesota Press, 2013), 3.

17. Cisneros's narrator is making a critique of capitalism when she asks us to look above the merchants, but she is also self-aware of the class and social structures in place that can undermine such a Marxist critique. A Marxist reading of "Tepeyac" here would fall short of understanding the nexuses of class, hierarchy, poverty, tourism, and consumerism alongside the reading of race, religion, ethnicity, language, and history.

18. Cisneros, "Tepeyac," 21 (emphasis added).

19. Mary Pat Brady, *Extinct Lands, Temporal Geographies: Chicana Literature and the Urgency of Space* (Durham, NC: Duke University Press, 2002), 113.

20. Cisneros, "Tepeyac," 22 (emphasis added).

21. Kaitlin M. Murphy, *Mapping Memory: Visuality, Affect, and Embodied Politics in the Americas* (New York: Fordham University Press, 2018), 11.

22. Cisneros, "Tepeyac," 23 (emphasis added).

23. Cisneros, "Tepeyac," 23.

24. Cisneros, "Woman Hollering Creek," in *Woman Hollering Creek and Other Stories*, 43.

25. Cisneros, "Woman Hollering Creek," 45. And yet, the title of this story can reveal a specific location to those familiar with the geographies of Texas, like the title of "Tepeyac" does, and it can also create distance and inaccessibility to those unfamiliar with this small town in Guadalupe County.

26. Cisneros, "Woman Hollering Creek," 45.

27. Cisneros, "Woman Hollering Creek," 54.

28. Cisneros, "Woman Hollering Creek," 52.

29. Cisneros, "Woman Hollering Creek," 46.

30. Refer to "Border Land: Interethnic Violence in Texas, 1820–1879," University of Texas at Arlington Libraries (website), accessed November 1, 2023.

31. Cisneros, "Woman Hollering Creek," 46.

32. Brady, "The Contrapuntal Geographies," 140.

33. Cisneros, "Woman Hollering Creek," 46.

34. Cisneros, "Woman Hollering Creek," 54.

35. Cisneros, "Woman Hollering Creek," 55.

36. Debra A. Castillo and María Socorro Tabuenca Córdoba, *Border Women: Writing from La Frontera* (Minneapolis: University of Minnesota Press, 2002), 55.

37. Castillo and Tabuenca Córdoba, *Border Women*, 232.

38. Pérez, *The Decolonial Imaginary*, 55.

39. Cisneros, "Woman Hollering Creek," 44.
40. Cisneros, "Woman Hollering Creek," 50.
41. Cisneros, "Woman Hollering Creek," 51.
42. Cisneros, "Woman Hollering Creek," 51.
43. Cisneros, "Woman Hollering Creek," 50.

PART II

Love, Shame, and Sinvergüenzas

CHAPTER 6

"LOVE THE ONLY WAY I KNOW HOW"
Cultivating Erotic Conocimiento in the Work of Sandra Cisneros

Belinda Linn Rincón

If we were to construct a literary hall of infamy for the mistresses in Sandra Cisneros's fiction, the star diva would, of course, be Clemencia in "Never Marry a Mexican."[1] What reader could forget the malevolent Clemencia, the seductress of two generations of men in one family who leaves strategically placed gummy bears in her wake? Then, too, we would have to include the disillusioned yet resilient Inés in "Eyes of Zapata"; Amparo, the stoic washerwoman in *Caramelo*; and the unabashed narrators in *Loose Woman* and *My Wicked Wicked Ways*. This collection of mistresses depicts how socially marginalized women often become emotionally vulnerable yet disruptive figures who upend sexual norms. It is from the position of marginalization and vulnerability that these figures often produce knowledge about society, gender, and desire. Yet, because of her position, the mistress is socially rendered as dangerous, disruptive, and immoral and therefore unreliable as a knowledge producer. Cisneros's mistresses and her larger body of erotic writing link desire and feminist epistemology as the foundation for erotic ways of knowing, or what I am calling erotic conocimiento.[2] The forms of knowledge range from the deliberately untaught knowledge of female genitalia and orgasm to the "sucia love," as Deborah Vargas calls it, of a nonromantic, nonmonogamous, racialized sexuality disruptive to capitalism and neoliberal control, to a reflective and transformative self-knowledge.[3] However, part of the radicality of erotic conocimiento is its status as perennially incomplete. Through analogic reasoning, Cisneros's erotic and mistress poetry fails—and deliberately so—to render complete knowledge about sucia love and bodies, doing so to hold open space for the discovery and invention of desires. This work is different from oppressive practices of epistemology such as willful ignorance, unlearning, or erasure; Cisneros gives us just enough information and wisdom to repair the wounds of epistemic violence and to imagine spaces of joy.

Elizabeth Grosz argues that traditional Western philosophy fails to recognize the "explicit sexualization of knowledges, [and] the relationship that models and goals of knowledges have to sexually specific (male) bodies."[4] Cisneros's writing addresses the disavowal of embodied knowledge by enunciating an erotic conocimiento, a term that links body, sexuality, and knowledge production. Moreover, Nancy Pineda-Madrid emphasizes how oppression functions through knowledge production and argues that a ChicanaFeminist epistemology often revolves around family and womanhood in order to offer epistemic interpretations of cultural symbols and norms that obstruct Chicanas' quest for full humanity.[5] Thus, Chicana knowledge production can offer liberatory (re)interpretations that facilitate the process of humanization. Cisneros is part of a larger tradition of Chicana/Latina writers whose work doubles as epistemological inquiry. Much of this work, along with that of Chicana/Latina theorists, decolonizes Christian and Spanish ideologies of gender binaries that erase Indigenous knowledges of female sexuality. For example, in her recounting of the virgen-puta (virgin-whore) dichotomy, Irene Lara proposes the term *panocha conocimientos* as a decolonial reclamation of untaught body knowledge. This inquiry into the panocha—a Mexican colloquial term, with Nahuatl roots, for vagina—requires women to ask what excites them, how and when they express erotic joy, and "who is invested in shaping our desires?" It is a "woman-loving, self-loving reclamation" made in the face of an "anti-sexual Christian legacy" that imposes shame and guilt onto women's sexual lives.[6] Following Audre Lorde, Laura E. Pérez reminds us that eros is "before, after, and within the erotic in sexuality." In Pérez's formulation of eros ideologies, eros names a decolonial project that presumes a subject in a state of constant becoming who recognizes their interdependence with other subjects and with nature. Moreover, eros ideologies are "socially consequential healing practices of loving awareness and respect of self."[7] My emphasis on conocimiento as opposed to ideologies stems from Gloria Anzaldúa's use of conocimiento to encompass more than the Spanish word for "knowledge." For Anzaldúa, "conocimiento" signals a skepticism of rationality and "questions conventional knowledge's current categories, classifications, and contents."[8] Key to achieving conocimiento is self-transformation resulting from knowledge produced through pain and reflexivity. Erotic conocimiento, therefore, refers to knowledge practices that explore unlearned, denigrated knowledges of women's bodies and desires and that often produce reflective and empowering self-knowledge that can lead to broader social change.

Cisneros's narrators ask questions, talk back, and talk dirty. For this behavior, most of them are socially marginalized, a status that is crucial to the

"LOVE THE ONLY WAY I KNOW HOW"

feminist knowledge they produce and embody. The pain of marginalization leads many narrators to develop self-reflexive knowledges of their bodies and desires that result in personal and social transformation. This is perhaps why Cisneros implies the ostracization and "immorality" of mistresses and sexually promiscuous women in the titles of *Loose Woman* and *My Wicked Wicked Ways*. Like puta, pachuca, mujer andariega, Malinche, and chingada, these figures serve as prototypes for Vargas's la sucia. When used to describe an individual's sexual behavior, *sucio/a* (dirty or filthy) signifies sexual deviancy, impurity, deficiency, and lack (lack of cleanliness, lack of control). For Vargas, lo sucio as a queer analytic draws on a range of racial and class discourses and emphasizes the neoliberal and state projects aimed at "cleansing" the taint of subjects who resist heteronormative regulation. This analytic helps us understand how Cisneros's sucias perform "nonnormative and delinquent modes of intimacy . . . that are tactically impure or nonredeemable within the logics of capitalism's constructions of love."[9]

UNLEARNING BODY IGNORANCE

Cisneros most explicitly addresses the consequences of ignorance in "Guadalupe the Sex Goddess" (1996), an essay that explores both processes of unlearning body ignorance and (re)learning body knowledge. Cisneros begins with her mother as a source of body ignorance because of her refusal to teach young Sandra about the female body or explain, for example, why tampons were forbidden. But Cisneros also recognizes how her mother and all female ancestors were deliberately kept ignorant about women's bodies by a religion and a culture that "creat[ed] a blur, a vagueness about what went on 'down there,'" and that this locked women in a "double chastity belt of ignorance and vergüenza, shame."[10] The negative value judgment associated with knowing one's body emblematizes how power inheres in the suppression of information for the specific purpose of controlling women's knowledge, autonomy, and pleasure. As Nancy Tuana reminds us, ignorance is not just a form of "not-yet-knowing," it is also the result of knowledges that were known but then devalued, deliberately forgotten, and unlearned.[11] In other words, women have not always been ignorant of their own bodies; rather, they have been taught to disregard the knowledge of female genitalia and women's capacity for pleasure. Cisneros shows how the lack of accurate terms for female genitalia produces a misunderstanding about how her own body works: "until I was an adult I had no idea I had another orifice called the vagina; I thought my period would arrive via the urethra or perhaps through the walls of my skin."[12] Cisneros describes the significant consequences of body ignorance, which include poor sexual health, the transmission of STDs, and unwanted pregnancy.

Through observing classmates in her high school locker room, reluctantly making appointments with gynecologists at university clinics, and watching porn, Cisneros gained knowledge about the female body. She achieved a deeper connection to her body and culture through self-directed research into pre-Columbian deities including Tlazolteotl, the filth goddess also associated with fertility and sexual passion. Lara explains how Catholic chroniclers branded Tlazolteotl and other revered goddesses as sucias, quoting Fray Juan de Torquemada: "[for] a goddess of loves and sensualities, what can she be but a dirty, filthy, and stained goddess?"[13] By unlearning body ignorance and Christian demonization, Cisneros produces a decolonial imaginary that challenges Western colonial epistemes and their promotion of the "virtuous virgin/pagan puta" dichotomy instilled by patriarchal coloniality.[14] But Cisneros's genealogical excavation into sex goddesses also produces an embodied knowledge. The goddesses become part of "who I am," influencing her rebellious dismissal of cultural norms. By the end of her essay, she adopts a culturally specific term to replace "down there": panocha. In the move from "down there" to vagina to panocha, Cisneros's body ignorance moves to body knowledge, self-acceptance and transformation.[15]

In unearthing the deliberately withheld knowledge of sexual desire and power represented by the goddesses, Cisneros eventually renames La Virgen de Guadalupe as a sex goddess rather than a virgin mother. This is a significant epistemological feat because, as Pineda-Madrid argues, cultural icons are critical in producing and transmitting knowledge.[16] Patriarchal interpretations of La Virgen throughout the centuries have promoted her as the idealized symbol of women's virginity and motherhood. Cisneros's reinterpretation produces new knowledge through the heuristic use of La Virgen's iconicity. This work of liberatory interpretation is critical at the cultural and personal level as it facilitates her self-understanding. She learns that both writing and sex potentially lead to profound introspection, beyond acquired, conscious knowledge and into ontological inquiry: "Like writing, [sex] could take you to deep and mysterious subterranean levels. With each new depth I found out things about myself I didn't know I knew. . . . I was no one, I was nothing, and I was everything in the universe little and large—twig, cloud, sky. How had this incredible energy been denied me!"[17] Once Cisneros learns about the power that inheres in her body, she gains cognitive authority and self-trust, which empower her with insight that she uses to write. In this way, body knowledge facilitates both personal and social transformation through narrative production.

"LOVE THE ONLY WAY I KNOW HOW"

DEMASTERED DESIRE AND CISNEROS'S ANTIHYMENEAL WRITING

While Cisneros seeks a more complete body knowledge, she also holds open a place for inscrutability and inexplicability within her project of erotic conocimiento, in which both the knower and the object of knowledge remain productively opaque. Sandra K. Soto's call to demaster racialized sexuality informs my understanding of erotic conocimiento's opacity. Demastery, a "structure of feeling whose force is precisely in its unintelligibility," does not have a precise definition but instead resonates as a willful refusal to acquire or wield authority, control, or power over an object of knowledge.[18] Mastery over knowledge, Julietta Singh argues, is an act of violence because mastery is "a splitting of the object that is mastered from itself, a way of estranging the mastered object from its previous state of being." Mastery is relational, either inter- or intrapersonal, and enacts a kind of ontological violence. For Singh, an attempt at self-mastery is akin to a "self-maiming, one that involves the denial of the master's own dependency on other bodies."[19] Judith Butler describes an ethical dimension to self-mastery by reminding us of our fundamental corporeal vulnerability to others and the way that our exposure to others—through the touch of grief, violence, or desire—means that we are partially constituted by something beyond our knowledge. In her words: "I am not fully known to myself, because part of what I am is the enigmatic traces of others."[20] Furthermore, demastery is critical to erotic decoloniality, which proposes subjects that are in a constant state of becoming. It is a process of "be-ing as ellipses, as points of suspension, as markers of the unfinished or inarticulate ending of the plot in the making that is our individual lives and our social lives together."[21] The unfinished nature of decolonial subjects and knowledges therefore presumes demastery. Cisneros's erotic writing vacillates between learning and unlearning and ultimately demonstrates a demastering of the desiring Latina body.

Demastery is most evident in poems such as "I Am So in Love I Grow a New Hymen" in *Loose Woman*, where Cisneros uses catachresis—the "use of a borrowed word for something that does not have a name of its own"—to gesture at disclosure yet playfully thwart comprehension.[22] Beginning with a description of past lovers, the poem then directly addresses a current lover and provides a catalog of disjointed and incongruous geographic locations and cultural associations to highlight the borderlessness of bodies and feelings:

No doubt you're Villa
and I'm Pershing's dizzy troops.
No doubt I'm eucalyptus and you

> a California conflagration. No doubt
> you're eucharist, Euclidean geometry,
> World War II's Gibraltar strait,
> the Chinese traders of Guangzhou,
> Zapatistas breakfasting at Sanborn's,
> Sassoferrato's cobalt blue,
> Museo Poldi Pezzoli's insurance rate,
> Gaudí's hammer against porcelain plates.[23]

The unruly list of associations conveys an impressive knowledge of the foreign and eclectic, thereby providing nonparochial expressions of desire not commonly found in romantic poetry's similes, metonyms, and tropes. Cisneros's use of catachresis in so much of her love poetry signals an important epistemological project of validating and inquiring into but never fully explicating Latina desire. We know that love poetry often relies on the metaphor to express emotion and meaning, by comparing two objects that are thought to have similar characteristics. Elena Tapia describes how the metaphor's reliance on a presumed preexisting similarity is further delimited by objectivist semantics, which maintain that "words must correspond to particular entities which have stable features" that exist independent of the person using them. Our understanding of metaphors comes from "embodied and/or culturally based experiences," making them an intuitive and subjective form of knowledge.[24] Yet Cisneros rejects the traditional use of metaphor, premised on resemblance, objectivist semantic epistemology, cultural familiarity, or intuition. Instead, by using catachresis, she privileges dissimilarity, ambiguous correspondences, and unfamiliarity.

In "I Am So in Love," Cisneros's speaker uses catachresis to associate both herself and her lover with arcane references to history, math, religion, war, trade, and art. Yet the associations between the source domains (Euclidean geometry, the Strait of Gibraltar, the Chinese traders of Guangzhou, etc.) do not clarify our understanding of the possible target domains (the speaker and her lover's mutual desire). I say "possible" because we are never really sure what the referents are referring to: do they refer to the speaker's and lover's bodies, their desires, or all of the above? The speaker's inability to name what she seemingly wants to clarify through figurative language, however, is not a failure of language, or if it is, it is a productive one. It just might be that a "'proper' proper name is lacking" for Latina desire, which makes catachresis a suitable linguistic vehicle.[25] Lisa Freinkel's description of catachresis helps clarify this point. She explains that metaphors involve "a judgment of similarity [that] requires at least two terms for comparison," but with catachresis, "one of these terms is missing. A word is transferred from one place to another—to a place that lacks a name of its own. Where metaphor anchors its transfers on the basis of resemblance, catachresis functions on the basis of sheer proximity. In place of no name, we adapt the nearest available term."[26] Poets have long turned to metaphor to elucidate the inenarrable nature of love, but Cisneros uses catachresis to maintain a certain inexpressibility of desire, using arcane referents to refer to an object that has no name.

The idea of borrowing "the nearest available," often contextually improper term suggests a deliberate misappropriation of words; hence, the Greek translation of "catachresis" is "abuse." It is therefore fitting that the speakers in Cisneros's erotic and mistress poetry, who are themselves deemed socially improper, frequently "abuse" language by utilizing a figure of speech marked by an "irreducible impropriety."[27] Many of Cisneros's speakers also incorporate world geography in their explorations of desire, drawing on a borderless knowledge that places the couple above nationalities. In her analysis of *My Wicked Wicked Ways*, Adriana Estill brilliantly traces the lyric narrator's progression from a young girl confined to a patriarchal domesticity and ethnic Chicago neighborhood to a self-possessed world traveler. For example, in "By Way of Explanation," the speaker chides her lover for not knowing her body's intricacies and then proceeds to associate different body parts with mostly Third World locations: Madagascar, the Amazon, Egypt, Tierra del Fuego, and Quintana Roo, among others. Estill notes that the speaker's turn to world geography "resists easy classifications" and "makes her less penetrable by the interlocutor's mind or eye."[28] Estill suggests that if the attempt to "know" the "authentic" Third World woman is an act of colonial violence, then the speaker's decentralized "geocorpus" thwarts her lover's efforts at objectification. Catachresis—which some have referred to as an "extravagant" metaphor, where extravagant literally means to wander out of bounds—similarly encourages a borderless knowledge that "disrupts the reassurances and taxonomic ordering of resemblance, offering instead a world where semantics has lost its bearings, where the foreign and faraway has collapsed in on the near and the neighborly."[29]

The inventory of recondite references that are likely not fully understood by lover or reader may suggest the speaker's mastery over knowledge and meaning. Estill argues that in "By Way of Explanation," the speaker essentially offers her lover a nonexplanation and that this ability to withhold knowledge endows her with power and control over the subject.[30] My reading of "I Am So in Love" aligns with Estill's contention that the speaker impedes full comprehension of the desiring Latina body, but further suggests that such complete knowledge is not even available to the speaker herself. Rather, the speakers in both poems exhibit a demasterful control over the subject matter, and, because their own knowledge is incomplete, the meanings they and we attribute to their bodies and desires can proliferate indefinitely. By relying on catachrestic (global) proximity rather than metaphoric resemblance and equivalence, Cisneros's speakers explore an irreducible Latina desire, using improper or extravagant associations to produce new meanings.

For all the opacity in "I Am So in Love I Grow a New Hymen," Cisneros is crystal clear on the effects of desire. The title's reference to growing a new hymen is both shocking and suggestive. The hymen, a specific part of genitalia that many women have, has been critical to how male medical and scientific communities have demarcated female "genital geography," privileging the reproductive organs inside the female body over the external and seemingly inessential clitoris.[31] The inside/outside distinction further supports what Sharon Marcus calls rape-as-invasion metaphors, which imagine female sexuality as a "delicate perhaps inevitably damaged and pained inner space."[32] Moreover, the hymen as closure has been fundamental to narratives of female virginity and male pleasure. With the former, the hymen checks of girls and young women are a degrading way for parents to check for virginity. With the latter, the act of puncturing the hymen is said to be both a sign of male conquest and a pleasurable act.[33]

Hymen is also the name of the Greek god of marriage, who is the namesake for hymeneal or bridal songs and epithalamium poems, performed to invoke good fortune for the bride and groom. Thus, the hymen's etymology makes evident the way a bride's loss of virginity (through the rupture of the hymen) signifies marriage itself. Yet Cisneros ironically uses *hymen* in her title not to represent marriage and virginity, but rather to celebrate nonmarital and nonvirginal sexual union and female pleasure. Cisneros rejects the male reduction of female genitalia to parts that protect the violable, penetrable, and "pained inner space" of the female body. Instead, her title emphasizes pleasure-induced regeneration ("growing" a new hymen) unassociated with biological reproduction, while privileging female desire over virginal purity.

Much of Cisneros's erotic poetry flaunts the epithalamium poetic form, virginity, and marriage altogether. In "Old Maids," the narrator defies the marriage imperative:

> My cousins and I,
> we don't marry.
> We're too old
> by Mexican standards.
> . . . .
> My cousins and I,
> we're all old
> maids at thirty.

"LOVE THE ONLY WAY I KNOW HOW"

> Who won't
> dress children[34]

Through a progression of present-tense contractions that include *don't, can't,* and *won't*, the narrator emphasizes a present and continual defiance, refusing to embark on the predetermined telos of virgin to wife to mother. Passing the age of reproduction (which the aunts determine to be the age of thirty), the nieces are "old maids," condemned to spinsterhood—a mark of womanly failure and a drag on the social order. Yet, after studying narratives of abandonment, confinement, sacrifice, and fidelity from diverse cultures, they have concluded that marriage facilitates women's oppression. They will remain in a permanent present state of nonreproductivity and never experience the futurity and regeneration promised through motherhood. John Alba Cutler explores this rejection of matrimony as indicative of an anti-assimilationist Chicana individualism that rejects the "demands that Chicanas speak only in the maternal role."[35] In Cisneros's antihymeneal poetry, we see how nonassimilating narrators expose the fault lines within marriage and motherhood and usually have fun doing it.

Cisneros's sucias—women who deliberately opt out of the social power that accrues to wedded and reproductive women—remind us why states and economies are heavily invested in the definition, practice, and consumption of love. By facilitating property transfers and inheritance and by promoting economic stability, marriage helps maintain a patriarchal society of theoretically self-sufficient consumers who reproduce themselves and enable the privatization of welfare and care—an unrecompensed labor that usually falls to women. The state grants legitimacy and recognition to married couples and rewards their responsible choice to wed, offering them an array of benefits, entitlements, and credits—from health insurance to more favorable tax codes to Social Security survivorship benefits. In the sucia's refusal of marriage, her desires imply her incapacity for proper citizenship. Cisneros's sucias and mistresses, to whom I will now turn, often stand as emotional and perhaps economic destabilizers of marriage and thus become disobedient citizens of the heteronormative state.

WORLD TRAVELING AND SELF-KNOWLEDGE

While society views sucias as unreliable knowers, Cisneros's sucias often seek to broaden their self-knowledge through self-inquiry rooted in painful reflections on racial, gender, and class marginalization. Her mistress narrators dwell on moments of symbolic violence and direct their narrative animosity toward mostly white wives of lovers. Clemencia's hatred toward Megan in "Never Marry a Mexican" is perhaps the most notable example. For example, Clemencia contemplates telling her lover's son: "I was sleeping with your father and didn't give a damn about that woman, your mother. If she was a brown woman like me, I might've had a harder time living with myself, but since she's not, I don't care. . . . She's not my sister."[36] She then examines the motives behind her callous actions: "Why do I do that, I wonder? Sleep with a man when his wife is giving life. . . . Why do that? It's always given me a bit of crazy joy to be able to kill those women like that, without her knowing it."[37] Whiteness and middle-class status are the two identity categories that remain out of reach for Clemencia, leading her to project her feelings of inadequacy onto the pristine whiteness of the unassuming wife, who has attained social legitimacy and security through marriage and motherhood. Jealousy is perhaps one motive for her rage, which results in acts of symbolic violence. Maythee G. Rojas argues that before Clemencia can begin the healing process, she must first appropriate "the dominant male's conquering mask and modus operandi as a means of liberating herself."[38] Thus, the references to killing are Clemencia's mimicry of patriarchy's violent rhetoric. But Clemencia's assault on Megan's material belongings can also be read as an aggression that stems from the human demand for recognition. In other words, Cisneros's mistresses "know to leave before being left and how to linger when left." As Vargas reminds us, lo sucio is a tactic for self-preservation and critique.[39] Therefore, when Cisneros's sucias leave their scent on bedsheets, fingerprints on bathroom mirrors, and gummy bears in diaphragms, their acts are traces of presence, experience, and knowledge. As the narrator of "The So-and-So's" tells her married lover, "I will not out so easily. / I was here. As loud as trumpet. / . . . / I want to be like you. A who."[40] The refusal to disappear is a demand for a recognized subjectivity and agency usually only afforded to men.

We can also read moments of mistress aggression as steps in the process of erotic conocimiento. First, the fact that many of Cisneros's mistresses direct their ire toward the unsuspecting white wives of their lovers reveals a complicated relationality. Following Norma Alarcón, Pineda-Madrid argues that a "woman becomes a woman not only in opposition to men but also in opposition to other women."[41] This recognition is key to ChicanaFeminist epistemology because it serves as a corrective to Anglo feminist binary thinking. Cisneros balances aggression with examples of how the mistress attempts to reconcile the rage that she projects onto the white wife. While the mistresses in *Loose Woman* take pleasure in their disdain for wives, *My Wicked Wicked Ways* portrays a mistress who is slightly more generous to the wife of her lover. The twenty poems collected as "The Rodrigo Poems" focus on the narrator's affair with a man named Rodrigo. Significantly, the series begins with a poem about Rodrigo's wife. In "A Woman Cutting Celery," we see a woman angrily chopping celery as she waits for her adulterous husband's return. In this opening poem, Cisneros privileges the wife's emotions and frames our understanding of the affair through *her* rage and pain. Although we do not get direct interior access through first-person narration, we do observe her pain from a distance and witness her gradual unraveling: "A thin blond vein / rises from the corner of her jaw / like a crack in a porcelain plate."[42] While the poem privileges a distant objectivity, this stanza is the only moment that encourages us to sympathize with the wife.

In one of the last poems, "New Year's Eve," the mistress encounters the wife at a party. Cisneros focuses on the mistress's preconceived assumptions of the wife, which are quickly dispelled as she realizes the ordinariness of her archrival: "From what I could observe / she is a woman risen from a rib / like any other— / two eyes, two breasts, one uterus."[43] Notably, the narrator's description does not refer to whiteness; rather, the mistress has now learned to see beyond race and class. Moreover, the wife is not as stately, as beautiful, as powerful as the mistress had presumed, and this revelation surprises her: "How did I fail to understand? / A female, like any common female. / For a common male."[44] If the wife is knocked from her pedestal, then so is the husband, Rodrigo. While the last line implies that Rodrigo's commonness is unremarkable and thus he no longer has power over her, it is the wife's commonness that allows her to see her lover with clear eyes.

These poems represent how mistresses attempt to understand wives by entering their world, an act of world traveling that María Lugones describes as critical to "cross-cultural and cross-racial loving."[45] For Lugones, it is our tendency to perceive others arrogantly that prevents us from forming the identifications that could eventuate in feminist solidarities. She writes, "there is a complex failure of love in the failure to identify with another woman, the failure to see oneself in other women who are quite different from oneself."[46] I read some of "The Rodrigo Poems" as initial gestures at this kind of love, as the mistress attempts to alter her arrogant perception of the wife to a loving one by traveling to the wife's world of failed marriage. I also see these poems as extensions of Cisneros's erotic conocimiento, in which the mistress narrators engage in a process of self-construction by confronting their own ignorance. Andrea J. Pitts argues that "forms of self-knowledge and self-ignorance are always accompanied by knowledge-of-others and ignorance-of-others."[47] In the examples just provided, we see narrators engaged in self-reflection, actively questioning their own motivations, choices, and actions. Whether it is Clemencia asking, "Why do I do that, I wonder?" or the narrator in "New Year's Eve" asking, "How did I fail to understand?," the mistresses' self-knowledge is shaped by what they know and don't know of their lovers' wives.[48] They take what Pitts calls an epistemic risk, in which knowers "face that they may be mistaken about their beliefs about themselves and about others."[49] By crossing the epistemic gap, the mistresses undergo self-transformation.

HUMANIZING DISCREDITED KNOWERS

Cisneros's autobiographical account of self-described sexual deviancy is also a frame for understanding the mistresses in her work. In a keynote address titled "A Woman of No Consequence: Una Mujer Cualquiera," delivered at the National Lesbian and Gay Journalists Association (NLGJA) 1995 conference in San Antonio and subsequently published, Cisneros begins by outing herself as a mistress. She tells her audience about her first affair as a teenager still living with her parents. She recounts meeting a lover who was "waiting for me in a bed still warm from where his wife rose and left it for me."[50] She then directly addresses her lover and declares herself to be "a woman who will take you there, and you have chosen me so different from that woman you share a life with, so other than she, you've chosen me . . . say you love me, say it, say it, lapping me up, lapping up the brown caramelo of my skin, say you love me, daddy, please. Yes, yes. Little nip of hurt, pedacito de mi alma, oh, I knew it, I knew you did."[51] Through an orgasmic exhortation to her lover, she plunges her audience into the intimate moment of extramarital and nonvirginal climax—in the process, breaking norms of propriety and discretion.

Importantly, the rhetorical context of her speech proves critical to further understanding her erotic conocimiento. Not only does she narrate orgasm onstage, but she details her affair in a seemingly inappropriate public venue. If Cisneros insists on being a valued knower, as someone with knowledge that has social import, then it may be ironic that she seemingly discredits herself first by naming herself a mujer cualquiera (woman of no consequence) and framing her sexual escapades as acts of criminality: "My life of crime began at nineteen when I had an affair with my first married man. I became a sexual outlaw then. . . . It was wonderful to be a sexual renegade. . . . I enjoyed being a sexual deviant."[52] Yet her description of sexual deviancy works as a gesture of identification and solidarity with her LGBTQ listeners, many of whom may have experienced the social ostracization or material consequences of having a legally criminalized sexuality. As a heterosexual cis woman, Cisneros is not a sexual minority, but through a description of her sucia practices, she signals her support for communities oppressed by heteronormativity.

Despite establishing that both Cisneros and her listeners belong to a community of devalued subjects and knowers, Cisneros implies that even her audience might regard the sucia/mistress as too deplorable for full acceptance. She describes her deliberate rhetorical strategy and her goal of gaining epistemic validity for sucias and others like herself: "All week I kept wondering what I could tell you that would make you hear me, that would make you listen with more than your ears, allow you to accept what I have to say, and ultimately open your heart and let me in." She goes on to say that if she told a good enough story, "It would change the way you think about women like me, and therefore change the way you look at the world."[53] The implicit logic behind her appeal is that listening opens the door to understanding, understanding can lead to empathy, and empathy for la otra and other marginalized figures could lead to social change. Cisneros's appeal most likely landed positively with an audience of wordsmiths who knew the importance of stories and their influence on public discourse and policy. The NLGJA had been founded five years earlier in response to what Leroy Aarons, its first president, described as a "mass media [that] are essentially conservative, frequently homophobic, yet extremely powerful opinion shapers." He described how NLGJA members struggled with "invisibility, fear of exposure, desire to influence fair coverage, and deep ethical questions."[54] Cisneros's call for a recognition of her humanity extended to her listeners and their struggle for epistemic validation not only as journalists, but as human beings. Recognition and validation, Heather Stewart argues, are fundamental to one's being: "Insofar as being regarded as a knower is central to human dignity and value, being undermined as a knower is a violation of the speaker's very humanity."[55] Cisneros's demand for humanization for herself and others through epistemic validity constitutes a key part of her erotic conocimiento, which recognizes one's interdependence with others.

Her 1995 keynote is not only about her sexual escapades. Rather, in the latter half she moves into a more reflective register as she recounts how she lived in Sarajevo in 1984 and befriended a woman named Jasna Karaula. Speaking during what would be the last stages of the Bosnian War (1992–1995), Cisneros describes being distraught over Jasna's predicament: "A bit of disbelief, of shock that this thing, this war is happening to you, is happening to someone you know personally. . . . I lived with the ache of not knowing whether she was alive or dead."[56] In an antiwar speech given on March 7, 1993, in San Antonio, Cisneros described Jasna as her *"hermana de mi corazón,* sister of my heart" and as "a woman I love as any woman would love a woman."[57] In "I Awake in the Middle of the Night and Wonder If You've Been Taken" from *Loose Woman,* a book that she dedicates to Jasna, we see how Cisneros's eros encompasses other forms of love beyond the romantic or erotic. The poem is located nearly midway through the book and features a narrator who awakens from her laced bedding, the site of desire in previous poems, to a nightmare about the possible death of a friend. In "I Awake," Cisneros describes her fear that Jasna will be killed. In Sarajevo, Jasna's life is worthless: "You don't count. You're not history." The last stanza ties the two women's social and political marginalization together: "I'm a woman like you. / I don't count either. / Not a thing I say. / Not a thing I do."[58] Unlike the mistresses in her writing, who refuse to learn about the white wives of their lovers and whose rejection of gender solidarity produces incomplete or imperfect self-knowledge, the narrator in "I Awake" recognizes the social positionality that many women share. This acknowledgment provides Cisneros with self- and social knowledge about the world and her interconnected place within it. It was during antiwar protests in San Antonio that she realized that her own intolerance contributed in small ways to larger acts of intolerance: "If I am holding a peace vigil for Bosnia then it is only logical that I cannot be fighting with my mother . . . or with anyone for that matter." She then asks her audience: "So what does Sarajevo have to do with sex and my talk this morning?"[59] Her answer is that the mujer cualquiera, the sucia who is always already prejudged and silenced, and her friend Jasna are all worthy of tolerance and compassion. Through erotic poetry, antiwar speeches, op-eds, and her keynote, Cisneros calls for epistemic humanization of all devalued subjects.

Cisneros's erotic and mistress writing emblematizes the expansive potential of erotic conocimiento—of knowing the self and others through, with, and from the body. She exposes how body ignorance is deliberately perpetuated and how sucia love can challenge heteronormativity's patriarchal institutions, practices, and knowledges. As her narrators seek self-knowledge, we see that erotic conocimiento is the foundation for a humanizing project where mistresses and sucias become validated epistemic agents with the potential to enact personal and social transformation. Cisneros's insistence on embodied knowledge and epistemic validity is particularly critical now, as sexual assault survivors continue to be gaslighted when making claims of sexual assault. While the #MeToo movement seeks to challenge such forms of "epistemic harm,"[60] Cisneros's writing reminds us of the need to end society's epistemic erasure of embodied knowledges produced by mistresses, sucias, and mujeres cualquieras, whose exuberant and demasterful descriptions of sucia love expose the fallacies of matrimony and plumb the depths of desire's potentialities.

NOTES

I give thanks to Geneva M. Gano and Sonia Saldívar-Hull for inviting me to be part of this amazing project and group of Cisneros scholars. I also want to acknowledge Lola, Stella, and Rodrigo for their support.

"LOVE THE ONLY WAY I KNOW HOW"

1. The chapter title quotes from Sandra Cisneros, "You Bring Out the Mexican in Me," in *Loose Woman* (New York: Alfred A. Knopf, 1994), 6.

2. I have elected to set Spanish words in roman type in order to normalize their usage throughout my analysis, though I have maintained the authors' original italicization in all direct quotations.

3. Deborah Vargas, "Sucia Love: Losing, Lying, and Leaving in Díaz's *This Is How You Lose Her*," in *Junot Díaz and the Decolonial Imagination*, ed. Monica Hanna, Jennifer Harford Vargas, and José David Saldívar (Durham, NC: Duke University Press, 2016), 351–376.

4. Elizabeth Grosz, "Bodies and Knowledges: Feminism and the Crisis of Reason," in *Feminist Epistemologies*, ed. Linda Alcoff and Elizabeth Potter (New York: Routledge, 1993), 188.

5. Pineda-Madrid writes *ChicanaFeminist* as one word to indicate a "critical consciousness" attuned to race, gender, class, and sexual orientation. See Nancy Pineda-Madrid, "Notes toward a ChicanaFeminist Epistemology (And Why It Is Important for Latina Feminist Theologies)," in *A Reader in Latina Feminist Theology: Religion and Justice*, ed. María Pilar Aquino, Daisy L. Machado, and Jeanette Rodriguez (Austin: University of Texas Press, 2002), 243.

6. Irene Lara, "Goddess of the Americas in the Decolonial Imaginary: Beyond the Virtuous Virgen/Pagan Puta Dichotomy," *Feminist Studies* 34, no. 1–2 (2008): 116, 118, 121.

7. Laura E. Pérez, *Eros Ideologies: Writings on Art, Spirituality, and the Decolonial* (Durham, NC: Duke University Press, 2019), 16.

8. Gloria E. Anzaldúa, "now let us shift . . . the path of conocimiento . . . inner works, public acts," in *This Bridge We Call Home: Radical Visions for Transformation*, ed. Gloria E. Anzaldúa and AnaLouise Keating (New York: Routledge, 2002), 541.

9. Vargas, "Sucia Love," 353.

10. Sandra Cisneros, "Guadalupe the Sex Goddess," in *Goddess of the Americas / La Diosa de las Américas: Writings on the Virgin of Guadalupe*, ed. Ana Castillo (New York: Riverhead Books, 1996), 46.

11. Nancy Tuana, "Coming to Understand: Orgasm and the Epistemology of Ignorance," *Hypatia* 19, no. 1 (Winter 2004): 195.

12. Cisneros, "Guadalupe the Sex Goddess," 48.

13. Torquemada, quoted in Lara, "Goddess of the Americas," 101.

14. Lara, "Goddess of the Americas," 103.

15. Cisneros, "Guadalupe the Sex Goddess," 46.

16. Pineda-Madrid, "Notes toward a ChicanaFeminist Epistemology," 260.

17. Cisneros, "Guadalupe the Sex Goddess," 49.

18. Sandra K. Soto, *Reading Chican@ Like a Queer: The De-Mastery of Desire* (Austin: University of Texas Press, 2010), 2.

19. Julietta Singh, *Unthinking Mastery: Dehumanism and Decolonial Entanglements* (Durham, NC: Duke University Press, 2018), 10.

20. Judith Butler, *Precarious Life: The Powers of Mourning and Violence* (New York: Verso, 2006), 46.

21. Pérez, *Eros Ideologies*, 6.

22. Lisa Freinkel, "Catachresis," in *The Princeton Encyclopedia of Poetry and*

Poetics, 4th ed., ed. Stephen Cushman et al. (Princeton, NJ: Princeton University Press, 2012), 209.

23. Cisneros, *Loose Woman*, 16–17.

24. Elena Tapia, "Beyond a Comparison of Two Distinct Things, or What Students of Literature Gain from a Cognitive Linguistic Approach to Metaphor," *College Literature* 33, no. 2 (Spring 2006): 137, 138.

25. Freinkel, "Catachresis," 210.

26. Freinkel, "Catachresis," 210.

27. Freinkel, "Catachresis," 210.

28. Adriana Estill, "Building the Chicana Body in Sandra Cisneros' *My Wicked Wicked Ways*," *Rocky Mountain Review of Language and Literature* 56, no. 2 (2002): 38–39.

29. Freinkel, "Catachresis," 211.

30. Estill, "Building the Chicana Body," 39–40.

31. Tuana, "Coming to Understand," 219.

32. Sharon Marcus, "Fighting Bodies, Fighting Words: A Theory and Politics of Rape Prevention," in *Feminists Theorize the Political*, ed. Judith Butler and Jean W. Scott (New York: Routledge, 1992), 398.

33. The male interest in vaginal closure has led to medical procedures such as the "husband stitch" or the "daddy stitch," in which "an extra stitch [is] given during the repair process after vaginal birth, supposedly to tighten the vagina for increased pleasure of a male sexual partner." Carrie Murphy, "The Husband Stitch Isn't Just a Horrifying Childbirth Myth," Healthline, September 21, 2018.

34. Cisneros, *Loose Woman*, 9.

35. John Alba Cutler, *Ends of Assimilation: The Formation of Chicano Literature* (New York: Oxford University Press, 2015), 121.

36. Sandra Cisneros, "Never Marry a Mexican," in *Woman Hollering Creek and Other Stories* (New York: Random House, 1991), 76.

37. Cisneros, "Never Marry a Mexican," 76–77.

38. Maythee G. Rojas, "Cisneros's 'Terrible' Women: Recuperating the Erotic as a Feminist Source in 'Never Marry a Mexican' and 'Eyes of Zapata,'" *Frontiers: A Journal of Women Studies* 20, no. 3 (1999): 145.

39. Vargas, "Sucia Love," 353.

40. Sandra Cisneros, *My Wicked Wicked Ways* (Bloomington, IN: Third Woman Press, 1987), 87.

41. Pineda-Madrid, "Notes toward a ChicanaFeminist Epistemology," 248.

42. Cisneros, *My Wicked Wicked Ways*, 70.

43. Cisneros, *My Wicked Wicked Ways*, 99.

44. Cisneros, *My Wicked Wicked Ways*, 100.

45. María Lugones, *Pilgrimages/Peregrinajes: Theorizing Coalition against Multiple Oppressions* (Lanham, MD: Rowman and Littlefield, 2003), 78.

46. Lugones, *Pilgrimages/Peregrinajes*, 82.

47. Andrea J. Pitts, "Gloria E. Anzaldúa's *Autohistoria-teoría* as an Epistemology of Self-Knowledge/Ignorance," *Hypatia* 31, no. 2 (Spring 2016): 357.

48. Cisneros, "Never Marry a Mexican," 76; Cisneros, *My Wicked Wicked Ways*, 100.

49. Pitts, "Gloria E. Anzaldúa's *Autohistoria-teoría*," 365.

50. Sandra Cisneros, "A Woman of No Consequence: Una Mujer Cualquiera," in *Living Chicana Theory*, ed. Carla Trujillo (Berkeley, CA: Third Woman Press, 1998), 80.

51. Cisneros, "A Woman of No Consequence," 80–81.

52. Cisneros, "A Woman of No Consequence," 81.

53. Cisneros, "A Woman of No Consequence," 78.

54. Leroy Aarons, "Letter from the President," *Alternatives* (NLGJA newsletter) 1, no. 1 (September 1991), n.p.

55. Heather Stewart, "'Why Didn't She Say Something Sooner?': Doubt, Denial, Silencing, and the Epistemic Harms of the #MeToo Movement," *South Central Review* 36, no. 2 (Summer 2019): 77.

56. Cisneros, "A Woman of No Consequence," 84.

57. Sandra Cisneros, *A House of My Own: Stories from My Life* (New York: Alfred A. Knopf, 2015), 111, 112.

58. Cisneros, *Loose Woman*, 64.

59. Cisneros, "A Woman of No Consequence," 84.

60. Stewart, "Why Didn't She Say Something Sooner?," 89.

CHAPTER 7

FROM MARGINAL TO SIN VERGÜENZA
Overcoming School-Inflicted Shame through Transgressive Literary Aesthetics in Sandra Cisneros's Life and Writing

Georgina Guzmán

Among the Sandra Cisneros Papers, in the Wittliff Collections at Texas State University, lie Cisneros's personal diaries, which she began penning in 1968. In my browsing of her diary pages from 1968 and 1969, when she was thirteen to fourteen years old, three themes emerged from the pages: school, clothes, and worry. Her nagging preoccupation is of looking poor and not having anything nice to wear, of feeling inferior to her classmates.[1] While ruminations on clothing may seem like a common theme for a teenager, in Cisneros's diaries, they are constant and poignant; her shame and worry about her family's financial means and her humble appearance seem to afflict her deeply. Today, over fifty years later, Cisneros continues to examine those worries to help other students heal from similar forms of shame. For example, in April 2019, speaking to an audience of students and community members at Heritage University in Toppenish, Washington (a place where many Mexican farmworkers labor in the fruit and vegetable fields surrounding the university), Cisneros read her story "Eleven" from her collection *Woman Hollering Creek*.[2] In that story, the eleven-year-old narrator's fifth-grade teacher and classmates assume that an ugly, smelly sweater left behind in the lost and found is hers, and this assumption causes a sense of painful humiliation in her so deep that she just cries and withdraws into herself, unable to speak up and tell them that the sweater is not hers. Janelle Retka, a reporter from the *Yakima Herald* who was in the audience, says that Cisneros explained that this story stemmed from "a childhood experience in which she was made to feel different or lesser than her classmates." Cisneros said that "they assumed the sweater was mine because that's the way they saw me, poor and raggedy."[3] She then went on to explain how storytelling can transform experiences rooted in shame into opportunities for healing:

> I think it's important for us to tell the stories that have taken our voices away, that don't allow us to speak. They harm us and stay in our heart like a little grain of sand . . . just like the oyster that has to survive the invasion of a little grain of sand. Each time you tell the story it becomes a different story and you keep healing yourself until finally, one day you've made this beautiful pearl that has nothing to do with the invading grain of sand and you can give it away—and that story was like that for me.[4]

This story serves as a point of entry into some of the central concerns that Cisneros repeatedly examines in her writings: the way that school serves as a primordial site of shame and injury for working-class students of color, the long-lasting traumas it can inflict, and the healing powers of storytelling, which can enable us to reclaim our lost voices and self-esteem.

Cisneros's stories of healing from scholastic trauma resonate deeply for many of us who have been made to feel other, marginal, inferior, or voiceless within educational institutions; they provide blueprints for self-healing for those of us who have had few models before us. Her *consejos* (wise tips) on how we may overcome feelings of shame and inadequacy by transforming those ugly stories within us into beautiful pearls of writing serve as healing words that provide us with models of a bold Chicana *sin vergüenza* aesthetics (aesthetics without shame). Forever teaching us to no longer allow ourselves to be shamed for our difference, she was one of the first Chicana writers to show us how we could instead embrace that difference as the source of our strength—as cultural capital—in our art and politics. In fact, her 2022 poetry book *Woman without Shame / Mujer sin vergüenza* demonstrates her lifelong dedication to overcoming shame in all its forms and providing mentorship in the art of harnessing its healing powers.[5]

Using as a theoretical lens bell hooks's critical observations in her essay "Moving beyond Shame"—on the strategies of shaming that subordinate students of color within the educational system—I examine Cisneros's racial, class, and gendered shame in school and her methods of overcoming shame in her writings and her biography.[6] I look especially at Cisneros's experiences of being shamed for being a female, working-class Mexican American, both in her K–12 education and beyond, as revealed in her personal diary entries and in her essays about her experiences attending graduate school at the University of Iowa. From there, I look at the evolution of her literary style—from the early, significantly less ethnic, minimalist style of *The House on Mango Street*

(1984) to the more oppositional Mexican American maximalism of *Caramelo* (2002)—to uncover how her process of healing from shame manifests through her aesthetics.[7]

Indeed, examining the minimalist vignette style of *The House on Mango Street* against the overflowing, footnote-rich maximalism of her 464-page novel *Caramelo* (replete with 86 chapters and about 100 footnotes about Mexican culture), I show how Cisneros's aesthetic moves mirror a therapeutic process of overcoming shame—that is, of becoming *sin vergüenza*, a woman without shame, someone no longer afraid of patriarchy, dominant society, or literary critics' judgment. *The House on Mango Street*, her first book, is not only a deeply minimalist text; it also tends to minimize explicit cultural or ethnic markers. In its vignettes, which she has called "small pearls of poems," she employs the distinctive markers of minimalist aesthetics: extremely sparse narrative, an economy of words, and no ornamentation. A lot is left unsaid, and one must fill in the gaps.[8] By *Woman Hollering Creek and Other Stories* (1991) and *Caramelo* two decades later, however, Cisneros is less reticent, no longer taking up as little space as possible or tending to hide a small voice and content behind those "small pearls"; she has now transformed those pearls into turquoise (a visible mark of ethnicity) and created veritable chunky necklaces with it, much like the Taxco turquoise and silver necklaces she proudly wears today. Her writing and her being have learned to take up more space.

Cisneros's bold literary style (and by extension her fashion style) does what Aída Hurtado and Norma E. Cantú articulate in *MeXicana Fashions: Politics, Self-Adornment, and Identity Construction*: it assertively "reclaims the right to self-adornment to highlight previously derogated social identities . . . to restitute the self on positive terms rather than the stigma assigned by society."[9] Her novel *Caramelo* represents the ultimate reclamation of cultural and literary styles that were previously derogated in the United States. It epitomizes the working-class, Mexican American aesthetic that Tomás Ybarra-Frausto describes as *rasquachismo*, or "an aesthetic representation that belongs to the barrio . . . in which too much is not enough, and all available spaces must be used."[10] Amalia Mesa-Bains states that along with maximalist ornamentation and a hybrid, inventive repurposing of everyday household items and discards, *rasquachismo* also has a political valence that helps articulate a self-affirming Chicano identity:

> the sensibility of rasquachismo is an obvious and internally defined tool of artist-activists. The intention was to provoke the accepted "superior" norms of the Anglo-American with the everyday reality of Chicano cultural practices. Whether through extensions and reinterpretations of domestic settings, the car, or the personal pose, rasquachismo is

a world view that provides an oppositional identity. Rasquachismo becomes for Chicano artists and intellectuals a vehicle for both culture and identity. This dual function of resistance and affirmation [is] essential to the sensibility of rasquachismo.[11]

An examination of Cisneros's evolving literary output indicates how she overcomes her racial and class stigma by embracing this Chicana maximalist use of cultural markers, accessing mental and spiritual liberation from shame, and learning to harness oppositional, *sin vergüenza* aesthetics in form, content, and everyday life.

ATTENDING TO THE INJURY IN ORDER TO HEAL: THE IMPORTANCE OF EXAMINING SHAME

Scholarship on affect studies can often feel rather abstract and divorced from the practical. But Cisneros's writings, to me, serve as practical case studies that illustrate the poignant effects of shame that affect theorists have articulated. Examining the nature of how affects operate is useful for the study of racial injury and trauma in Chicana/o literature and everyday life, because, as Gloria Anzaldúa reminds us, it is vital to "let the wound caused by the serpent be healed by the serpent."[12] Chicana literary critics have thus turned to these questions in recent years, exploring racial shame, injury, and soul sickness in Chicanx/Latinx literature. Stephanie Fetta's *Shaming into Brown: Somatic Transactions of Race in Latina/o Literature* (2018) explores painful scenes of racialization. Drawing at times from Silvan Tomkins's work on shame, Fetta's work is of primal importance in the way it centers "soma—the physical, emotive, and social register of our subjectivity" to show how shame is registered in the body and how hegemonic exertions of social power affect racialized subjects.[13] Countering the potentially illness-inducing "'mind/body fragmentation' of academia" that Lara Medina and Martha R. Gonzales explore in their anthology *Voices from the Ancestors: Xicanx and Latinx Spiritual Reflections and Healing Practices* (2019), Christina Garcia Lopez's *Calling the Soul Back: Embodied Spirituality in Chicanx Narrative* (2019) explores the trauma, grief, and soul sickness that Chicana narratives illuminate and the way their storytelling serves as medicine within "institutions of the academy that have typically insisted on a rational mind disconnected from matters of soul or spirit."[14] She explores how "these narratives [are] deeply engaged in restorative work, healing the wound of spiritual trauma" that arises in the academic setting.[15] She delves into how writers like Cisneros, Anzaldúa, and Helena María Viramontes take up Chicana spirituality, *curanderismo*, and ancestral/

Indigenous knowledge to create decolonial, shamanic narratives that enable collective healing. Her work brings attention to processes of injury and narrative healing in Chicana literature. I seek to complement these scholars' work by going the route of affect and aesthetics—examining how the adoption of oppositional and political *sin vergüenza* style can also carry out some of that healing work within academia and beyond.

CISNEROS'S EARLY EDUCATION AND THE SHAMING OF HISTORICALLY MARGINALIZED STUDENTS

In "Moving beyond Shame," bell hooks provides us with a critical lens to understand how shame affects students of color within school settings. She writes:

> Throughout the history of civil rights struggle to end racial discrimination, exploitation, and oppression, freedom has often been determined by the degree to which people of color have access to the same privileges as white peers. Embedded in this notion of freedom is the assumption that access is all that is needed to create the conditions for equality. The thinking was: Let black children go to the same schools as white peers and they will have all that is needed to be equal and free. Such thinking denies the role that devaluation and degradation, or all strategies of shaming, play in maintaining racial subordination, especially in the area of education.[16]

hooks's words shed light on Cisneros's educational experiences as a Chicana scholarship girl attending mostly white, private Catholic schools in Chicago in the 1960s. As the daughter of a Spanish-speaking Mexican immigrant who worked as an upholsterer and an English-speaking Chicana who was a stay-at-home housewife and caretaker to her seven children, Cisneros was a child of modest means. Her family frequently had to move from one apartment and school to another because of their poverty. She was allowed entrance into those private Catholic schools on financial aid, but her experiences of shaming there constantly reminded her of her subordinate place within Chicago's racial and class hierarchies.

As bell hooks states, there is "a need for critical vigilance when marginalized students of color enter environments that continue to be shaped by the politics of domination. Without critical vigilance, shaming as a weapon of psychological terrorism can damage fragile self-esteem in ways that are irreparable."[17] Cisneros was subject to these kinds of injurious forces as a student on scholarship at Saint Aloysius School and then Saint Callistus Catholic Elementary in 1960s Chicago. She recalls that the nuns made her conscious of being a minority and one of the poorer children in her class: "it was a very racist Catholic school. There were a lot of Italian kids, and Latinos were the minority."[18] She also remembers how "the nuns at her school were majestic at making one feel little" and how her teachers' "cruelty" led her to lose her spirituality—it was them and their bad treatment of her "that made her lose her faith."[19]

In the Sandra Cisneros Papers, we find that Cisneros's personal diaries from her childhood reveal that when she was a young student, her self-esteem was constantly plagued by feelings of class shame and inadequacy, particularly with regard to her scholarship status and her humble clothing. For example, on January 5, 1968, she wrote:

> Dear Diary, I'm quite troubled and have been lately. Entrance exams are being taken this month but I don't know what high school I'm going to. Papa wants me to go to Josephinum but that's so expensive. The uniform alone cost 40 dollars. Papa is so fixed on the idea to send me there and I know we can't afford it. Papa is going to talk to the priest and see if I can get in anyhow and somehow I hope I get to go there because of the drama club and because it's only four blocks away. Yours, Sandra[20]

Cisneros's father was determined to get his daughter the best education possible at a majority white, private Catholic school, but his daughter was conscious that it was beyond the family's means and that it would place a strain on them. Her father had to resort to imploring the priest for charity, placing him in a lowly position vis-à-vis the institution. For this young student, that self-knowledge and awareness—even before stepping onto the campus—led to a self-consciousness, a knowledge that she did not really financially belong there. Later journal entries, written after Cisneros had enrolled in Josephinum, show that she was confident in her studies and felt that she belonged there because she was academically qualified, but also that she fretted about her appearance and about standing out as the poor student in comparison to her classmates. On February 13, 1968, she wrote:

> Dear Diary, Tomorrow we're having a St. Val. Day Party at school and we don't have to bring our uniform. Even though my friends like this, I don't. I only have one pink dress and it was worn at our Xmas Party. I wish I had more clothes. My friends said, "What are you going to

wear?" I answered casually with a smile, "Oh, I have to see." I do have to see but see what? I don't know what I'll do since I haven't any clothes except for the pink one. Yours, Sandra[21]

For her classmates, the choice to wear whatever they wanted for Valentine's Day was a fun and welcome occasion, but for Cisneros, it was a source of fear, shame, and anxiety. Like for many students today, uniforms served as an equalizing garment that helped her mask her poverty and blend in. Once that equalizing agent was gone, she was mortified to wear the one, same dress she had worn before because it would reveal her poverty. She kept cool and pretended that she had fashion options to protect her already damaged self-esteem.

bell hooks enables us to see how these kinds of moments of shame in the classroom can become residual in our lives and can lead to cumulative trauma. Instances at school such as these serve as "moments of shame and humiliation so painful or as indignities so profound that one feels one has been robbed of her dignity or exposed as basically inadequate, bad, or worthy of rejection."[22] And just as hooks posits that only "by entering that experience long enough to endure it, deliberately, and consciously in order to transform it can we ever re-create who we are," Cisneros continues to show that only by writing through those painful school experiences can we heal.[23] She has been entering those experiences since her own diary pages and her earliest works. In *The House on Mango Street*, the teacher/nun from Esperanza's school passes by her family's boarded-up apartment building, looks up, and asks whether Esperanza lives *there*, making Esperanza feel ashamed as she is judged in relation to her poor living conditions:

"You live *there*?"
    There. I had to look at where she pointed—the third floor, the paint peeling, wooden bars Papa had nailed on the windows so we wouldn't fall out. You live *there*? The way she said it made me feel like nothing. *There*. I lived *there*. I nodded.
    I knew then I had to have a house.[24]

Cisneros shows us how teachers can incite ugly feelings of judgment that linger within a young girl's view of herself in the world. In fact, the narrative arc of *The House on Mango Street*—Esperanza's longing to have a house—is a direct result of her teacher shaming her: "I knew then I had to have a house." It is this pivotal shaming that etches in her mind the desire to own a pretty house so that she may be regarded as someone of worth by her teacher. But in the end, writing and storytelling set her free from that shame: "I put it down on paper and then the ghost doesn't ache so much. I write it down and Mango says goodbye sometimes. She sets me free."[25]

SHAME AND THE RACE AND CLASS INJURIES OF GRADUATE SCHOOL

For Cisneros, though, the injuries of grade school continued even into graduate school, so that process of healing and writing through trauma was indefinitely prolonged. In 1976, she went off to graduate school in Iowa, at the Iowa Writers' Workshop—one of the most prestigious graduate writing programs in the United States—and was forced to relive her otherness. Having lived at home while earning her undergraduate degree in English at Loyola University Chicago (1972–1976), she was at the time she left for Iowa the first in her family to leave home without being married—something unheard of in her generation. Cisneros relates: "I had marched off to college and, with relief, left my father's house, that frying pan, only to leap into the fire of an all-Anglo writers' workshop. The move forced me to have to deal with my 'otherness' for the first time—my race and class difference—and to develop, at long last, a feminist consciousness."[26] Interesting that Cisneros describes being confronted with her otherness for the first time in graduate school, after having experienced so much of it in her K–12 education. What is certain is that at this juncture in her life, her gender difference figured more prominently in her intersectional identity and oppression. Cisneros felt that her father's home was inhospitable to her woman-identified self, but it was a "frying pan" in comparison to the alienating firestorm she faced in graduate school.

In Iowa, Cisneros was the only Chicana in her graduate cohort, where the only other women of color were Joy Harjo and Rita Dove. Most classmates were white and wealthy, and Cisneros felt out of place and insecure, leading her to lose her voice and question "her right to a life of letters." In her 1995 essay "A Woman of No Consequence: Una Mujer Cualquiera," she recounts:

> I am famous now for being an *hocicona* (a big mouth), but when I was attending graduate school at the Iowa Writers Workshop, I was too afraid to even speak. Partly because I was young, and partly because I was other and didn't know it. What I did know was a terrible source of shame. The language for that shame I carried with me for so many years in the form of things I did not talk about or want known about me; I'm not certain I was aware of it in a conscious way, but it was there nonetheless like a fine shard of glass that had healed under the flesh;

poke and it hurt. It did not clarify itself into words until that graduate seminar when we were talking about houses. A house, or lack of one, became my subject. Once I could name that smudge as a shame, as shame of my working-class home, neighborhood, of my doubt about my right to a life of letters, of my fear of not being as good as my classmates, of not being smart enough, I became angry. Fueled with that anger, the poems and stories came in a torrent.[27]

Like a practical theorist explaining how affect theory works on the ground, Cisneros uses clear language to illustrate the acutely self-conscious and embodied nature of the debilitating feelings that can stem from experiencing marginality and alienation. She shows how the experience of being shamed or judged as inferior for one's ethnic background can lead to a self-doubt that breeds and festers within us, causing us to feel inferior and internalize a virulent, ever-flaring case of imposter syndrome. She likens internalized shame and inferiority to "fine shards of glass" that painfully remain embedded in the body, are hard to extricate, and continuously hurt inside; yet they remain hidden injuries because of the overwhelming desire to hide these defects that one sees within oneself.[28]

For Cisneros, it was the act of identifying, naming, and confronting that shame and self-doubt that enabled her to extricate that glass from within her flesh and begin to heal. Fired up with indignant anger and a renewed sense of self-worth, Cisneros found her political consciousness catalyzed: "my political consciousness began the moment I could name this shame."[29] She became determined to make her writing have a political purpose, and now, endowed with an oppositional racial, class, and gender politics, she wielded a transgressive aesthetics to arrive at her aims.

MANGO STREET: TRANSGRESSIVELY USING MINIMALIST AESTHETICS TO CRITIQUE MARGINALITY

One thing Cisneros gained from her studies at the University of Iowa was her adept use of minimalist aesthetics in her writing. In crafting *The House on Mango Street*, she took the minimalist form—underscored by extremely sparse narrative, an economy of words, repetition, no ornamentation, and gradual variation—and adapted it into an oppositional poetics to inscribe the historically marginalized experiences of working-class women of color within American literature. If Ernest Hemingway was the forefather of this aesthetics of literary omission—used to "strengthen the story and make people feel more than they understood"—Cisneros endowed it with a mestiza poetics fueled by social justice.[30] By inscribing into *Mango Street* narratives of those who are unable to realize their potential, such as sequestered and abused women (Rafaela, Minerva, and Sally), forgotten immigrants (Geraldo), and impoverished students with patriarchs at home (Alicia), she examines lives that were previously omitted from American literature.

In *Mango Street*, Cisneros also uses minimalist narrative to heal the trauma of her own mother Elvira's lack of schooling. In her 2015 memoir, *A House of My Own*, Cisneros shares many details about her mother's unfulfilled life, confessing: "I became a writer thanks to a mother who was unhappy being a mother. She was a prisoner-of-war mother banging on the bars of her cell all her life."[31] Her mother felt trapped because she had no education, was dependent on her husband, and was charged with raising seven children, but was an artist at heart. It was Cisneros's mother who helped give her daughter the privilege of obtaining the education she never could: she would take young Sandra to the library, museums, and the opera, nurturing her daughter's artistic spirit, and giving her freedom from domestic drudgery to develop her craft as a writer. Cisneros states: "I'm here because my mother let me stay in my room reading and studying, perhaps because she didn't want me to inherit her sadness and her rolling pin."[32] In the vignette "A Smart Cookie," we see Elvira's imprint in references to kitchen implements, sighs, and sorrows.

The power of minimalist aesthetics is harnessed in "A Smart Cookie" when Esperanza's mother reveals that she was pushed out of school because she was made to feel ashamed of looking poor. Esperanza's mother begins the story by telling her daughter, "I could've been somebody, you know?"[33] It is a simple statement that encapsulates so much regret and the lost possibilities of a lifetime: an education and its many benefits lost, all because of the irremediable effects of shame. Esperanza takes over the narrative and elucidates, "She can speak two languages. She can sing an opera. She knows how to fix a TV. She used to draw when she had time."[34] Esperanza recognizes her mother's multifaceted talents, despite her lack of formal education and the child-rearing duties that sideline her art. Her mother then says, "out of nowhere":

> Shame is a bad thing, you know. It keeps you down. You wanna know why I quit school? Because I didn't have nice clothes. No clothes, but I had brains.
>
> Yup, she says disgusted, stirring again. I was a smart cookie then.[35]

All her mother says about her life prior to dropping out (or being pushed out) of school is expressed in the latent lamentation, "I was a smart cookie then." That is the last sentence of the vignette—no follow-up, no details, just a succinct statement resounding with grief and regret. The simplicity of the statement makes us want to know more and pulls at our heartstrings. Esperanza's mother's lesson is haunting: Esperanza will need to go to school and study hard so that she does not end up like her mother—an organic intellectual who is full of artistic talent but who is reduced to singing operas while stirring a pot of oatmeal for her hungry kids. The omission of further details in the minimalist story leads us to fill them in ourselves, with our own stories, and in doing so we are able to intimately read her mother as representative of all mothers before us who were shut out from obtaining an education through institutional violence and the emotional toll it took on them. The style and voice that these self-reflections employ—a child's short, syntactic sentences with deceptively simple language—highlight their poignancy and immediacy.

As we can see from "A Smart Cookie," *Mango Street*'s deployment of the minimalist form heightens its politics. Part of the reason Cisneros's text is so poignant in its characterization of the underprivileged is that through its concise form, it swiftly paints people as infinitely interesting even as it also indicates that they are infinitesimal specks liable to be forgotten in the larger scheme of society. Cisneros's vignettes can stand on their own or be read within a sustained narrative of socioeconomic, sexual, or autonomous poverty; as she says, "you can understand each story like a little pearl or look at the whole thing like a necklace."[36] Whether read as pearls or a necklace, the vignettes of *Mango Street* nonetheless still deploy an aesthetic of marginality; Cisneros's scarce and economical language underscores the paltry conditions that she is writing about.

As Cisneros shows, for the Chicana writer, omission isn't solely an aesthetic practice; it is a social reality she must contest. Pushed out of school, marginalized, and excluded from literary discourse, her community risks being written out of narratives and wrongly pathologized as not valuing school. By showing Esperanza piecing her mother's story together and gathering the crumbs of her mother, the smart cookie, Cisneros uses her Chicana daughter-narrator to write and reclaim Chicana women's school and societal experiences in their own educational counternarratives.

WOMAN HOLLERING CREEK: "MORE IS MORE" BECOMES AN ANTIDOTE TO FEELING LESS THAN

By 1987, when Cisneros received her second National Endowment for the Arts grant, she seems to have found the validation to delve deeper into her Mexican culture, aesthetics, and *rasquache* sensibilities than ever before. In many ways, *Woman Hollering Creek* is a transitional text in terms of style: it still works minimalism into stories like "Eleven," but it also demonstrates an adventurous foray into the possibilities latent within Mexican maximalism. Cisneros's evolving style and narratives in this stage of her writing suggest that she had the realization that "more is more" can be an antidote to being made to feel less than; the stories seem to demonstrate that *la cultura cura* (culture cures), and that she accessed this curative culture not in school, but through the education she received by living in the community of San Antonio, Texas.

In the stories in *Woman Hollering Creek*, Cisneros *manda* (sends) the aesthetic lessons she learned at the Iowa school *al carajo* (to hell) and infuses her style with the once-Mexican city of San Antonio; racial, geographic, cultural, religious, and linguistic specifics overflow in every story. It is an explosion of all things Mexican: the stories invoke the Alamo, Lucía Méndez and her telenovelas, La Virgen de Guadalupe, Zapata, La Malinche, El Cristo Negro de Esquipulas (from the San Fernando Cathedral in San Antonio), Maya kings, Pedro Infante, and Popocatépetl and Iztaccíhuatl, among others. Almost every story draws from the rich racial, cultural, and spiritual diversity of Mexicans and Chicana/os in or around Texas. And her extravagant tapestry of all things Mexican is *rasquache* to its core.

In her memoir, *A House of My Own*, Cisneros shows us how the experience of living in San Antonio helped imbue her writing with these Mexican American aesthetics of maximalism. She writes: "across a table of *sopa de conchitas* at Torres Taco Haven, this question: 'What is the Mexican American aesthetic?' A San Antonio architect is asking. He's trying to translate the private Mexican housescape to the public building. What is the Mexican American aesthetic? I think and then respond, 'More is more.'"[37] For her, in San Antonio, "more is more" becomes the guiding force of her aesthetics, a Chicana defiance of the once-imposed Iowan constrictions of minimalism. That Cisneros is able to define her politics and aesthetics while sitting, chatting, and eating *sopa de conchitas* at this famed San Antonio taqueria highlights how the location, food, company, and culture she found in that city helped her embrace the *sin vergüenza* style and subject matter that would propel her art from that point forward.

CARAMELO: RESISTANCE, *RASQUACHISMO*, AND THE CHICANA SCHOLARSHIP STUDENT COUNTERNARRATIVE

Cisneros's novel *Caramelo* represents a culmination of that literary maximalism, at 464 pages in length, with 86 chapters, about 100 footnotes, transnational settings, multiple narrators, and a historical chronology/glossary. In conceptualizing the difference between short story and novel forms, Cisneros explained in 1994: "You don't start out by building a house if you haven't learned how to build a room.... At this point in our career and our craft we're learning how to build the rooms before we can build a house."[38] With *The House on Mango Street*'s minimalist assemblage of textual blocks, Cisneros certainly practiced learning how to build her rooms. In *Caramelo*, she has built nothing short of a *rasquache* mansion. If Cisneros's highly sparse and restricted form in *Mango Street* simulated the impoverished and confining conditions her characters were living in, *Caramelo*'s intentional disregard of boundaries, margins, and borders reflects the full realization of the Chicana subject *sin vergüenza*—hybrid, endlessly creative, empowered, and defying all limits and expectations.

As Mesa-Bains reminds us, the intention of *rasquachismo* is "to provoke the accepted 'superior' norms of the Anglo-American with the everyday reality of Chicano cultural practices."[39] Cisneros's maximalist incorporation of Mexican and Chicano popular culture in *Caramelo* counters hegemonic notions that Mexicans are from a "cultural wasteland of non-achievement" that we should be ashamed of.[40] Through the cornucopia of talented artists from Mexican popular culture that *Caramelo* invokes—artists like Pedro Infante, Agustín Lara, Lola Beltrán, María Félix, Lupe Vélez, and Tin Tan—Cisneros takes us with her on her counterhegemonic pilgrimage of recovering and valorizing Mexican culture. She even includes a historical chronology at the end of the book to firmly situate her story within a historical context. As Gabriella Gutiérrez y Muhs has noted, "this compendium makes *Caramelo* an interactive/didactic novel that forces the reader to continue investigating for her/himself the previously unfamiliar cultural iconic characters in the American mainstream that Cisneros highlights as if part of a spiritual quest."[41] This reclaiming and embracing of forgotten Mexican artists is part of the spiritual work of Chicana healing, of recovering culture that we were made to feel did not exist, or that we regarded as a stigma or tried to bury in our efforts to assimilate. The recovery of our rich culture, Cisneros suggests, is the first step in our recovery from a soul sickness that can arise out being made to feel like we have no culture.

Perhaps just as importantly, in *Caramelo*, Cisneros uses the spirit of Chicana/o resistance and affirmation accessed through *rasquache* aesthetics to provide an antiracist counternarrative of working-class Chicana education in Catholic school. As we have seen, this is a traumatic subject for Cisneros, one that is still palpable, as though it were yesterday. In *Caramelo*, systemic racism within the US educational system is named, critiqued, and challenged, and Cisneros is able to access healing from school injury for her protagonist, Lala. These kinds of difficult conversations about systemic racism in school were elided in *The House on Mango Street*. Perhaps the critical lens and the language were not there yet, or it was not politically safe to articulate those kinds of critiques yet. In *Mango Street*, Esperanza's mother blames herself for dropping out of school. She succinctly states that she was poor and felt out of place in school because of her working-class clothes and appearance; she has internalized her class injury and blames herself instead of "the overt and covert forms of psychological terrorism and the role shame and shaming plays as a force preventing marginalized students from performing with excellence."[42]

In *Caramelo*, on the other hand, Lala's mother, Zoila, shares hooks's analysis of the ways students of color are set up to fail in the educational system. In chapter 62, "A Godless Woman, My Mother," the Reyes family has returned from Mexico in late August and Lala is now at the age in which she must enroll in high school. Zoila is not religious and is in fact "suspicious of anyone who represents the church."[43] Yet, she has decided that Lala will attend Immaculate Conception Catholic High School because of the superior education she will receive there:

> Not for any love of Church, believe me, but because the public schools, in her own words, are a piece of crap. —The whole system is designed to make you fail, Mother says. —Just look at the numbers dropping out. But until it's the güero kids who are failing in as many numbers as us, nobody gives a damn. Listen to me, Lala. Better to be beaten by priests and nuns than to get a beating from life.[44]

Zoila does not hold her tongue: she openly discusses race and racism within the educational system, and she critiques the systemic violence of an educational system that fails its Latinx students and proceeds with zero accountability because no one cares about Latinx student success. Only when poor schooling affects white children does anybody "give a damn." The mother character is no longer taking blame for dropping out of school. Rather, she shows how racism within the educational system serves as a mechanism to push Latinx students such as herself and her children out. This mother is teaching her Chicana daughter a very different lesson about the racist realities of education in the United States and the uphill battle Latinx students face to receive the education due to them. She is critical of the church and the public schools but feels she has to make the hard decision to place her daughter in a Catholic school, where she may suffer physical punishment, rather than placing her in the public schools, where she will certainly suffer institutional violence and a lifetime of missed possibilities.

Because Zoila's critique of the US educational system is wedged into a detailed description of the Mexican *rasquachismo* of the Reyes family's decor, Cisneros's narrative placement and stylistic choices suggest that, as Mesa-Bains says, the sensibility of *rasquachismo* can provide "a combination of resistant and resilient attitudes devised to allow the Chicano to survive and persevere with a sense of dignity."[45] That is precisely what the household decor appears to provide to the family. This chapter begins with a description of "a framed portrait of La Virgen de Guadalupe" that made its way to the family home via Lala's Awful Grandmother, who purchased it

> from a Villita vendor in front of the very hill where the Indian madonna made her miraculous apparition, blessed by the basílica priest, wrapped in a fresh copy of ESTO sports newspaper, tied taut and double-knotted with hairy twine, stuffed alongside a bottle of rompope rum eggnog, bags of Glorias—Father's favorite chuchulucos, a year's worth of La Familia Burrón comic books in an ixtle shopping bag.[46]

Then, immediately following Zoila's critique of institutions, in the very next paragraphs, the book goes on to describe the house and all the pictures the family has on the walls: "a 1965 Mexican calendar . . . [with] a white horse, a handsome charro, and in his rapturous arms, a swooning beauty, her silk rebozo and blouse sliding off one sexy shoulder."[47] Why have such excessive aesthetics lodged before and after Zoila's critique? This parallel structure suggests that suffusive Mexican/Chicanx *rasquache* aesthetics in the home can provide Mexicans/Chicanxs with affirmation, critical consciousness, and a powerful self-grounding that helps them clearly read and interpret American narratives and incisively critique them. In effect, *rasquachismo*, for Lala's family, "brings an integral world view that serves as a basis for cultural identity and a sociopolitical movement."[48] Zoila suffers no fools and has no shame. She emblazons the house with Mexican culture, calls things out for what they are, and has passed that defiance down to her daughter. Her narrative transmits powerful aesthetic and political lessons that serve us well in our own journeys of healing and resistance.

HEALING THE SELF TO HELP HEAL OTHERS

With many years having passed since Cisneros's school days, the qualities and actions that critics and academics try to shame her for have evolved, but her methods of healing from that opprobrium have remained consistent. In *Woman without Shame*, Cisneros fully embodies the rich, fulfilled life of living *sin vergüenza*, providing maximalist details of her life observations and love life while basking in the cultural abundance of living in Mexico. Her interviews, too, increasingly reveal that she cares not for people's opinions of her. By taking away people's power to shame her or make her feel less than, she can no longer be hurt by anyone's judgment. She can be free to just be—and she passes on those lessons to others. For example, in a 2023 podcast interview with Carlos Frías, Cisneros shows how she embraces her role as a healer who uses her past traumatic experiences to help others overcome their trauma:

> Books are medicine. . . . Authors, we are doctors. We are healers. In a different age, we would've been shamans. The *curanderos*. The healers of the community. The visionaries. We are working from an intuitive place. In writing, we are healing our own wounds. When you look at societies who have the healers, they're often the medicine men and women who have had a trauma and survived it and are illuminating the path for others who are going through that process of trying to heal. That is what I think my job is. It's one of service. And it's very important that my books be out there.[49]

Using her stories to teach us how not to allow other people or institutions to shame us, and helping us "move beyond shame to a place of recognition that is humanizing," Cisneros shows us how we may in effect reclaim our dignity, self-worth, and brilliance within spaces where we have historically not been welcomed.[50] Her writings help us value what was once devalued and recover our own power and self-determination, helping us heal from scholastic injury through the power of taking up space and telling our own transgressive, culturally rich counternarratives.

NOTES

Infinite thanks to Geneva M. Gano for the invitation to participate in the Cisneros symposium (2019) and colloquium (2022), and for her continuous, insightful feedback and endless hospitality. Sonia Saldívar-Hull—thank you for being my first mentor and supporter. I sincerely thank Teresa Hernández and Olga L. Herrera for their invaluable feedback on this essay; they helped improve it tremendously. Raúl Moreno Campos—always my first reader and companion. Gracias.

1. Sandra Cisneros, diary, box 12, folders 1, 2, 13, 14, Sandra Cisneros Papers, Wittliff Collections, Texas State University.

2. Sandra Cisneros, *Woman Hollering Creek and Other Stories* (New York: Random House, 1991).

3. Janelle Retka, "Author Sandra Cisneros Shares Stories of Belonging and Overcoming Fear," *Yakima Herald*, April 16, 2019.

4. Retka, "Author Sandra Cisneros Shares Stories."

5. Sandra Cisneros, *Woman without Shame: Poems* (New York: Alfred A. Knopf, 2022).

6. bell hooks, *Teaching Community: A Pedagogy of Hope* (New York: Routledge,

2003), 93–104.

7. Sandra Cisneros, *The House on Mango Street* (New York: Vintage Books, 1984); Sandra Cisneros, *Caramelo or Puro Cuento* (New York: Vintage Books, 2002).

8. Quoted in Feroza Jussawalla and Reed Way Dasenbrock, "Interviews with Writers of the Postcolonial World," in *Writing Women's Lives: An Anthology of Autobiographical Narratives by Twentieth Century American Women Writers*, ed. Susan Cahill (New York: HarperCollins, 1994), 467. Ernest Hemingway, for example, known as the father of minimalism, wrote in *Death in the Afternoon* in 1932, "If a writer of prose knows enough about what he is writing about he may omit things that he knows and the reader, if the writer is writing truly enough, will have a feeling of those things as strongly as though the writer had stated them. The dignity of movement of an ice-berg is due to only one-eighth of it being above water." Hemingway, *Death in the Afternoon* (1932; New York: Scribner, 1999), 153–154.

9. Aída Hurtado and Norma E. Cantú, *MeXicana Fashions: Politics, Self-Adornment, and Identity Construction* (Austin: University of Texas Press, 2020), 5.

10. Quoted in Jesús Rosales, *Thinking en Español: Interviews with Critics of Chicana/o Literature* (Tucson: University of Arizona Press, 2014), 220.

11. Amalia Mesa-Bains, "Domesticana: The Sensibility of Chicana Rasquache," *Aztlan: A Journal of Chicano Studies* 24, no. 2 (Fall 1999): 158.

12. Gloria Anzaldúa, *Borderlands/La Frontera: The New Mestiza*, 4th ed. (1987; San Francisco: Aunt Lute Books, 2012), 68.

13. Stephanie Fetta, *Shaming into Brown: Somatic Transactions of Race in Latina/o Literature* (Columbus: Ohio State University Press, 2018), xviii.

14. Christina Garcia Lopez, *Calling the Soul Back: Embodied Spirituality in Chicanx Narrative* (Tucson: University of Arizona Press, 2019), 14; see also Lara Medina and Martha R. Gonzales, eds., *Voices from the Ancestors: Xicanx and Latinx Spiritual Reflections and Healing Practices* (Tucson: University of Arizona Press, 2019).

15. Garcia Lopez, *Calling the Soul Back*, 4.

16. hooks, *Teaching Community*, 93–94.

17. hooks, *Teaching Community*, 99.

18. Melita Marie Garza, "Author Sandra Cisneros Tells Her Story to Latino Schoolchildren," *Chicago Tribune*, December 28, 1992.

19. Kim Sagel, "Sandra Cisneros," *Publishers Weekly*, March 29, 1991, 74; Diane Scharper, "Flair for Details, Spiritual Insight Enliven Collection," *National Catholic Reporter*, February 3, 2016.

20. Cisneros, diary, January 5, 1968, box 12, folder 1, Sandra Cisneros Papers.

21. Cisneros, diary, February 13, 1968, box 12, folder 1, Sandra Cisneros Papers.

22. hooks, *Teaching Community*, 94.

23. hooks, *Teaching Community*, 103.

24. Cisneros, *The House on Mango Street*, 5.

25. Cisneros, *The House on Mango Street*, 110.

26. Sandra Cisneros, "My Wicked Wicked Ways: The Chicana Writer's Struggle with Good and Evil, or Las Hijas de la Mala Vida," presentation, Modern Language Association (MLA) Convention, Chicago, December 1985, and MLA at Yale, 1986, 2–3, box 39, folder 4, Sandra Cisneros Papers.

27. Sandra Cisneros, "A Woman of No Consequence: Una Mujer Cualquiera," in

Living Chicana Theory, ed. Carla Trujillo (Berkeley, CA: Third Woman Press, 1998), 82.

28. Cisneros, "A Woman of No Consequence," 82.

29. Sandra Cisneros, *A House of My Own: Stories from My Life* (New York: Alfred A. Knopf, 2015), 126.

30. Charles M. Oliver, *Ernest Hemingway A to Z: The Essential Reference to the Life and Work* (New York: Checkmark Press, 1999), 75.

31. Cisneros, *A House of My Own*, 291.

32. Cisneros, *A House of My Own*, 75.

33. Cisneros, *The House on Mango Street*, 90.

34. Cisneros, *The House on Mango Street*, 90.

35. Cisneros, *The House on Mango Street*, 91.

36. Quoted in Jussawalla and Dasenbrock, "Interviews with Writers of the Postcolonial World," 467.

37. Cisneros, *A House of My Own*, 186.

38. Quoted in Jussawalla and Dasenbrock, "Interviews with Writers of the Postcolonial World," 467.

39. Mesa-Bains, "Domesticana," 168.

40. Ngugi wa Thiong'o, *Decolonising the Mind: The Politics of Language in African Literature* (Suffolk, UK: James Currey, 1986), 3.

41. Gabriella Gutiérrez y Muhs, "Capirotada: A Renewed Chicana Spirituality through a Chicana Literary Lens," in *(Re)Mapping the Latina/o Literary Landscape: New Works and New Directions*, ed. Cristina Herrera and Larissa M. Mercado-López (New York: Palgrave Macmillan, 2016), 148.

42. hooks, *Teaching Community*, 98.

43. Cisneros, *Caramelo*, 312.

44. Cisneros, *Caramelo*, 312.

45. Mesa-Bains, "Domesticana," 158.

46. Cisneros, *Caramelo*, 311–312.

47. Cisneros, *Caramelo*, 312–313.

48. Mesa-Bains, "Domesticana," 158–159.

49. "Sandra Cisneros on Living 'Sin Vergüenza,' but Not Being a 'Sinvergüenza,'" interview by Carlos Frías, *Sundial* (podcast), April 12, 2023, 49:50.

50. hooks, *Teaching Community*, 103.

CHAPTER 8

THE LOOSE WOMAN AND THE MEN OF ILL REPUTE

Richard T. Rodríguez

> I was born under a crooked star.
> SANDRA CISNEROS, "HIS STORY"

"His Story," a poem in Sandra Cisneros's 1987 poetry collection *My Wicked Wicked Ways*, finds the speaker recounting how her "unlucky fate" is sealed: not only was she "born woman in a family of men," but she belongs to a genealogy of star-crossed women (including one "arrested for audacious crimes that began by disobeying fathers" and another "three times cursed a widow") who, coincidentally, also possess the name "Sandra Cisneros." Yet while relishing her status as a self-anointed wicked woman whose misfit foremothers helped pave the way for her departure from the family home, the speaker-poet makes it clear that this is a story not merely about herself but also about her father. Indeed, as the title of the poem discloses, "His Story" works as a dual recounting of the daughter's gendered misalignment as "a crooked star" and the father's paternal "sorrow" because his only daughter has gone astray.[1]

I begin with this poem as it illustrates how Cisneros's writing frequently doubles as both an autobiographical recollection and an opportunity for mutually relating with those similarly misaligned and pulled into her personal-literary orbit. For just as "His Story" is as much her father's story as it is the poet's, the life and work of Cisneros generate a potent cross-identification with ostracized Others.[2] In "His Story," such cross-identification prompts not understanding between father and disorderly daughter but a retelling of "his story" vis-à-vis his daughter's. In Cisneros's life and work, in contrast, her politics of defiance unsettles normative kinship relations at the same time as it facilitates bonds with those in the shadows of conventional cultural and historical narratives. Here I examine how this cross-identification operates between Cisneros and Latino gay men. By tracing the bonds between the two with respect to their shared status as outsiders and outcasts from commonly repressive institutions (namely the family and the church) and the attendant sexual practices these institutions sanction, I build on the foundational insights of Chicana feminist critic Catrióna Rueda Esquibel to identify a queer connection between a self-identified "loose woman" and the gay men (relatedly bearing the status of ill repute) inhabiting her world. Thus, elaborating on Cisneros's well-known refusal of an identity cast within the terms of nuclear and procreative family formations ("she is nobody's mother and nobody's wife"), we might see how Cisneros's feminist and sexual politics facilitates deep, mutual attachments between "the queen bee" and "her drones" on the page and beyond it while catalyzing Latino gay male cultural expressions.[3]

MIRACLES AND THE MARLBORO MAN

In "Memories of Girlhood: Chicana Lesbian Fictions," Esquibel astutely argues that Cisneros's first novel, *The House on Mango Street* (1984), is a Chicana lesbian text as it centers "intense girlhood friendships" that "inscribe a desire between girls," a desire the critic elects to name "lesbian."[4] What I find most striking in this formulation, compelling for how it contests a ready-made definition of "lesbian," is Esquibel's assessment of the protagonist's resistance to "forced heterosexualization."[5] Not wishing to maintain that Esperanza is Cisneros (which she is and isn't, as Cisneros has repeatedly asserted), Esquibel matches her assessment of the former to the persona of the latter, who has recurrently refused customary ties to husband and children that fulfill not only the expectation of normative womanhood but also the formula to guarantee a "straightened" orientation as opposed to one "crooked."[6]

Woman Hollering Creek and Other Stories (1991), Cisneros's third book, extends the resistance to "forced heterosexualization" identified by Esquibel in *The House on Mango Street* by spotlighting a number of desirous bonds—bonds that are amorous as much as they are unrequited—that refuse the gender roles circumscribing traditional family forms. This refusal manifests most powerfully when Cisneros intimately writes about a range of individuals whose identities and social statuses render them outside the norm. Indeed, the intimacy the reader feels between Cisneros and her subjects is the product of the way her work hinges on the ability to "cross over." Katherine Rios argues that "*Woman Hollering Creek* offers a collection of stories about 'crossing over' in all its manifestations: across geographical borders and borders of culture, class and color; through language and writing; and even across theoretical borders, braving the 'crossfire' between hegemonic theoretical discourses."[7] Another form of "crossing over," to build on Rios's insights, manifests by way of the cross-identification established between Cisneros and those about whom she writes, including Latino gay men. Through this cross-identification, Cisneros's writing, as Rios contends, "discloses the self-consciousness of the Chicana's betrayal and transgression as she attempts to interpret, translate, and cross cultures."[8] In particular, two stories from *Woman Hollering Creek*—"Little Miracles, Kept Promises" and "The Marlboro Man"—intimate this cross-identification.

Consider, then, a letter written by one man (albeit authored by Cisneros) in support of another and included in the story "Little Miracles, Kept Promises." This "story" consists entirely of written requests by patrons of a Catholic church in Texas that are placed on a shrine dedicated to La Virgen de Guadalupe. In the letter, Benjamin T. requests assistance from the Miraculous Black Christ of Esquipulas to watch over a man whom he loves dearly but who is currently stationed overseas. Benjamin T.'s letter stands out from the others not only for its unique request but also for its distinctive use of code. This may be due perhaps to nonfunctional keys on the typewriter on which the letter is written, but most likely it is a means to maintain discretion—based on the self-professed shame of the letter writer—in light of Catholicism's downcast eyes on same-sex desire. Thus, signed "B2njIm3n T." (Benjamin T.) to "M3rlc5145s Blıck Chr3st 4f 2sq53p5lıs" (Miraculous Black Christ of Esquipulas), the letter reads as follows: "3 ısk y45, L4rd, w3th ıll my h2ırt pl2ıs2 wıtch 4v2r Mınny B2nıv3d2s wh4 3s 4v2rs2ıs. 3 l4v2 h3m ınd 3 d4n't kn4w whlt t4 d4 lb45t ıll th3s l4v2 sıdn2ss ınd shım2 thıt f3lls m2." (I ask you, Lord, with all my heart please watch over Manny Benavides who is overseas. I love him and I don't know what to do about all this love sadness and shame that fills me.)[9]

As with other examples of Cisneros's writing that aim to reconfigure religious icons for those whom the Catholic Church has historically and ideologically excluded (consider, for example, her 1996 essay "Guadalupe the Sex Goddess"), the letter from Benjamin deploys a strategy identified by the late queer theorist José Esteban Muñoz as "disidentification," which "works on and against dominant ideology." As Muñoz further explains, "this 'working on and against' is a strategy that tries to transform a cultural logic from within, always laboring to enact permanent structural change while at the same time valuing the importance of local or everyday struggles of resistance."[10] Akin to the impulse of disidentification, the cross-identification that underscores the twenty-three letters in "Little Miracles, Kept Promises" forcefully enacts a collective bond based on shared "everyday struggles of resistance." Albeit disparately situated based on respective social stature and geographic location, the assemblage of letters and letter writers in Cisneros's narrative documents a palpable, collective longing for and procurement of the lost, the disparaged, the exiled, and the nearly impossible.[11]

These letter writers, whose impassioned pleas are infused with the utmost profundity, exist as more than one-dimensional fictionalized figures; they are skillfully sketched personages possessing a range of empathetically relatable plights with whom Cisneros patently identifies (or, rather, cross-identifies) in her own role as scribe. The writers featured in "Little Miracles, Kept Promises" include a remorseful wife whose love for her husband has lamentably faded, an unemployed man in search of a job with benefits, and a pair of grandparents imploring the Miraculous Black Christ of Esquipulas for their grandson's kindness, drug rehabilitation, employment, and ultimate departure. Here, the glue connecting the letters adheres as well to a collective yearning for miracles granted by a responsive Christ or saint, often to save the forlorn within this lot of imploring individuals, who are rendered as poor, adrift sinners in a Catholic context.

Benjamin's letter further illustrates obliged negotiations within multiple institutions that, as ideologically repressive and state sanctioned as they are, often offer hope (or at least the promise of it) to the destitute. Benjamin's love for Manny is mediated not just by the jarring terrain of the Catholic Church and affectionate public relationships that necessitate anchoring within heterosexual coupling and reproduction, but also by the military and its disavowal of queer service members.[12] Characteristic of Cisneros's work, this letter speaks to Latinx readers who transgress heteronormative sexual mores. Cisneros is acutely aware of the complicated situation in which Benjamin is placed, as is evidenced by the style in which his letter is delivered and, moreover, the specific feelings that charge his epistolary plea: love, sadness, and shame. Indeed a "crooked star" to those institutions that revile his love and denounce its public accession, Benjamin stands as a queer figure in the pantheon of Cisneros's literary landscape registering those eclipsed by forced heterosexualization.

On a personal note, since the first time I read Benjamin's letter, I felt an even deeper connection to Cisneros's writing, based on an evident fellowship with Benjamin in light of the patriarchal repression and heteronormative expectation with which he is forced to contend. Yet what I find most compelling about Cisneros's desire to bond with gay men in her writing is not a simple bid for queer representation; instead, it is how her texts, via literary form, signal that "affirmative" representations cannot be simply asserted when repression, exclusion, and violence incessantly contour queer lives. In other words, while we may regard Benjamin's appearance in Cisneros's work as an act of representational solidarity, the distinct form his letter takes discloses a concentrated awareness of how the amorous bond between two men can only be written in code, which in turn necessitates an against-the-grain reading practice to throw light on that proverbial love that dares not speak its name.[13] Cross-identification in this instance exceeds a simple comparison of identities to instead consider the means by which the legibility of similarly repressed voices might manifest vis-à-vis nonnormative narrative practices.

This strategy is also adopted in "The Marlboro Man." Although the story reads as a conversation between two women friends, the figure on which this conversation decidedly pivots is the eponymous cowboy at the center of the advertising for the Marlboro brand of American cigarettes. The woman who begins the narrative—whose focalized voice is discernable by the bold type in which it appears on the page—recounts her friend Romelia's relationship with a man named Durango, who is assumed to be the titular Marlboro Man. The other woman engaged in the conversation, however, expresses doubt that Durango was indeed the Marlboro Man, given her knowledge of the openly gay model and actor Christian Haren, who played this role in ads for Marlboro cigarettes and died of AIDS-related complications in 1996.

On the surface, one might regard this story as an opportunity offered to the reader by Cisneros to be let in on some juicy *chisme* shared by two *comadres* about a third woman (Romelia) romantically involved with and done wrong by her skirt-chasing man (Durango). But this man's hypermasculinity, which causes him to be mistaken for the figure of the Marlboro Man, is overwhelmed by a queer narrative about a man whose visual manliness eclipsed his nonheterosexual status. That is, the narrative of a tumultuous relationship between a philanderer and his beguiled girlfriend cannot exist without attachment to Haren, a man whose sexuality was overshadowed by heteronormative presumption based on masculine presentation. The doubling effect here works as an act of cross-identification whereby the one man's duplicitous behavior is contrasted with another's struggle to survive, live, and love despite the virtually insurmountable pressure to stay hidden, particularly in the face of homophobia and the devastation wrought by the AIDS pandemic. At the end of the story, the second woman, calling on the authority of journalist and news anchor Dan Rather, maintains that Haren was indeed "the *original* Marlboro Man." Her friend seems to finally concede the point, declaring: "The original, huh? . . . Well, maybe the one I'm talking about who lived with Romelia wasn't the *real* Marlboro Man."[14]

Cisneros here is aiming to dislodge the figure of the cowboy from the culture of straight masculinity and, more specifically, the heterosexual relationship. Moreover, the common tethering of the cowboy to white manliness is undone, all while the two Marlboro Men in the story stand as doubles, impossible to disaggregate from each other. And while Haren's history is briefly alluded to ("The Marlboro Man was working as an AIDS clinic volunteer and he died from it even"), it ultimately looms large in Cisneros's literary landscape, particularly for how the outcast figure is not only the disparaged woman but also, inextricably, the defamed gay man, whose story might be misconstrued or otherwise go untold.[15] Another "crooked star," this time one whose celebrity and life were cut short by aspects of his life that were rendered socially unacceptable, he is in alignment with those many with whom Cisneros stands in solidarity; it is a fellowship, as it were, between straight women and gay men.

Fittingly, these two stories appear under the section titled "There Was a Man, There Was a Woman." The conjoining of man and woman, however, hardly unites the two under the banner of heterosexual romance or conjugality. Instead, the categories of man and woman remain divided by the comma on the page even as they are united by a queer politics of "crossing over" that—in the literary *and* lived worlds fashioned by Cisneros—brings these two together, although modified by an adamant refusal of normative gender and sexual conventions, by way of a cross-identification based on institutional marginality and a mutual resistance to it. And yet the goal of cross-identification as an analytic framework is not to merely signal a shared politics of marginality and resistance. Instead, cross-identification operates as an incendiary method for self-declaration, particularly as it relates to and jump-starts the assertion of the sexual self.

ASSOCIATIONS AND PROVOCATIONS

In "The Artist and the City," published in the February 2013 issue of *Texas Monthly*, journalist Jeff Wilson mentions to Sandra Cisneros that he learned from artist Franco Mondini-Ruiz that upon her relocation to San Antonio, "the group Cisneros fit into most easily was the gay community, . . . [like] 'the queen bee finding her drones.'"[16] Mondini-Ruiz's categorization of Cisneros indicates the long-standing intimate relationships Cisneros has held with queer communities over the course of her personal and professional history, a fact even when one takes stock of the cultural workers with whom she kept company from her early days in Chicago, her time in the Bay Area, and her subsequent relocation to and residence in San Antonio. One may indeed trace the ties Cisneros cultivated with Chicana lesbian artists and writers like Diana Solís and Carmen Abrego in Chicago vis-à-vis Norma Alarcón's foundational journal *Third Woman* (first published in Bloomington, Indiana, where Alarcón was a graduate student at Indiana University), and Cherríe Moraga, Ester Hernández, and Lourdes Portillo in San Francisco while Cisneros was a visiting professor at the University of California, Berkeley.[17] While Cisneros maintained connections to Chicana lesbian friends and colleagues, her move to San Antonio marks a time when her closest interlocutors and allies were the gay men who indelibly formed her most intimate network.

The friendship between Mondini-Ruiz and Cisneros is one example; another is Cisneros's collaboration with visual artist Ralfka Gonzalez. A San Antonio–based artist who would subsequently relocate to the San Franciso Bay Area, Gonzalez was commissioned by Cisneros to design the cover of her second book of poetry, 1994's *Loose Woman*.[18] The cover illustration, an expansive collage that covers the entirety of the book jacket, save the text and the author's photo appearing on it, encompasses an array of figures culled from Mexican, Catholic, and popular culture. While La Virgen de Guadalupe, Frida Kahlo, and a circle of naked men make an appearance, the one figure that appears at least a couple of times is Saint Sebastian. According to Flora Doble, Saint Sebastian operates as a "gay icon" as a result of how "the Christian fixation with the desirable bodies of its saints and the permeable boundaries between the bodily flesh and the divine have been seen as homoerotic or queer."[19] In one particular image of the saint on the front cover of *Loose Woman*, Sebastian, represented as always with arrows piercing his flesh as his scantily clad body appears in full view, might be understood as "inviting voyeurism to the beautiful male nude."[20] Yet it is not only the desirability of Saint Sebastian's fully exposed body that makes him an ideal "crooked star" for the cover of Cisneros's poetry collection about the affirmative embrace of sexual promiscuity (how else to define a self-declared "loose woman"?), but also his status as an outcast queer figure (emblematized, for example, in the 1976 film *Sebastiane* by the late gay British filmmaker Derek Jarman), which makes him a spiritual ally and a fitting affiliate in the pantheon of Cisneros's figures of resistance.[21]

Cisneros's introduction to Mondini-Ruiz, it turns out, was facilitated by another gay Latino artist: Rolando Briseño. And through Briseño, Mondini-Ruiz, and others belonging to the tight-knit San Antonio community of Latino intellectuals and artists (many of them gay men), Cisneros would meet Ángel Rodríguez-Díaz, a Puerto Rican painter and Briseño's partner, during her tenure in the Lone Star State. Briseño explains:

> I was in this group that Sandra Cisneros started that was called the Grupo de Cien and it was a bunch of artists and intellectuals that would meet—what was it? Once a month? Every Saturday? I don't know— anyway, we would meet and have brunch and talk about things that needed to be changed in San Antonio, like public radio. These entities are operating here as if they were in Minnesota or they could be in, you

know, Wisconsin. I mean, totally white, totally ignoring the, you know, over fifty percent of the population is Mex-American—and who knows how many illegal Mexicans too. You know, it's come on.[22]

Recounting how he met Cisneros through Briseño, Rodríguez-Díaz explains how this introduction would subsequently lead to Cisneros expressing admiration for his *Goddess Triptych* (1991–1994) and him painting what is now one of her most recognizable portraits.

> So he introduced me to her, and we had hit it off nicely. We became very good friends . . . then I suggested doing her portrait. She had seen some of my work and she liked it very much and she had seen the first goddess.
>
> And so that was the first one—*The Myth of Venus*—and she saw it and loved it because she—then she came over to my studio in New York; she was doing reading of her book—what was her book? *Woman Hollering Creek.* . . . And it was one of the bookstores there. So they taxied her—you know, the limo came and brought her over, and then—to my apartment. You know, I told her what to bring and what kind of things to bring because I had seen her dress up her. And so oh, I like this skirt, then I like the bustier, or that top that you wore, and you know, she had very cropped hair then.
>
> And then what I did was base the portrait on one of her characters—especially one—the woman in the story of the "Eyes of Zapata"—almost como los de Zapata, which is a very intense, tender, and very woman—you know, something about womanhood in that story that is beautiful. And I—it's sort of like—we use that character to create her portrait and that is why she is standing the way she is standing and that is why, you know, the whole demeanor of it—because I wanted to paint the heroine in that story. And actually, it's one of my favorite stories because it's one of the stories where I find that she is the mature woman. And we could go on to other issues about her writing, which I read before doing the portrait so I could sort of get a feeling for her artistic inquiries or things that moved her.[23]

Rodríguez-Díaz's portrait, *The Protagonist of an Endless Story* (1993), features Cisneros with arms crossed, dressed in black, and staring icily yet self-assuredly at the painting's viewer (see figure 8.1). The painting also showcases what writer Héctor Tobar identifies as the artist's propensity for "dreamscapes, finely detailed oils that depict Latinos against dramatic, iridescent skies."[24] Yet what I find most compelling is how *The Protagonist of an Endless Story* manifests as

Figure 8.1. Ángel Rodríguez-Díaz, *The Protagonist of an Endless Story*, 1993, oil on canvas, 72 x 57⅞ in. (182.9 x 147.0 cm). Smithsonian American Art Museum, purchase made possible in part by the Smithsonian Latino Initiatives Pool and the Smithsonian Institution Collections Acquisition Program, 1996.19.

the result of the inspiration Rodríguez-Díaz draws from Cisneros's work. Noting the affirmative embrace of womanhood at the heart of "Eyes of Zapata," the painter reads Inés, the story's protagonist, as Cisneros's literary double. With her example and writing serving as catalysts for Rodríguez-Díaz's painting, this may also be read as yet another example of the cross-identification taking place between Cisneros and Latino gay men. Indeed, *The Protagonist of an Endless Story*—which centers a protagonist who, for all parties involved, embodies the relatable enduring struggle for love in the face of family and patriarchy—takes shape as the result of each artist's admiration for their interlocutor's respective work.[25]

In a 2021 tribute honoring Cisneros as the recipient of the Fuller Award for Lifetime Achievement by the Chicago Literary Hall of Fame, San Antonio–based artist David Zamora Casas reflects on the impact of her writing on him as a Latino gay man as well as on her living example as an artistic peer and friend. Casas writes:

> As a maricon American Mexican "penniless painter," I have been inspired, sometimes delightfully shocked, and happy to know Sandra Cisneros since first reading *My Wicked Wicked Ways*. I was blessed to watch her fly high like a lechuza magically from *Mango Street* through the romantic eyes of Zapata and the tearful eyes of La Llorona from *Woman Hollering Creek*.
>
> Early on, I observed La Sandra editing my very first artist statement and became aware of the importance of telling our multifaceted stories con orgullo y sin vergüenza. My shameless pride was ignited.
>
> Her actions fueled my strong impulse to honestly explore my personal sexual identity as well as that of la Virgen de Guadalupe. It is embedded in a surreal memory of La Sandra reaching the sublime.[26]

Oscillating between Cisneros's influence as a writer and her formidable presence in San Antonio, Casas ultimately notes how the "dear gays supported La Sandra and La Sandra supported nosotros los maricones, las mariposas y las monfloras de San Antonio."[27] A queer San Antonio mutual support network was thus born.

Cisneros's support (particularly as it is grounded in a San Antonio context) and cross-identification with gay men, queens, and lesbians is further reflected in her essay "A Woman of No Consequence: Una Mujer Cualquiera." Initially delivered as a keynote speech for the third annual conference of the National Lesbian and Gay Journalists Association, on February 18, 1995, in San Antonio, Cisneros's essay centers her outsider status as *la otra*, the other woman. She begins:

> I've always been la otra. The other woman. Even when my lovers didn't have a wife. Even when they didn't climb out of my bed to climb that same night into another's. I've been la otra. The one they sought when the one at home didn't understand them.
>
> It's not to say I understood them any better. But they didn't need to understand me, understand? That was the difference.
>
> So I don't count. Una mujer cualquiera. A woman of no consequence. That's me.[28]

It is quite fitting that Cisneros begins her essay by declaring herself *la otra*, not merely for the way she elects to affirmatively identify as a woman who refuses to adhere to the strictures of sexual decorum (including a virtuous respect for monogamy) but because of the grammatical and situational proximity between *la otra* and *los otros*. A term often used in a Mexican context to refer to queers (signaling their otherness, of course), *los otros* is frequently deployed by queer US Latinx communities to index a sense of community persisting against the grain of heteronormativity.[29]

No doubt aware of this, Cisneros used her address to her gay and lesbian audience in San Antonio as an opportunity to create an intimate alignment between herself as a woman of no consequence and those additionally cast as such—willingly, to be sure, in their self-identification as *los otros*. This is clear as her essay comes to a close, when she begins to wax powerfully on the subject of humanity. Cisneros writes: "I want to be humane to counter all the inhumanity on the planet. I want to *not* be ashamed to call myself a human being. For the sake of those I love too dearly, my friend in Sarajevo, my gay and lesbian friends, my family, it is not enough to write from my ego."[30] For me, Cisneros's refusal "to write from my ego" underscores more than a plea for some vacuous notion of humanity devoid of difference; it signals her aspiration to stake a claim for solidarity with others of an outsider alignment and to foster mutual support.

In addition, this mutual support, or what I have been calling the cross-identification between Cisneros and her queer compatriots, is intimately felt both as a means of mutual uplift and as a co-constitutive rousing force to situate oneself in relation to a similarly situated other and against the grain of gender and sexual norms. As Casas makes clear, "The day I read her words, 'Lipstick on a penis,' I thought, 'You bring out the queer in me, you bring out the Truth in me. You bring out the caballero in me. You bring out the gentle man in me. You bring out the pierce-my-cock-with-an-obsidian-knife in me, you bring out the gender fluid in me.'"[31] Cisneros's words animate an incentivizing drive not only to bring her queer readers out from the depths of the proverbial closet, but also to surface various ways to identify against the normative grain (an obsidian knife–pierced cock, a gentle man, a gender-fluid queer, to name a few) that conspires against the illicit behaviors and subjectivities of loose women and gay men of ill repute alike.

BRINGING OUT THE QUEER

Casas's words—inspired by Cisneros's verse—augment the substance of this cross-identification between Cisneros and Latino gay men and its ability to induce a declaration of one's queer sexual self. To be sure, it is Cisneros's poetry that inspires Casas to bring out all the things that might otherwise remain hidden or, more to the point, closeted. The line that induces Casas to name those things—"Lipstick on a penis"—comes from her poem "Still Life with Potatoes, Pearls, Raw Meat, Rhinestones, Lard, and Horse Hooves," from the collection *Loose Woman*.[32] Fittingly dedicated to Mondini-Ruiz and thus marking another example of cross-identification between Cisneros and Latino gay men, the poem further adopts a "crooked star" status but charges it with unflinching sexual desire and unshakable self-assuredness. With a bar in the city where Cisneros then resided functioning as the poem's mise-en-scène ("Look, I hate to break this to you, but this isn't Venice or Buenos Aires / This is San Antonio"), Cisneros's speaker addresses someone whom I read as a gay male ally ("You and me. I'll buy you a drink. / To a woman who doesn't act like a woman. / To a man who doesn't act like a man"). Here the speaker not only waxes defiantly and vivaciously erotic (indeed, one way to bond a morally insubordinate woman with an avowedly homosexual man), but she also aligns herself with powerful cinematic women whose gay male fan bases are well known and widely detailed ("I'll be Mae, Joan, Bette, Marlene for you—").[33] As the poem concludes, the speaker expresses anger toward the "pretty blond boy [bartender who] is no longer serving us." She responds with a two-pronged inquisitorial and incisive fury:

> Doesn't he know who we are?
> *Que vivan los de abajo de los de abajo,*
> *los de reinda suelta*, the witches, the women,
> the dangerous, the queer.
> *Que vivan las perras.*
> "*Que me sirvan otro trago . . .*"[34]

Another poem from the collection *Loose Woman*, however, more closely aligns Casas with Cisneros, as reflected by his naming of what the Chicana writer has brought out in him. This poem, "You Bring Out the Mexican in

Me," is unquestionably one of Cisneros's most recognized poems and one that has inspired many like Casas to adopt its confessional tone and poetic structure as apt expressive vehicles for relating one's personal story—another version, if you will, of "his story," albeit from a decidedly gay male perspective. In her reading of the poem, Suzanne Chávez-Silverman rightly identifies how Cisneros's engagement with "notions of power and danger (nuclei of potential empowerment or containment in discursive constructions of sexuality) are relativized and inverted in relation to their meaning in dominant discourse." But for Chávez-Silverman, the poem's potency is undercut by what she calls "the deployment of an unproblematized, essentialist trope of 'Mexicanness.'"[35] While my interpretation of the poem stands in solidarity with Chávez-Silverman's regarding how "You Bring Out the Mexican in Me" wields a counterdiscourse via sexuality, particularly for how it serves as a catalyst for queer Latinx artists and writers, I disagree with her take on Cisneros's embrace of "Mexicanness." Chávez-Silverman's assessment inadvertently reinstates a national culture that can only prove problematic or essentialist from the purview of a Chicana. Indeed, she reads Cisneros's embrace of Mexicanness—curiously untethered from her sexuality—as drenched in majority white demands for ethnic otherness. As she writes, "I do not think it coincidental that Cisneros has been embraced by the literary mainstream in this country, for in *Loose Woman* particularly, she is giving back to the dominant culture something comfortable, something familiar: what they (think they) already know about Chicanas."[36] This tired take (which recalls Mexican critic Ilan Stavans's cringeworthy, sexist, and elitist disdain of Cisneros's writing) forecloses consideration of what a book like *Loose Woman* and a poem like "You Bring Out the Mexican in Me" mean (as if such significance is attributable to a fatally flawed false consciousness) to queer and straight Chicanas and Latinas as well as Latino gay men.[37]

Cisneros's work has undeniably inspired a younger generation of Latinx queer writers. Consider Lorenzo Herrera y Lozano's poem "You Bring Out the Joto in Me." Riffing on Cisneros's poem of feminist empowerment, Herrera y Lozano's poem (not unlike Casas's tribute) seizes on the loaded meaning of *out* in Cisneros's title and draws influence from the emboldening charge of Chicana self-revelation and sexual liberation. In turn, Herrera y Lozano—a poet with roots in California and ties to Texas—builds on "You Bring Out the Mexican in Me" to fashion a self-assured Latino gay male sexual politics. Just as Cisneros's poem references Golden Age of Mexican Cinema diva Dolores del Río, Herrera y Lozano conjures up María Félix to tap into the example of a powerful Mexican woman figure, not to essentialize cultural difference but instead to fashion an alter ego that runs counter to heteropatriarchal Mexicanness and normatively white Americanness.

Begin, then, with the first stanza of Cisneros's rousing poem:

You bring out the Mexican in me.
The hunkered thick dark spiral.
The core of a heart howl.
The bitter bile.
The tequila *lágrimas* on Saturday all
through next weekend Sunday.
You are the one I'd let go the other loves for,
surrender my one-woman house.
Allow you red wine in bed,
even with my vintage lace linens.
Maybe. Maybe.
For you.[38]

While following in its literary forerunner's footsteps, Herrera y Lozano's poem imitates not so much the form of Cisneros's poem but instead its confessional tone. His poem begins as follows:

You bring out the Joto in me.
The María Felix eyebrows.
The sexually confused macho.
The Tecate & lime.
The Saturday morning shock
of hickies and phone numbers.
You are the one I would hold hands
in public with, while cruising down my old barrio.
Allow you other men in bed, still believing
promises of monogamy and forever.
Definitely. Definitely.
For us.[39]

Although Herrera y Lozano replaces Cisneros's "Mexican" with "Joto," the terms are united by a shared effort to foreground a discerning sexual politics with which to rail against heteronormative expectation. This is true despite the clear distinctions between one's alcoholic drink of choice (tequila or Tecate beer) and the movement toward or away from sexual monogamy. Although Cisneros's "Maybe. Maybe." and Herrera y Lozano's "Definitely. Definitely." also distinguish the two poems, I read the "For you" that completes her poem's first stanza as an invitation to Herrera y Lozano and other queer poets to regard her poem as a template for the creation of their own poems.[40] Undoubtedly, this prompting of "For you" is intended not merely for the amorous addressee of "You Bring Out the Mexican in Me," but also for those whose (mis)aligned sexual subjectivities require bringing out onto the page. And while Herrera y Lozano's poem upholds antimonogamy (which Cisneros's poem does as well, before the promise of letting go of "the other loves"), the first stanza of "You Bring Out the Joto in Me" ends with "For us," the prospect of a solid bond with a man that exceeds sexual possessiveness, but also a way to acknowledge Cisneros's invitation and accept both the implicit provocation and explicit potentiality for queer cross-identification. As each poem unfolds, we see how the two poets call on marginalized icons and denigrated figures (for example, Tlazolteotl, the "filth goddess," for Cisneros; "the psycho who stalks your home at night" for Herrera y Lozano) as respective sources of affirmation and empowerment against the norm.

One may indeed readjust the interpretive lens to assess how gay men have provided Cisneros with a way to fashion her own sexual self in terms of cross-identification (and one immediately thinks of her poem "Tea Dance, Provincetown, 1982," in which Cisneros writes, "It was easy to be half naked / at a gay beach. Men / didn't bother to look. / I was in training to be a woman without shame").[41] I wish to conclude, however, by highlighting Cisneros's undeniable influence on the proliferation of gay Latino expression. By considering Herrera y Lozano and Cisneros together, we witness the profound declarations of the self that entwine the men of ill repute and the loose woman from whom they draw inspiration. For while their genealogies are unquestionably distinct, the two are bonded in difference, thanks to the points of convergence facilitated by the cross-identification this essay has attempted to ascertain between Cisneros and the Latino gay men beholden to our dear queen bee.

NOTES

My gratitude to Adriana Estill and Audrey Goodman for their careful readings of this essay, which helped make its overall argument stronger and more convincing. Geneva M. Gano and Sonia Saldívar-Hull encouraged me to write the essay and unconditionally supported me while I did.

1. Sandra Cisneros, *My Wicked Wicked Ways* (Bloomington, IN: Third Woman Press, 1987), 36–37.
2. For another example of Cisneros's father's persistent influence, see Sandra Cisneros, "Only Daughter," in *Máscaras*, ed. Lucha Corpi (Berkeley, CA: Third Woman Press, 1997), 119–123.
3. Cisneros's identification as "nobody's mother and nobody's wife" first appears in the author bio for *Woman Hollering Creek and Other Stories* (New York: Random

House, 1991), 169; Jeff Wilson, "The Artist and the City," *Texas Monthly*, February 2013.

4. Catrióna Rueda Esquibel, "Memories of Girlhood: Chicana Lesbian Fictions," *Signs: Journal of Women in Culture and Society* 23, no. 3 (1998): 645.

5. Esquibel, "Memories of Girlhood," 656.

6. Cisneros has repeatedly declared that *The House on Mango Street* is not autobiographical, although aspects of Esperanza's story contain elements of her coming-of-age in Chicago.

7. Katherine Rios, "'And You Know What I Have to Say Isn't Always Pleasant': Translating the Unspoken Word in Cisneros' *Woman Hollering Creek*," in *Chicana (W)Rites on Word and Film*, ed. María Herrera-Sobek and Helena María Viramontes (Berkeley, CA: Third Woman Press, 1995), 202.

8. Rios, "And You Know What I Have to Say," 202.

9. Sandra Cisneros, "Little Miracles, Kept Promises," in *Woman Hollering Creek and Other Stories*, 122–123.

10. José Esteban Muñoz, *Disidentifications: Queers of Color and the Performance of Politics* (Minneapolis: University of Minnesota Press, 1999), 11–12. See also Sandra Cisneros, "Guadalupe the Sex Goddess," in *Goddess of the Americas / La Diosa de las Américas: Writings on the Virgin of Guadalupe*, ed. Ana Castillo (New York: Riverhead Books, 1996), 46–51.

11. Here I am reminded of a footnote in Teresa de Lauretis's *The Practice of Love: Lesbian Sexuality and Perverse Desire* (Bloomington: Indiana University Press, 1994), in which she writes: "Another male spectator has suggested that possible reasons for male homosexual identification with the [Bette] Davis persona and with Charlotte Vale [from Irving Rapper's 1942 film *Now, Voyager*] in particular include 'the ability to be expressive during the repressive 1940s and 1950s, sense of style, sexual self-assuredness, and (somewhat tragically or ironically) the fact that women like Charlotte don't get the man *either*'" (137n30). Earl Jackson Jr. is credited by de Lauretis for this insight, and it is one that guides my analysis for how gay men intimately relate to Cisneros's writing. For a related conversation on gay male connections to Hollywood divas, see Richard Dyer's classic study *Heavenly Bodies: Film Stars and Society* (New York: St. Martin's Press, 1986).

12. Interestingly, Cisneros's story was initially published in a 1990 issue of the journal *Grand Street*, three years before the Clinton administration proposed the "Don't Ask, Don't Tell" policy, which, implemented in early 1994, prohibited discrimination against closeted military service members.

13. This interpretive move draws inspiration from Ralph E. Rodriguez's call to read Latinx literature against the normative grain, particularly with respect to identity politics; see Rodriguez, *Latinx Literature Unbound: Undoing Ethnic Expectation* (New York: Fordham University Press, 2018).

14. Sandra Cisneros, "The Marlboro Man," in *Woman Hollering Creek and Other Stories*, 60.

15. Cisneros, "The Marlboro Man," 58.

16. Wilson, "The Artist and the City."

17. Cisneros's powerful poem "Down There" proves a necessary contribution alongside works by Cherríe Moraga and Gloria Anzaldúa in the collection *The*

Sexuality of Latinas, ed. Norma Alarcón, Ana Castillo, and Cherríe Moraga (Berkeley, CA: Third Woman Press, 1989).

18. Sandra Cisneros, *Loose Woman* (New York: Alfred A. Knopf, 1994).

19. Flora Doble, "Saint Sebastian as a Gay Icon," Art UK (website), January 20, 2020.

20. Doble, "Saint Sebastian as a Gay Icon."

21. The year after *Loose Woman* was published, Cisneros would contribute an introduction to the book *Mi primer libro de dichos / My First Book of Proverbs* (San Francisco: Children's Book Press, 1995), a collaborative endeavor between Ralfka González and Ana Ruiz. The notion of figures of resistance borrows from Teresa de Lauretis's essay "Figures of Resistance," which, in contrasting experience with ideology to break the rules of identification, offers a model whose parameters I extend here to consider the intimate connection between a Chicana feminist writer and Latino gay men in literature, language, and other expressive forms. See de Lauretis, *Figures of Resistance: Essays in Feminist Theory* (Urbana: University of Illinois Press, 2007), 235–260.

22. Rolando Briseño, oral history interview by Cary Cordova, March 16–26, 2004, Smithsonian Archives of American Art (online).

23. Ángel Rodríguez-Díaz, oral history interview by Cary Cordova, April 23–May 7, 2004, Smithsonian Archives of American Art (online). See also Sandra Cisneros, "Eyes of Zapata," in *Woman Hollering Creek and Other Stories*, 85–113.

24. Héctor Tobar, "A Cultural Diamond in the Rough," *Los Angeles Times*, August 2, 1999. Tobar's article is also an excellent account of the vibrant Latinx arts scene in San Antonio, of which Cisneros, Rodríguez-Díaz, Mondini-Ruiz, and Briseño were a part.

25. Ángel Rodríguez-Díaz passed away at the age of sixty-seven on March 31, 2023.

26. David Zamora Casas, "Rainbow-Colored Lipstick Kisses," in *Sandra Cisneros: Fuller Lifetime Achievement Award*, program (Chicago: Chicago Literary Hall of Fame, 2021), 51.

27. Casas, "Rainbow-Colored Lipstick Kisses," 52.

28. Sandra Cisneros, "A Woman of No Consequence: Una Mujer Cualquiera," in *Living Chicana Theory*, ed. Carla Trujillo (Berkeley, CA: Third Woman Press, 1998), 78.

29. For the use of *los otros* in a Mexican context, see Joseph Carrier's classic study *De Los Otros: Intimacy and Homosexuality among Mexican Men* (New York: Columbia University Press, 1995).

30. Cisneros, "A Woman of No Consequence," 86.

31. Casas, "Rainbow-Colored Lipstick Kisses," 52.

32. Cisneros, *Loose Woman*, 108–110. For an excellent piece on gay men and the classic Hollywood diva, see Daniel Harris, "The Death of Camp: Gay Men and Hollywood Diva Worship, from Reverence to Ridicule," *Salmagundi* 112 (1996): 166–191.

33. Cisneros, *Loose Woman*, 108.

34. Cisneros, *Loose Woman*, 110.

35. Suzanne Chávez-Silverman, "Chicanas in Love: Sandra Cisneros Talking Back and Alicia Gaspar de Alba 'Giving Back the Wor(l)d,'" *Chasqui* 27, no. 1 (1998): 36; see also Cisneros, *Loose Woman*, 4–6.

36. Chávez-Silverman, "Chicanas in Love," 45.

37. Ilan Stavans, *The Riddle of Cantinflas: Essays on Hispanic Popular Culture* (Albuquerque: University of New Mexico Press, 2012), 114–119.

38. Cisneros, *Loose Woman*, 4.

39. Lorenzo Herrera y Lozano, *Amorcito Maricón* (San Francisco: Kórima Press, 2014), 23.

40. Consider as well Guatemalan American queer poet Maya Chinchilla's "Homegirl," which is written "after Cisneros" and begins: "You / bring out the homegirl in me / The one who has your back / My inner cha-cha chola / The big hoop girl / burgundy lips and sticky gloss kisses." Chinchilla, *The Cha Cha Files: A Chapina Poética* (San Francisco: Kórima Press, 2014), 76.

41. Sandra Cisneros, *Woman without Shame: Poems* (New York: Alfred A. Knopf, 2022), 5.

CHAPTER 9

WILD, WICKED, AND CRAZY BRAVE TONGUES

Locating the Collaborative Origins of Sandra Cisneros's and Joy Harjo's Poetic Voices

Audrey Goodman

> Write with your eyes like painters, with your ears like musicians, with your feet like dancers. You are the truthsayer with quill and torch. Write with your tongues of fire. Don't let the pen banish you from yourself.
> GLORIA ANZALDÚA, "SPEAKING IN TONGUES"

> Without desire, you can't invent anything.
> SANDRA CISNEROS, "NO PLACE LIKE HOME"

> A poem exists because it says: "I am the voice of the poet or what is moving through time, place, and event; I am sound sense and words; I am made of all this; and though I may not know where I am going, I will show you, and we will sing together."
> JOY HARJO, *POET WARRIOR*

In the September 16, 2020, episode of the *New Yorker: Poetry* podcast, Mvskoke poet Joy Harjo read and commented on "Still-Life with Potatoes, Pearls, Raw Meat, Rhinestones, Lard, and Horse Hooves," a poem by Sandra Cisneros published in the May 23, 1994, issue of the *New Yorker* and included in the last section of Cisneros's second book of poetry, *Loose Woman*, published that same year.[1] Harjo explained in the accompanying conversation with poetry editor Kevin Young that she chose this poem because she appreciated its "wildness," its willingness to question the terms of what a poem can be, and its location in a place at once intimate and public, particular and symbolic, real and fantastic. The poem creates "a place to go in and shift your perspective,"

Harjo explained, and it invites the reader to "move through generations in a couples of lines." Furthermore, "it's a place that can hold what is unspeakable" and contain "contradictions and contradictory history."[2] In a letter to Cisneros responding to the entire collection of poems in *Loose Woman*, Harjo wrote, "I love your work and I'm so damned proud of you, my sister. I also love your wild streak which picks up power like a tornado, a tornado of laughter and love."[3]

"Still-Life with Potatoes" exemplifies Cisneros's poetic voice: one that speaks fearlessly of desire from the liminal places where the speaker works, dreams, drinks, and writes, places where people encounter and transform one another's perspectives and languages. As it expresses the pleasures of discarding decorum, embracing artifice, and creating art from life, this voice also traverses literal and symbolic contact zones. Consider the locations, real and imagined, and the exuberant clash of cultures evident in "Still-Life." While the poem is set in a bar in San Antonio, Texas, its first half evokes distant and often glamorous cultural traditions: refined still-life paintings, the Venetian legends of Casanova, the Italian neorealist films of Pier Paolo Pasolini, the Argentine music of Astor Piazzolla, and the feminine icons of early Hollywood films. Quickly and gleefully, however, Cisneros's speaker punctures any illusion of refinement her readers might bring to these references: "Look, I hate to break it to you, but this isn't Venice or Buenos Aires. / This is San Antonio," her proud and humble home.[4] Acutely aware of the physical and cultural distances between the speaker's imaginative sources and her present perch, the poem bridges those distances and brings them into dramatic and intimate relation. In speaking with Harjo, Young commented that the poem asks readers to think about who in society "gets to say what something is." He reads the poem as "saying that beauty is all these different things and some of them might not obviously belong together, but the poet, the artist, the human eye . . . really is able to put it all together." Harjo commented in turn that Cisneros is "at the edge of awareness of America," inhabiting that edge and claiming her power to find joy and beauty there.[5] Cisneros shifts the center of cultural authority from distant arbiters of taste and value to the speaker, whose liminal position becomes a new and powerful site for speaking.

Like Audre Lorde, who believed in the capacity of language to "break that silence" and generate self-determined action, Cisneros confronts implicit expectations regarding women's behavior and speaks truths about women's desires in her poetry.[6] She accesses not only the knowledge of her subjects' bodies but also the power of language, poetic form, and genres of art, reinventing them to serve her own needs. In "Still-Life with Potatoes," Cisneros explicitly contends with the genre of the still life. Paintings so categorized typically give precedence to the organic shapes of fruit, vegetables, and everyday things. Yet, as Claudia Tobin explains in *Modernism and Still Life*, modern versions of the still life can be rife with paradox. The still life is located "at the borders of private and public space, nature and culture, vitality and mortality," and the genre's "very designation conjures word play and duality."[7] In her still life, Cisneros sketches an especially unlikely assemblage, and the poem's body juxtaposes ordinary and precious materials, natural and artificial objects, real and idealized bodies, English and Spanish words. The poem pictures a once-beautiful Contessa who now sports "a wart the size of this diamond." It reveals that the speaker's mink is "genuine acrylic." No subject or observation is off limits: when the speaker offers to dance a tango, it could be "in a lace G-string / stained with my first-day flow." Anything but still, the poem opens life's big questions: "What's natural?" "Life?" "What's beauty?" And, with creative exuberance, it invents an irreverent and fearless poetic persona who casually orchestrates the arrangement and turns it into a performance. As long as her companion provokes laughter, she will adorn him as "sequin and bangle" and "be anything you ask." At the end of the poem, she proposes that she and her companion leave that bar and go to another, "where they'll buy us drinks / if I wear my skirt on my head and you come in wearing nothing / but my black brassiere."[8]

Harjo's choice to read and comment on "Still-Life with Potatoes" and to respond at the end of the podcast by reading her own poem "Running" attests to the strength and impact of her long friendship with Cisneros and to their common need to create and affirm distinctive poetic voices. When *Loose Woman* was published, Harjo's acclaim appeared on the second page: "I love these poems! Sandra Cisneros has attained a sureness possible when someone faces down the terrors of intimacy, the push-pull of relationships. These poems are firecrackers and tequila, with a little candlelight and lace linen."[9] Her blurb for Cisneros's 2022 collection of poems, *Woman without Shame / Mujer sin vergüenza*, explicitly connects their shared journey and their writing lives: "These new poems by Sandra Cisneros prove that a mystic poet can be an aging brown-skinned woman shameless in her being." Harjo views Cisneros's bravery as matched by her wisdom and spiritual knowledge, claiming, "These poems are prayers for understanding this earthly journey of mystery and beauty. These poems cross the road with impunity."[10] The two writers, who connected first as MFA students at the Iowa Writers' Workshop, still searching for the right teachers and forms for their work, have maintained over the course of their long and active careers a friendship and a correspondence that recognize wild and incendiary streaks in themselves and in each other.[11] Harjo agreed to be judge at the 2006 Macondo Writers Workshop, which Cisneros organized, and attested afterward in a thank-you note to her friend: "Macondo has changed me; *you* have changed me. Thank you so much for the opportunity, the helpful criticism, and the *affirmation & encouragement.* I want to come back every year!"[12]

This essay explores the generative potential of the intimate contact zones where Cisneros and Harjo work and where they developed formative relations with their teachers. It identifies key elements of their creative networks, arguing that such extended and deep relationships have infused not only their physical encounters but their imaginative lives as well. In *Imperial Eyes*, Mary Louise Pratt adapted the notion of the contact zone from the field of linguistics, "where the term contact language refers to an improvised language that develops among speakers of different tongues who need to communicate with each other consistently, usually in the context of trade."[13] My approach to Cisneros's poetry further adapts Pratt's terminology and critical approach as I consider Cisneros's formation as a writer in relation to creative friendships with other poets, most notably Harjo, and to institutional structures. As Pratt explains, "A 'contact' perspective emphasizes how subjects get constituted in and by their relations to each other."[14] Susan Stanford Friedman's work in *Mappings* also provides a model for my locational approach. Friedman focuses on how the academy, along with its institutions, "produces, preserves, collects, organizes, passes on, and constantly re-forms old and new knowledge."[15] Both Cisneros and Harjo found themselves on the margins of white patriarchal culture, forced to contend with the continuing effects of racism and coloniality on their writing lives; through forging alliances with each other and with other Chicana, Latina, Black, and Indigenous artists, they created the spaces from which their own poetic voices could emerge. In their poetry, liminal sites such as bars, city streets, hotel rooms, kitchen tables, and ceremonial grounds become contact zones where the cultures and knowledges passed down by ancestors, teachers, and allies intermingle. Through mapping their relationships with each other and with other artists, I sketch an ongoing, intimate history of creative and collaborative feminist production.

BREAKING THE SILENCES

In their essays and memoirs, Cisneros and Harjo reflect on the process of finding the teachers, artists, and sources of inspiration that would allow them to reject institutional notions of "mastery" and lay the foundations for their own transformations and creative expression. In *Mappings*, Friedman contends that in many literary histories and theories, "women writers as producers of culture remain invisible" and "the feminine exists under constant threat of erasure or appropriation."[16] Such invisibility and erasure in the academy were especially pronounced in the 1980s and 1990s, and especially for Chicana and Native women. Because of their shared experience as outsiders at the Iowa Writers' Workshop, Cisneros and Harjo sought out teachers and models beyond those canonical writers and professors who were upheld at Iowa.

The epigraphs, allusions, and letter poems in the 1987 collection *My Wicked Wicked Ways* indicate the range of writers Cisneros claimed as her essential teachers.[17] The epigraph to part 1 comes from Gwendolyn Brooks's poem "a song in the front yard," and it confirms Cisneros's indebtedness to Brooks for the locations of her poems and her distinctive use of language. The rhymes, alliteration, assonance, and word play in the poems in *My Wicked Wicked Ways* also take formal cues from the radical verse of Emily Dickinson and share one of Dickinson's central subjects, the ferocious, violent power of desire. Inspired and fortified by the models of the writers she chose as kin, Cisneros in these early poems communicates the pleasures of impromptu performance and confronts the dark side of her struggle to find her way as a writer. The last poem in the collection, written and printed in Spanish, "Tantas Cosas Asustan, Tantas," lists the many things that scare the poet and acknowledges the weight of those fears. However, because the list proceeds through even pairings of opposite actions, the poem creates a sense of balance, and it moves toward the idea that fears really are a matter of perspective. Anything *can* be scary (such as being alone)—but so can the reverse of that thing (such as being with someone forever). And if fear is a part of life, so is the possibility of happiness, which emerges at the end as something surprising, present, but indeterminate, like a kite soaring in the wind. An appropriate conclusion to this first volume of poetry, shaped by the writer's struggle to free herself from the constraints of familial, cultural, and academic expectations, this parting image of the kite suggests that happiness comes through letting go and letting ideas take their own direction.

For Harjo, other poets, the elders in her family, her parents, the spirits of her ancestors, the natural world and the oceans, and the words, stories, and songs of friends and other artists served as foundational teachers. In her 2021 memoir *Poet Warrior*, she pays tribute to her many "poetry ancestors," offering an open catalog of her sources of inspiration:

> My poetry would not exist without Audre Lorde's "Litany for Survival," without Mvskoke stomp dance call-and-response, without Adrienne Rich's "Diving into the Wreck," without Meridel LeSueur or N. Scott Momaday, without death or sunrise, without Walt Whitman, or Navajo horse songs, or Langston Hughes, without rain, without grief, without—[18]

The final dash indicates that this list stretches to infinity, an idea emphasized in the expansive list of experiences that serve as additional "beloved teachers," including encounters with the Pacific Ocean, the fire burning at ceremonial grounds, and the deaths of her parents. Harjo insists, "The best teachers are exacting. There is no end to learning."[19] Musicians were also at the origins of Harjo's poetry: Miles Davis and John Coltrane inspired her from the start, as did Native jazz musicians, such as trombonist "Big Chief" Russell Moore and Kaw/Mvskoke saxophone player Jim Pepper, who synthesized sources and used his horn to express "what his heart couldn't speak."[20] In Harjo's tribute poem to Pepper, "The Place the Musician Became a Bear," her speaker mixes a vision of the moon with sounds of the subway as she experienced them when visiting Pepper in Brooklyn. Together they "listened to the sax gods of Ben Webster, Cannonball Adderley, and his other inspirations and influences, talked Oklahoma and home," and heard "the subway beneath his apartment building shaking the world like a huge underground snake" when "he'd disappear for his fix."[21] Riffing on the original and incorporating her own senses, sounds, and poetic voices, Harjo's written version of the song, too, rearranges sources and sensations to dramatize her struggle to accept the uncertainty and constant motion of contemporary life. Pepper's model further propels her own saxophone playing: "When I pick up my horn and blow," she explains, "I stand near him, an echo, a new song, in this postcolonial world."[22]

Academic institutions, by contrast, impeded creativity. Although the Iowa Writers' Workshop promised to provide Cisneros and Harjo with advanced training in their craft, access to a professional network, and a prestigious credential, they found the workshops to be conformist, combative, and silencing. According to David Dowling, Cisneros and Harjo sat together at the back of the classroom; along with Rita Dove, they were among the first women of color and among few working-class poets accepted to the program. They tried to speak in their own poetic languages and to create their own poetic forms, but their efforts often met with silence from their classmates and dismissal from their teachers. Students from privileged backgrounds knew and conformed to "the intimate language of the workshop," Harjo claimed; she and Cisneros faced criticism for resisting, but they lacked alternative models for either their work or their working lives. "Both met crushing silence when their work was circulated, as was the case when either of them made a comment," says Dowling.[23] Their experience at Iowa and beyond confirmed that "survival is not an academic skill," as Lorde explains in "The Master's Tools Will Never Dismantle the Master's House," and they discovered that their creative survival required "learning how to stand alone, unpopular and sometimes reviled."[24] In the process of "navigating transformation," they learned to wield the tools that would give them access to "that deep place of knowledge" inside themselves.[25]

Officially a poet for the purposes of her MFA, Cisneros was "gravitating" back toward fiction but hadn't yet found the story cycles, the forms for narrative sketches, or the work of those who might have shown her how to live as a woman writer. Cisneros claims, "I like to tell people I'm a writer *despite* the University of Iowa Writers' Workshop. It taught me what I didn't want to be as a writer and how I didn't want to teach."[26] Her adviser, Donald Justice, would not count the fictional sketches she was writing as part of her poetry thesis, and no one else there had tried to combine fiction and poetry writing. The writers she discovered through reading, such as Jorge Luis Borges, offered the best formal inspiration and showed her that narrative fragments can make "stories that ignore borders between genres, between written and spoken, between highbrow literature and children's nursery rhymes, between New York and the imaginary village of Macondo, between the United States and Mexico."[27] Although Marvin Bell, who would eventually become her adviser, provided some support for her narrative experiments, Cisneros maintains, "Maybe Iowa was a family for some, [but] it wasn't *my* family. I felt homeless."[28] In Dowling's summation, "The Workshop, for all its sins, paradoxically inspired Cisneros's *Mango Street*, if only as a counterpoint written with a survivor's grit in opposition to the forces that threatened to destroy her creative spirit during peer critiques."[29] Other scholars who have studied Cisneros's experience in the MFA program have emphasized the empty promises her male teachers made that finding the right teacher would secure her success.[30] Harjo recalled in a letter she wrote to Cisneros in 1985, "I was worried about you at Iowa. I knew you could go either way. What I mean is that I saw a lot of spirit, life in you, but your direction wasn't clear. I'm real proud of who you have become, who you are."[31]

Harjo's teachers at Iowa criticized her work as well, in part because she did not reference traditional Western poets; she did not yet feel surrounded and empowered by "that wide circle of ancestors who gave me inspiration and strength to continue."[32] Although she arrived at Iowa with an undergraduate degree in creative writing from the University of New Mexico, financial backing from Leslie Marmon Silko, and a chapbook published with Puerto del Sol, she could not yet support herself and her two children from her work as a writer. Rather than find external affirmation from her official teachers, who rarely addressed poetry's power to speak truth and live in the present, Harjo had to teach herself. She had to find her own way to listen to voices on the page and "to that small, inner voice that told me that poetry was the path, even when I had different plans."[33] It took time to learn to place herself in the presence of teachers in the broadest sense: the writers, musicians, storytellers, and spirits who could share wisdom. In *Poet Warrior* she admits that "when I began teaching in the university system, I lost myself" because she lacked the confidence to adapt Indigenous teaching methods that prioritize orality. "It's better to tend to cultivating knowledge, to learn from all of the many teachers who are part of the catalog of wisdom from which the voice of knowing emerges," she finally realized.[34]

In "Arts of the Possible" Adrienne Rich claims, "Every real poem is the breaking of an existing silence, and the first question we might ask any poem is, *What kind of voice is breaking silence, and what kind of silence is being broken?*"[35] Rich's essay explores the "cartographies of silence" that control women's speech in institutional settings and tests the ways that poetry emerges through silence, especially "for women and other marginalized subjects and for disempowered and colonized peoples generally, but ultimately for all who practice any art at its deepest levels."[36] To break the silences they encountered at the University of Iowa and other academic institutions, Cisneros and Harjo looked deeply into their own family histories, forged their own communities, claimed their own teachers, and learned to "hear each other and see each other," as Toni Cade Bambara expresses of feminist aesthetic activism in her foreword to *This Bridge Called My Back*, the anthology first published in 1981 by Kitchen Table Press.[37] Following Gloria Anzaldúa's advice to "forget the room of one's own," they found ways to "write in the kitchen" and dream their own creative spaces instead.[38] For example, the 1997 anthology Harjo edited with Gloria Byrd, *Reinventing the Enemy's Language*, "was conceived during a lively discussion of native women meeting around a kitchen table."[39] Inspired by the powerful voices of their ancestors and of this generation of feminist poets, Cisneros and Harjo kept breaking institutional silences and loosening their wild tongues.

WILD NIGHTS

As they found locations and created rituals for working with other artists, both poets confronted the difficulties of solitude and silence on their own, often at night. In "Poem as Preface," the introduction to the second edition of *My Wicked Wicked Ways*, Cisneros states that when she started to live and work alone, "Sometimes the silence frightened me. / Sometimes the silence blessed me. / It would come get me. / Late at night. / Open like a window, / hungry for my life."[40] In "Night Madness Poem," included in *Loose Woman*, the speaker accepts that the charge of creativity that drives her to write all night might make her appear intoxicated or "rumpled." Unable to turn away from her inner self and silence the poems in her head, she willingly takes on the labels "crazy lady," "witch woman," and "woman delighted with her disasters." In exchange for the temporary madness of a night of writing, she realizes the power of her tongue as weapon. She dares her reader to "choose your weapon" and claims her own: "the telephone, my tongue. / Both black as a gun." She concludes,

> I have the magic of words,
> The power to charm and kill at will.
> To kill myself or to aim haphazardly
> And kill you.[41]

This poem links desire, creativity, and violence, and it does so in solitary spaces over which her speaker asserts absolute control. The two poems that conclude *Loose Woman*, "Vino Tinto" and "Loose Woman," dramatize the poet's inner world and her fierce public persona. In its central stanza, "Vino Tinto" dwells in the spaces and times of desire and creation, the midnight hours in which the poet creates her own temporality, "nights that swell like a cork." As tangible memories of her lover fill those hours, prompted by sips of dark wine, they alternately intoxicate and threaten to suffocate her. The drops of burgundy or cabernet "spiral like Egyptian silk, / blood bit from a lip, black / smoke from a cigarette," creating a visceral pull back to the nights when they touched each other and trembled. The memories pull her tight, but they also vibrate like a string. "Love, how it hummed," the speaker remembers.[42] By contrast, "Loose Woman" shouts out all the names that might have been hurled against the speaker, claims them as compliments, and launches her own words as weapons. Beast, bitch, witch, *macha*, hell on wheels, boogeywoman, rowdy lesbian . . . she'll take them all. While she rejects the epithets wielded by others, writing that they are not "sticks and stones" that break her bones and "do me in," her own words pack a punch: "when I open my mouth," her would-be oppressors "wobble like gin." Her words sparkle and shine: "Diamonds and pearls / tumble from my tongue."[43] The poem ends with a defiant catalog of all the ways the speaker is a "loose" woman: one able to speak fast, "shoot sharp," and "let-loose."[44]

A more recent poem by Cisneros, "Smith's Supermarket, Taos, New Mexico, at the Fifteen Items or Less Checkout Line" (2018), confirms the poet's commitment to protect the spaces needed to write freely while also negotiating the power of everyday encounters and the risk of speaking of intimate desires. Set in an ordinary supermarket in the middle of the day, the poem focuses on the conveyor belt that transports groceries and alcohol toward the register, a space in motion, divided and redivided by each customer. It speculates on the life of the young man in front of the speaker, a "baby-faced cholo," sketching his portrait in quick strokes in stanzas one and three and offering precise details about his identity, his skin, and his purchases. His movements are "gentle" but decisive with respect to the item that will soon be put into his shopping bag: "a plastic bottle of store-brand vodka." The transparent container of potent alcohol counters the rich red color of the wine that speakers in Cisneros's poems typically prefer, the "vino tinto" that flows through her speakers' nights of romance, passion, anguish, anger, and creation. The contents of this young man's bottle seem to be purely destructive. By contrast, Cisneros's speaker has gathered all the items she needs to fuel her writing: she puts on the belt "a six-outlet surge / protector for my computer / and a fireproof glass cup / for my Lux Perpetua candle." Prosaic, essential, and symbolic, these objects promise to charge, protect, and illuminate her spaces of creation. It will be the votive candle that burns itself out when the speaker writes "till the dark descends," not the poet.[45]

However, this is not just a poem declaring its speaker's hard-won knowledge about self-protection and productivity and her distance from the rough life of the young man in front of her. Although at first their lives seem utterly divided, the fourth and fifth stanzas of the poem explore unexpected affinities as the poem's speaker lavishes attention on the young man with her second look. With rich alliteration and a slow, appreciative rhythm, she describes his clothing: "Baseball cap bad-as backwards. / Black leather from neck to knees." She admires the adornment of his brow and ear, those intimate parts of the body here "stitched with silver." We are getting closer, surprisingly, to this young man who seemed at the beginning of the poem to be just a type ready to grab his drink and go elsewhere for his "happy hour." And then closer again. The speaker describes the tattoo ringing his neck, his woman's name ("Rufina"). This cholo may be claimed, but the speaker fantasizes about stepping toward him and transgressing that claim to kiss the "wispy / ink." She addresses his absent lover in a way that shows her sympathy, her experience of being in that woman's place, drinking with him or drinking for him: "Fool, / it takes one to know one." And she wonders whether the woman, too, wants to lose herself by sharing "his bottle of forget," or whether the woman is part of what the man regrets and wants to leave behind.[46]

The mobility of Cisneros's identification with the absent woman opens the scope of this poem to other, overlapping intimacies. If "Still-Life" was a wild poem "about being at the edge of ruin and discovery," as Harjo claims, "Smith's Supermarket" is a poem that both acknowledges the thrill and danger of desire and affirms the greater power of creative control.[47] At age forty Cisneros declared with pride, "I can live *sola* and, as much as I complain, the truth is, I really do love to work. In fact, I'm at my healthiest, happiest when

I'm working." Included in a keynote speech for the national conference of the Women's Caucus for Art, held in San Antonio in 1995, this statement expresses a mature sense of purpose with force and clarity: "I like to think I'm inventing the truth. I'm listening to voices nobody listened to, setting their lives down on paper how many years later? And that writing is a resistance, an act against forgetting, a war against oblivion, against not counting, as women."[48]

Many of Harjo's night poems also create stages for exploring inner darkness, doubt, and despair as well as external threats of violence and destruction as they explore the sources of creativity. As they dramatize her desire to emerge into and inhabit other worlds, they create rituals for confronting and speaking back to fear. Harjo writes in her 2012 memoir *Crazy Brave*, "I often painted or drew through the night, when most of the world slept and it was easier to walk through the membrane between life and death to bring back memory. I painted to the music of silence. It was here I could hear everything."[49] She recounts two key moments at night when she contemplated running from violence and toward freedom: as a teenager, when she sought to escape her stepfather's violence; and as a young mother, when she sought to escape her own abusive partner. In those moments, she sensed the force of darkness like a tornado that "coiled around me and opened uncountable hungry mouths."[50] On another night, she was sitting in her quiet house when she envisioned a shaman who danced and "became the poem he was singing . . . a transmitter of healing energy, with poetry, music, and dance." At this moment, Harjo attests, she "became aware of an opening within me" and "knew this is what I was put here to do: I must become the poem, the music, and the dancer."[51] While she had come to sense the spiritual proximity of her powerful ancestors—including her grandmother, the painter Naomi Harjo Foster, and her great-uncle, the Seminole warrior Osceola, who never surrendered to the US government—she realized she had to summon within herself the power to open herself to the songs and stories that could heal her.

Harjo wrote one of her first and most enduring poems, "I Give You Back" (1983), after a decisive night in which she dreamed that she was cornered by a monster. In this dream vision, the speaker summons the courage to confront the embodiment of fear and discovers her ability to transcend it; suddenly, the monster vanishes. The poem refuses the fear that used to be the speaker's "beloved / and hated twin," claiming that it is no longer her blood, and returns it to the soldiers who seized her ancestors' houses and removed them from their homelands, to those who hated her for her poverty or the color of her skin, and to those who attacked her.[52] Banished from the speaker's body, the fear becomes an external and distant being. The poem concludes with the speaker inviting the now-diminished fear to return and witness her as finally, fully alive, capable of welcoming back even her most powerful enemy. In a 2001 letter written in support of Harjo's professorship at the University of California, Los Angeles, Cisneros revealed that she uses this poem in every workshop she teaches. "I consider her 'I Give You Back' magical, and try to open my classes with that poem as prayer."[53]

Harjo concluded the *New Yorker: Poetry* podcast in which she read "Still-Life with Potatoes" by reading a poem of her own, "Running" (2018). This poem also begins in a bar, and it uses the liminal space and time of the after hours to locate the speaker at the threshold between past and future, in "the doorway between panic and love."[54] In her poem, Harjo juxtaposes people and spirits, present and past, inner knowledge and outer realities as she confronts the darkness of the speaker's inner life and the histories of violence that threaten to trap her in a cycle of destruction. "I don't know how I'm going to get out of here," one line reads. The speaker describes the sensation of entrapment as like being stranded in the water, lacking a boat to get her across the river that separates her from home; she feels surrounded by "the fog of thin hope." The world she sees seems to be a false version, one "made with the enemy's words."[55] While Harjo has spoken elsewhere (in the introduction to *Reinventing the Enemy's Language*, in other poems, and in the *New Yorker: Poetry* podcast) about how English functions as a "trade language" for Native people, one that allows them and other colonized people to bridge linguistic and cultural differences, here the enemy's language threatens to eclipse the truth of the present and obscure the way forward. Thrust out from the bar into the dark streets of the city, where "there are no Indians anymore," the speaker considers the tools she will need to survive. She measures the distance between her own awareness of her inner fears, figured as a dark mouth "with its shiny moon teeth" that utters "no words, just a hiss and snap," and her recognition of the threats that lurk in the night streets: a violent boyfriend, racism, ugliness, and lack of spiritual vision.[56] Through the will of her imagination, she transcends the physical blow and rises with a new identity: the daughter of a warrior supported by the knowledge of her elders, now capable of running and "breaking free" from the violent cycle of history.

DREAM ZONES

The essays collected in the 2015 volume *A House of My Own* reveal that Cisneros's dreams have long fueled her work. As a child, she was chastised by her teachers for being a "daydreamer." While living in Hydra, Greece, she felt that she was "somewhere between reality and the imagination," as in the dream she had one night of swimming alongside dolphins in the Aegean Sea.

She describes the experience of leaping "in and out of the water joyously like a needle stitching the sea," creating imaginative connections between fluid elements. Borges's book *Dreamtigers* gave her "permission to dream in the same way that Kafka gave Gabriel García Márquez permission to dream, that Thomas Wolfe gave permission to Betty Smith." In a letter to Gwendolyn Brooks, she refers to writing as "dreaming on paper." And in the last paragraph of the book's concluding essay, she joyfully recounts the experience of taking a nap and inviting what she calls her "night dreams." In the dreams that came to her then, she saw a multitude of stories fluttering and whirling around her like butterflies, "stories without beginning or end, connecting everything little and large, blazing from the center of the universe into *el infinito* called the great out there."[57]

Harjo writes in *Poet Warrior* that she created her own spaces for dreams to live in the pages of her poems. When she wrote during the darkest of nights, she built "a dreaming house" made of words and images "on a tangled rectangle of a page."[58] Her journals and letters, meanwhile, allude to the dreams she and Cisneros shared, and at times Cisneros appears in her transcribed dreams. In an entry from 1994, Harjo records the following vision:

> Sandra Cisneros is holding a turtle. I am aware that turtles can snap, bite hard, but this turtle reaches out his head to nudge me. The turtle then turns into a baby boy in a high chair. Or he appears to be a baby boy in a high chair. He's pissed because he's a fully conscious human in a baby's body. I tell him he can pass as a dwarf once he can walk.[59]

The next year, Cisneros visited Harjo's class at the University of New Mexico; Harjo wrote to thank her because "you touched them, changed them, & inspired. I'm so proud of you."[60]

The dreams Cisneros and Harjo exchanged generated new poems, too. In the 2015 volume *Conflict Resolution for Holy Beings*, Harjo offers a line from Cisneros as an epigraph to "Speaking Tree": "I had a beautiful dream I was dancing with a tree." In this poem, the speaker declares herself "a woman longing to be a tree, planted in a moist, dark earth / Between sunrise and sunset—." Unlike the many poems Harjo set in darkness and night, restlessly seeking a way home through many different realms, this poem speaks of the desire to put down roots and live in place. She imagines holding close the dream to walk "just a little ways, from the place next to the doorway— / To the edge of the river of life, and drink—." Earlier in the poem her speaker alludes to her ability to hear "cries of anguish" from trees when their branches break, and the songs they sing "when they are fed by / Wind, or water music—." She claims to have heard trees murmuring their longing "to dance close together

/ In this land of water and knowledge."[61] By linking the imagination of trees dancing close together to Cisneros, Harjo recalls and animates memories of the times they danced together. She translates Cisneros's beautiful dream of dancing with a tree into her own dream of inhabiting the earth, sharing the sensations and languages of nonhuman beings, and creating an expanded sense of home. "Speaking Tree" proclaims that Harjo has learned to listen to all her teachers and create poems that can hold disparate voices, human and nonhuman. It recalls the movement toward imagining what it would be like to merge with and emerge from the earth evident in much of her earlier work, including the 1983 poem "Remember," the 1989 photo text *Secrets from the Center of the World*, and her stories of traveling through the night and emerging to map new worlds at dawn.[62] In 2014, likely around the time of composing "Speaking Tree," she wrote to thank Cisneros for a recent card and tell her she broke down when reading her friend's declaration that Harjo will always have a home with her. "I needed to hear your words," she claims; "You were the angel who walked me over the bridge."[63]

Gloria Anzaldúa advises, "Write of what most links us with life, the sensation of the body, the images seen by the eye, the expansion of the psyche in tranquility: moments of high intensity, its movement, sounds, thoughts."[64] Anzaldúa chose the form of the letter for this intimate and urgent address because she found a long poem to be unwieldy and an essay to be "wooden, cold." A letter allowed to her speak of her own struggle to write from her "deep core," to serve "for the center of the self," and she urged other women writers of color to "throw away abstraction and the academic learning, the rules, the map and compass. Feel your way without blinders. . . . Find the muse within you."[65] Cisneros and Harjo enacted her advice. While claiming poetry as the most authentic expression of their experience, they addressed their inner struggles candidly in letters. Cisneros asserts, "poetry is the art of telling the truth, and fiction is the art of lying. The scariest thing to me is writing poetry, because you're looking at yourself *desnuda*. You're always looking at the part of you that you don't show anybody."[66] The correspondence she and Harjo exchanged similarly confronts the fear of telling the truth, as these documents lay bare anxieties, desires, and ambitions. The letters between Cisneros and Harjo included in the Sandra Cisneros Papers in Texas State University's Wittliff Collections convey the poets' individual struggles and their strong encouragement to each other to sustain their friendship and their wild and brave creative work. In one letter from November 19, 1991, Harjo wrote, "Dear Sandy—Wish we had more time together—When you read the pieces about your wild girlfriends I knew I must have known them—have been there, here." A postscript invited Cisneros to come back and suggested that next time they "go dancing—visit laugh & tell stories."[67] In the 2001 letter of support for

Harjo's professorship, Cisneros wrote that her friend "showed me a poetry that could be socially-minded and grounded in the language of working-class people" and thus helped her find her way as a writer. "Joy has always been a maverick, a mentor who has impacted my life and the life of my students," she confirmed. "In a letter ten years ago, I wrote to her that I continued to read her poetry as 'tonic and torch.' I meant that she fortified and guided me. She still does."[68] This reciprocal process of teaching, writing, and reading continues to connect and transform not only these poets and their audiences but the cultural and academic institutions that support them as well.

In 1996, Harjo sent Cisneros a postcard from her home in Albuquerque, New Mexico, that pictured stallions from Wyoming; the caption read, "Roaming Free." Harjo wrote, "I heard you were in Paris. Perhaps the Crazy Horse Bar? Singing opera & drinking champagne."[69] Going back into the archives and reading such exchanges in conversation with their published writing provides a means of recovering what Anzaldúa has called a critical "intimacy and immediacy."[70] Through the intimate forms of their poetry and the private language of their letters, Cisneros and Harjo foreground the vitality and malleability of the writing process, rather than the printed object of the book. Such conversations and correspondence invite readers to consider how poetic expression emerges in many kinds of texts, to compare narratives of creative development, and to map the overlapping and intersecting networks that connect poets across generations, sexualities, races, and cultures.

NOTES

Many thanks to the Sinvergüenza Collective for sharing ideas, inspiration, and editing suggestions and to the Wittliff Collections at Texas State University for supporting my research with the Sandra Cisneros Papers. I am especially grateful for archivist Katie Salzmann's help in providing copies of essential letters during the COVID-19 pandemic.

1. Sandra Cisneros, "Still-Life with Potatoes, Pearls, Raw Meat, Rhinestones, Lard, and Horse Hooves," *New Yorker*, May 23, 1994; Sandra Cisneros, *Loose Woman* (New York: Alfred A. Knopf, 1994), 108–110; "Joy Harjo Reads Sandra Cisneros," *New Yorker: Poetry* (podcast), September 16, 2020, 37:14; the poem was also reprinted in the *New Yorker*'s special archival issue organized around "Voices of American Dissent," July 27, 2020.

2. "Joy Harjo Reads Sandra Cisneros," *New Yorker: Poetry*.

3. Joy Harjo to Sandra Cisneros, July 19, 1993. All letters cited in this chapter are collected in box 120, folders 4 and 5, Sandra Cisneros Papers, Wittliff Collections, Texas State University.

4. Cisneros, *Loose Woman*, 108–110.

5. "Joy Harjo Reads Sandra Cisneros," *New Yorker: Poetry*.

6. Audre Lorde, "The Transformation of Silence into Language and Action," in *Sister Outsider* (1984; New York: Penguin Books, 2020), 32.

7. Claudia Tobin, *Modernism and Still Life: Artists, Writers, Dancers* (Edinburgh: Edinburgh University Press, 2020), 1–2.

8. Cisneros, *Loose Woman*, 108–110.

9. Cisneros, *Loose Woman*, n.p.

10. Sandra Cisneros, *Woman without Shame: Poems* (New York: Alfred A. Knopf, 2022), n.p.

11. A joint interview with Garrison Keillor in 2005 offered both writers a public occasion to converse and reflect on their friendship. "I'm rethinking the connections between us, who we were and are in our time and in that place. Mostly I'm looking forward to getting to visit." Joy Harjo to Sandra Cisneros, May 15, 2005, Sandra Cisneros Papers.

12. Joy Harjo to Sandra Cisneros, August 21, 2006, Sandra Cisneros Papers.

13. Mary Louise Pratt, *Imperial Eyes: Travel Writing and Transculturation*, 2nd ed. (New York: Routledge, 2008), 8.

14. Pratt, *Imperial Eyes*, 8.

15. Susan Stanford Friedman, *Mappings: Feminism and the Cultural Geographies of Encounter* (Princeton, NJ: Princeton University Press, 1998), 7.

16. Friedman, *Mappings*, 32.

17. Sandra Cisneros, *My Wicked Wicked Ways*, 2nd ed. (1987; New York: Vintage, 1997).

18. Joy Harjo, *Poet Warrior* (New York: Norton, 2021), 183.

19. Harjo, *Poet Warrior*, 163.

20. Harjo, *Poet Warrior*, 139.

21. Joy Harjo, *How We Became Human* (New York: Norton, 2002), 224.

22. Harjo, *Poet Warrior*, 139.

23. David Dowling, *A Delicate Aggression: Savagery and Survival in the Iowa Writers' Workshop* (New Haven, CT: Yale University Press, 2019), 194, 203.

24. Audre Lorde, "The Master's Tools Will Never Dismantle the Master's House," in *Sister Outsider*, 102.

25. Harjo, *Poet Warrior*, 108; Lorde, "The Master's Tools," 103.

26. Quoted in Dowling, *A Delicate Aggression*, 206.

27. Sandra Cisneros, *A House of My Own: Stories from My Life* (New York: Alfred A. Knopf, 2015), 276.

28. Quoted in Dowling, *A Delicate Aggression*, 205.

29. Dowling, *A Delicate Aggression*, 207.

30. Corey Hickner-Johnson describes Cisneros's painful recognition that she lacked connection with those held up as model writers and theorists, such as Gaston Bachelard, and encouragement from her teachers, especially Justice. Hickner-Johnson also notes that Mark McGurl's influential study *The Program Era: Postwar Fiction and the Rise of Creative Writing* (Cambridge, MA: Harvard University Press, 2009) itself barely explores "the extent to which Cisneros was lost in a space that marginalized her femininity as well as her Latina identity." Hickner-Johnson, "Not with the Program: Sandra Cisneros on Feeling and Being a Latina Writer in the Program Era," *Tulsa Studies in Women's Literature* 37, no. 2 (Fall 2018): 379.

31. Joy Harjo to Sandra Cisneros, November 24, 1985, Sandra Cisneros Papers.

32. Harjo, *Poet Warrior*, 106.

33. Harjo, *Poet Warrior*, 44.

34. Harjo, *Poet Warrior*, 45.

35. Adrienne Rich, "Arts of the Possible," in *Essential Essays: Culture, Politics, and the Art of Poetry*, ed. Sandra M. Gilbert (New York: W. W. Norton, 2018), 329.

36. Rich, "Arts of the Possible," 329.

37. Toni Cade Bambara, foreword to *This Bridge Called My Back: Writings by Radical Women of Color*, 2nd ed., ed. Cherríe Moraga and Gloria Anzaldúa (1981; New York: Kitchen Table, 1983), vi. Lorde and Barbara Smith founded the activist publishing company Kitchen Table: Women of Color Press in 1981, putting their everyday working spaces at the center of their collaborative venture. See Smith, "A Press of Our Own Kitchen Table: Women of Color Press," *Frontiers* 10, no. 3 (1989): 11–13.

38. Gloria Anzaldúa, "Speaking in Tongues," in Moraga and Anzaldúa, *This Bridge Called My Back*, 168.

39. Joy Harjo and Gloria Byrd, eds., *Reinventing the Enemy's Language: Contemporary Native Women's Writings of North America* (New York: W. W. Norton, 1997), 19. This collection developed from conversations that took place in person, through letters, and in the form of notes scribbled on yellow legal pads or typed by hand. "No matter," Harjo and Byrd assure the reader in their introduction, "the kitchen table is everpresent in its place at the center of being" (19).

40. Cisneros, *My Wicked Wicked Ways*, xi.

41. Cisneros, *Loose Woman*, 49–50.

42. Cisneros, *Loose Woman*, 111.

43. Cisneros, *Loose Woman*, 112.

44. Cisneros, *Loose Woman*, 114–115.

45. Cisneros, *Woman without Shame*, 54.

46. Cisneros, *Woman without Shame*, 54.

47. "Joy Harjo Reads Sandra Cisneros," *New Yorker: Poetry*.

48. Cisneros, *A House of My Own*, 140.

49. Joy Harjo, *Crazy Brave: A Memoir* (New York: W. W. Norton, 2013), 150.

50. Harjo, *Crazy Brave*, 151.

51. Harjo, *Crazy Brave*, 154.

52. Joy Harjo, *She Had Some Horses* (New York: Thunder's Mouth Press, 1983), 73.

53. Sandra Cisneros to Thomas Wortham, November 20, 2001, Sandra Cisneros Papers.

54. Harjo, *Crazy Brave*, 163.

55. Joy Harjo, "Running," *New Yorker*, July 2, 2018.

56. Harjo, "Running."

57. Cisneros, *A House of My Own*, 17, 38, 97, 267, 374.

58. Harjo, *Poet Warrior*, 114.

59. Quoted in Stephen Kunsisto, Deborah Tall, and David Weiss, eds., *The Poet's Notebook: Excerpts from the Notebooks of Contemporary American Poets* (New York: W. W. Norton, 1995), 87.

60. Joy Harjo to Sandra Cisneros, March 31, 1995, Sandra Cisneros Papers.

61. Joy Harjo, *Conflict Resolution for Holy Beings* (New York: W. W. Norton, 2015), 118–119.

62. I have written elsewhere about Harjo's planetary poetics; see Audrey

Goodman, *A Planetary Lens: The Photo-Poetics of Western Women's Writing* (Lincoln: University of Nebraska Press, 2021).

63. Joy Harjo to Sandra Cisneros, September 22, 2014, Sandra Cisneros Papers.

64. Anzaldúa, "Speaking in Tongues," 170–171.

65. Anzaldúa, "Speaking in Tongues," 167, 171.

66. Quoted in Carmen Haydée Rivera, *Border Crossings and Beyond: The Life and Works of Sandra Cisneros* (Santa Barbara, CA: Praeger, 2009), 75.

67. Joy Harjo to Sandra Cisneros, November 19, 1991, Sandra Cisneros Papers.

68. Sandra Cisneros to Thomas Wortham, September 20, 2001, Sandra Cisneros Papers.

69. Joy Harjo to Sandra Cisneros, March 31, 1996, Sandra Cisneros Papers.

70. Anzaldúa, "Speaking in Tongues," 163.

CHAPTER 10

"HAY QUE INVENTARNOS / WE MUST INVENT OURSELVES"
The Impact of Norma Alarcón and Sandra Cisneros's Friendship on Chicana Feminist Literature

Sara A. Ramírez

Chicana feminist poet and philosopher Norma Alarcón is best known as the founder of Third Woman Press and as a critical activist-scholar in the fields of decolonial/US Third World (especially Chicana/Latina) feminist literature and philosophy. While scholars tend to focus on Sandra Cisneros's innovative contributions to fiction, we need to consider her similarly radical role as a literary activist who, along with Alarcón, has promoted the value of literature as a vehicle for sociopolitical justice and has responded critically and creatively to the literary publishing world's exclusion of writings by women of color. In this chapter, instead of delving into Cisneros's published writings as revolutionary contributions to the field of Chicana/Latina feminist literature, I highlight how she and Alarcón helped shape this field, particularly through their publication and international promotion of *Third Woman* journal and the subsequent establishment of Third Woman Press, one of the first and the longest-running (1981–2001) Latina-led publishing efforts focused on the work of women of color writers and artists in the United States.

Early in their careers, Alarcón, Cisneros, and their contemporaries took note of the racist exclusionary practices (or what Richard Jean So describes as the "redlining culture") of major publishers like Random House, which have overwhelmingly focused on the publication and promotion of books written by white writers.[1] While Latino-led small presses and journals existed in the 1960s and 1970s as a result of civil rights arts movements, there were few literary publishing efforts led by Latina feminists in the United States. None existed in the Midwest.[2] For this reason, activist Diana Solís organized a session titled "Taller de Escritoras Latinas / Latina Writers Workshop" during the Chicago Women Writers' Conference, which took place at the Chicago Public

Library Cultural Center on September 13, 1980.³ Here, a group of about ten Latinas declared that it was necessary to forge a Latina-led path in arts and letters, and the journal *Third Woman* was conceived. The group of women who showed up to Meeting Room 3 included Solís, Cisneros, Alarcón, Ana Castillo, and Salima Rivera.

Although this meeting occurred in 1980, promotional materials for Third Woman and most published mentions of the press indicate 1979 as the year Third Woman was founded. As the person in charge of revitalizing the press, I once asked Alarcón why 1979 had been documented as the founding year and not 1981, and she answered that it felt like "a good year." Through my research into Alarcón's and Cisneros's archives, however, I have learned that there was more to the year 1979 than Alarcón's whim; it was the year that she and Cisneros began their insurrectionary correspondence.

The two Chicanas first met during a van ride from a conference celebrating poet and writer Carl Sandburg in 1978, near Chicago. Nicolás Kanellos, coeditor of *Revista Chicano-Riqueña* and the future publisher of *The House on Mango Street*, was the driver. Alarcón remembers meeting Cisneros in the van:

> She was wearing a miniskirt and a black Parisian beret, a bit chic metropolis. Upscale Bohemian sort of thing. Nick [Kanellos] introduced us.... I think at that moment she was busy noting something in her journal. We are both shy people, so it was hard to get discussion going. Nick helped out by saying to Sandra that I was a grad student at [Indiana University], then he turns to me and says maybe you can take her down for a reading.⁴

Cisneros and Alarcón did not meet again until late the following year. Like many intelligent young women of color, Cisneros and Alarcón had come to associate their own oral speech acts with an interrupting and silencing, white supremacist, heteropatriarchal, and capitalist culture. They learned to navigate this culture through writing. Thus, the friendship between these two shy, emergent literary activists befittingly blossomed in the epistolary format, as each woman found in the other another Chicana feminist who shared the lived experience of "Third World women colonized in the belly of the imperial beast" and could appreciate the nuance of language in her writing.⁵ Unlike speaking, the familiar genre of writing enabled each woman to share her most intimate thoughts and feelings with her new friend, someone who strove to navigate an oppressive system as a Chicana in the US Midwest.

Cisneros and Alarcón's archived correspondence between 1979 and 1985 offers a narrative of a life-changing and field-changing friendship. These letters reveal how their connection influenced the process and creation of a Chicana/Latina feminist literary field. Significantly, these letters articulate the guiding principles that have sustained their friendship: generous support, reciprocity, and the erotic; a shared commitment to self-invention in the name of social justice; and a mutual regard for each other as deeply connected kin. These guiding principles were valuable for two women who faced the dominant culture's efforts to dehumanize them, and they are key to sustaining and growing a Chicana/Latina feminist literary field that is consistently threatened with delegitimizing imperatives.

"A COMMUNITY OF POETS BY LETTER": GENEROSITY, RECIPROCITY, AND THE EROTIC

After their initial meeting in 1978, Cisneros and Alarcón became reacquainted during Cisneros's visit to do a poetry reading in Bloomington, Indiana, in October 1979. At the time, Cisneros was an artist in residence for the Illinois Arts Council in Chicago and Alarcón was a doctoral student at Indiana University Bloomington, working with Kanellos and Luis Dávila on *Revista Chicano-Riqueña*. In what appears to be her first letter to Cisneros, dated October 17, 1979, Alarcón mentions a forthcoming payment for the poetry reading at Bloomington and suggests that Cisneros's visit has inspired a discussion about the need to foster a community of poets. Alarcón writes, "I would be pleased to share my work with you. We can certainly discover just how feasible a community of poets by letter might be."[6] Their subsequent written exchanges over the next couple of decades demonstrate that, for these friends committed to social justice, "community" means support not only for each other and other artists but, significantly, for an entire field dedicated to the study and proliferation of these artists' work.

In her response, dated October 26, 1979, Cisneros expresses her appreciation for the visit to Bloomington, generously details her publications as per Alarcón's request, and encourages her new friend to submit work to various publishers. She encourages Alarcón to submit to the magazines and journals in which she has been published (except *Nuestro* magazine because they "still owe me money") and five other (primarily women's) magazines with whom she (Cisneros) has not been published. Cisneros shows care by providing complete mailing addresses. She also takes the time to distinguish "women magazines" using an asterisk.[7] This sincere encouragement and shared commitment to feminist writing and publishing persist throughout the archived letters between them. For example, within a few months after their first exchange, Cisneros sends Alarcón a photocopy of *Radical Teacher*'s call for articles on women's studies and a very short handwritten note, asking her, "Are you still writing? Finding time for poetry?"[8]

Similarly, Alarcón encourages Cisneros's pursuit in the field of arts and letters. In a letter dated February 1, 1985, Alarcón expresses this encouragement as deliberate, writing, "This is an Emergency/Urgent letter to [help] create a positive atmosphere for you, and for your most serious work, the writing" (see figure 10.1).[9] The letter constitutes an "emergency" effort to reciprocate Cisneros's support and to envelop her with positivity amid discouragement she was facing while working as literature director at the Guadalupe Cultural Arts Center in San Antonio, Texas, between 1984 and 1985 (Cisneros was at the time the first and only woman to hold a leadership role there). Alarcón suggests that Cisneros feels charged with appealing to and appeasing everyone, including "the people at the center." However, Alarcón indicates, that expectation is misplaced on the writer, especially the Chicana writer, whose power emanates from the specificity in which she grounds her work. Alarcón reminds Cisneros of her poem "A Woman Cutting Celery," in which the protagonist no longer tolerates the behavior of an "errant [male] lover."[10] While it is possible that "the people at the center" to whom Alarcón refers are the people at the Guadalupe—with whom Cisneros had a falling out in 1985—it is also possible to interpret the "center" in its deconstruction sense: as a metaphor for dominant culture. Alarcón extends the metaphor by comparing "the people at the center" to "a bad [male] lover," underscoring that heteropatriarchy is inherent in the center—and, by extension, the Guadalupe Cultural Arts Center in 1985.[11] Playfully and grandly, Alarcón proclaims that their voices will be heard and brings attention to the positionality of the margin vis-à-vis the center. As a "luminous ring" enclosing the center, the margin is positioned to overtake the center by outshining it.[12] The letter illuminates important aspects of this Chicana feminist friendship, as it demonstrates the writers' faith in each other by taking each other's efforts seriously, especially vis-à-vis a heteropatriarchal culture that does not genuinely support their ideas or work.

This encouragement via letter is not unusual of their interactions. It is, indeed, quite typical and consistent, as it stems from their evident love for each other and for writing. Alarcón writes to Cisneros in a letter dated April 15, 1982:

> I know I am happy when we share our poetry, and ourselves and when I write letters to my friends and when the lot of us reads, at Northeastern I and Chicago Circle, and in the living room, and in Bloomington's La Casa, and when Beatriz [Badikian] says I want to talk with you,

2/1/85

Dear Sandra:

It was a good surprise to hear from you last night. I'd been thinking about you and had wanted to call, but like you I've been trying not to make too many calls, I have to save my money for the summer. Perhaps our greatest disease is that we don't take ourselves seriously enough -- To take oneself seriously is not only hard work and painful, but it also means that you have to be convinced that what you have to say is a matter of life and death. That is why I thought last Spring when you invited me and Beatriz and others to read in San Antonio, and you called the reading Poemas de Emergencia - that it had been a very appropriate title -- I find that when I write anything that sounds good to me, and even to others -- that indeed they were representing an emergency. We have learned not to take ourselves seriously, because most people have never taken us seriously, and it is very damaging to our psyches, we learn to postpone, to sacrifice, because a time will come for us -- but the time never comes, you seize it -- Lately I feel like a thief a lot, because I seize here and there, and strangely enough like a thief I feel guilt, as if I should be doing something else -- for someone. This is an Emergency/Urgent letter to ehlp create a positive atmosphere for you, and for your most serious work, the writing. You have given me one of the greatest gifts that I have ever received in my life, and I shall never forget it -- your faith in me, and I hope that I have reciprocated. One might hope that the whole world can read one's work and enjoy it or come away with something from it, but when we sit at the typewriter, we usually write for someone, or a small group of people at most, the rest of the world overhears it, and goes away with the illusion that it was written for them, but that is not the way it happened on paper, on paper it was for a very exclusive ear, at least that is the way I feel about it foten. My head is terribly muddled today because of the cold I have, but I think at least for today I have told you what I wanted. Think of the strength of your Celery poem, you have hundreds of them inside you, let me read them. The people at the center are very negative, and you have risked enough being around them -- you should get away from them soon -- they too are a bad lover! We shall prevail, our voices will resound, and our dreadful marginality will be the ring, the luminous ring that dulls the center -- whatever that is.

Figure 10.1. Letter from Norma Alarcón to Sandra Cisneros, February 1, 1985. Image courtesy of the Sandra Cisneros Papers, Wittliff Collections, Texas State University.

and when Diana Solis hugs me hello and goodbye, and when Margie [Margarita Lopez Perez] hugs me hello and goodbye and I hug them back, and when I hug Sandy [Sandra Cisneros] hello/goodbye/hello again and when I look into all of our eyes and our "bones are one long strand" (paraphrase) Third Woman Collective—The three of cups to us from the Tarot, a great card![13]

The Three of Cups Tarot card is magically accurate for these women. The number three is significant for the Third Woman Collective, and the card signifies reunion or celebration.[14] Interconnected as if their "bones are one long strand," the group identifies strongly with their poetry; when they share poetry, they share themselves.[15] This long and euphoric sentence illuminates the love between them in even simple exchanges such as greetings and farewells. Alarcón even refers to the letter's addressee in the third person, "Sandy," as if she is announcing these sentiments to the world; she wants everyone to know of the joy that their reunion inspires.

In response, Cisneros expresses her own joy and reciprocates Alarcón's love in a letter dated May 18, 1982 (see figure 10.2).[16] Significantly in this letter, Cisneros's description of a "religious feeling" echoes what Audre Lorde names as "the erotic" and its uses. Lorde identifies the erotic as "an assertion of the lifeforce of women; of that creative energy empowered, the knowledge and use of which we are now reclaiming in our language, our history, our dancing, our loving, our work, our lives." Lorde also argues that the erotic has been used against women by men.[17] While Cisneros names this feeling "camaraderie" (or "comradery"), she, like Lorde, senses that men have kept women apart so that they could never share that feeling.[18] Lorde explains further, "The erotic is not a question only of what we do; it is a question of how acutely and fully we can feel in the doing. Once we know the extent to which we are capable of feeling that sense of satisfaction and completion, we can then observe which of our various life endeavors bring us closest to that fullness."[19]

Both Lorde and Cisneros suggest that cultivating this feeling of the erotic is imperative for women, as it allows them to focus on endeavors that will help them create a world outside of white supremacy, heteropatriarchy, and capitalism.[20] Alarcón's letter to Cisneros so precisely conveys the erotic, that deep feeling of interconnection, that Cisneros senses that the note's audience is not only herself but the group of interconnected women (including Salima Rivera, Beatriz Badikian, and Yolanda Santiago) who have helped foster this feeling together. The erotic strengthens the group so that together "[they] are might."[21] In this way, Cisneros illuminates the deep feelings of the erotic as a significant element of Chicana/Latina feminist friendship and collaboration.

```
                                                         5/18/82

Norma, do you know

how much you mean to us?  I told Rodrigo I never felt as close to my women friends
as I do now, and I suppose and rightly so, that it's all due to the
collective and 3rd WOMAN.

I mean, Salima and I were friends but not close, Not like we are today.
And Beatriz and Yolanda surely would not have been my confidantes, my
comrades and encouragers as they are now had it not been for that religious
feeling we experienced when we read together.  Somehow it seeems men have
kept us apart  from each other, have split us so that we could never share
that comraderie that they, men, were famous for.

Therefore I don't assume the letters you send are simply for me and I share
them with the other women and we all benefit from your strength and you from
ours and each from the other and together we are mighty.  I loved your letter.
I began a poem or two that perhaps you'll see someday.  And, Norma, we are
lucky to have you as our friend.  I wanted to tell you that today.

Your letter echoes in my head.  I wanted to write sooner but April has been
mad.  And now May is here and half gone and I'm packing already.  Looks like
I'll be gone by May 31st or June 10th or thereabouts.  All tenuous because
I may get a ride east with a buddy or go out to NYC with Rodrigo, but it
all depends on whether they drive or don't drive or what.  I should know
by next week or so.  In the meantime we are planning a big bash!  A hell
of a party!  Ill send you an invite but for now know that it's scheduled
for May 30th.  Can you come?

Such short notice!                              avísame,

P.S.

I've seen Third Woman being sold for the outrageous amount of five dollars.
Please print the price on the cover.  Let Prarie News know their mistake.
THey've been telling bookstores $5 is the individual price not the individual
subscription.
```

Figure 10.2. Letter from Sandra Cisneros to Norma Alarcón, May 18, 1982. Image courtesy of the Norma Alarcón Papers, Department of Special Research Collections, University of California, Santa Barbara, Library.

THE IMPETUS TO "SHED USELESS SKIN" AND REINVENT THEMSELVES

Cisneros and Alarcón's correspondence reveals that as their friendship deepens over time, their relationship is not a surface-level collaboration. The exchanges between the two women reveal that their discussions and work affect each other at deep, psychic levels. Writing on April 15, 1982, Alarcón expresses:

> Sandra, in your own way you have shown me that I wanted to be brand new more than anything, that's why I took to English so well when I arrived in Chicago at the age of 11—Speaking English would serve so that I could dress myself up and be a newly minted coin—At the age of 11 my heritage (female) was already flattening my spirit, I didn't know it then, consciously, but I know it now—that I saw my salvation in language, except I made the mistake of thinking that exchanging one language for another would do it, when all the time it's the very use of it, whichever one it is, that helps shed useless skin.[22]

Thinkers such as Alarcón and Cisneros, who experience life in the interstices between Mexican and US American patriarchal cultures, find salvation in their use of language. Language facilitates the shedding of "useless skin," or what Gloria Anzaldúa describes as "a conscious rupture with all oppressive traditions of all cultures and religions."[23] Both Alarcón's and Cisneros's career trajectories were shaped by this impetus to "shed useless skin" and the desire to reinvent themselves and, by extension, history and the field of Chicana/Latina writing.

Alarcón's feminist path was inspired by the work of Mexican feminist poet, novelist, and short story writer Rosario Castellanos, which she studied as a graduate student. In the first issue of *Third Woman*, Alarcón explains Castellanos's influence on the title of the journal. In her play *El eterno femenino: Farsa* (The eternal feminine: Farce), Castellanos remarks on the various paths available to women to reach liberation from the oppressive intersection of racism, elitism, and sexism. She names reformist and revolutionary routes, yet she advocates for a third way. Alarcón takes note:

> That third way is *Self-Invention*, Castellanos felt, and I as well as those associated with Third Woman agree, that it is not enough to imitate models that are proposed to us and that are responses to circumstances other (different) than ours, furthermore, it is not even enough to discover, to recognize, to know what or who we are. We have to invent ourselves.[24]

"HAY QUE INVENTARNOS / WE MUST INVENT OURSELVES"

The motivation to invent themselves is evident throughout Cisneros's and Alarcón's archived and published work. For instance, Cisneros remarks on Castellanos's and Alarcón's influence on her own self-invention:

> Because I knew no Latinas who could guide me, I had to invent myself, or reinvent myself, as Mexican feminist Rosario Castellanos so aptly put it. Until I met Norma Alarcón, then just a graduate student at Indiana University, I didn't realize how difficult it had been for me to break out of that Bastille, my father's house. My Chicana feminism began with Norma, by sharing our stories, comparing our escape routes out of our fathers' houses, and claiming the right to a life of letters.[25]

Their friendship thus appears to be based on a deeply shared commitment to a life of letters as a route to escape patriarchy. Still, they remained mindful of and respected the complex particularities of their individual lived experiences. In a speech honoring Cisneros's lifetime achievements, Alarcón remembers that Cisneros had the boldness to live alone:

> Once she invited me to her apartment on Paulina Street, where this photo [popularized image of Cisneros sitting in front of her typewriter, from the cover of the first issue of *Third Woman*] was taken by Diana Solís. I asked her, "Do you live alone?" which surprised her, but the fact that she was living alone surprised *me*; I had always wanted that, too.[26]

This exchange and the differences in their personal lives amid their friendship suggest that the ages of eighteen to twenty-five are critical in a Mexicana/Chicana's life, especially before and during the 1960s and 1970s. Like most Mexicanas and Chicanas living under patriarchy, Alarcón never had a chance to live alone, as she transitioned from her father's house to a home with a husband before she was twenty. Alarcón's question "Do you live alone?" was rooted not in patriarchal assumptions but instead in sincere awe that patriarchy had not succeeded in ensnaring a young woman during a critical period in her life. Cisneros's life was beginning to model what is possible when we reinvent ourselves to escape the claws of patriarchy.

One of the most concrete ways in which the friends reinvented themselves was through the use of pseudonyms, a strategy that circumvented racist and patriarchal accusations of vanity. As Latinas, Alarcón and Cisneros did not have the white privilege of being perceived as individuals. The ethnic label "Latina" can be a double-edged sword: despite the reclamation of this ethnic identity to dispel stereotypes and assert individuality, it categorizes women as a homogenous racialized and gendered group and not as individuals within that group. For this reason, a Latina critic might be able to positively review the work of a Latina writer with whom the critic is not acquainted, but racist and patriarchal readers will deem the review suspect: can the critic be objective, given that she is reviewing the work of someone from her ethnic group? Moreover, positively reviewing one's acquaintances' works within one's ethnic and gendered community is tantamount to self-promotion, a strategy for success that we have been taught is "unbecoming" for women but not for men.

Cognizant of these racist and patriarchal literary norms, Alarcón used the pseudonym "Marisa Cantú" for a series of reviews in the first issue of *Third Woman*.[27] Cantú reviewed three texts: *From the Midwest to the West*, edited by Patricia Montenegro and Marjorie Agosin, which includes poems by Alarcón and Cisneros; *Eluder* by Rina Rocha; and *The Invitation* by Ana Castillo. Cantú's biographical note describes her as "Chicana poet and free-lance writer residing in the Chicago Area. Has published poems in *Odds and Ends* and *Verano*."[28] Alarcón explains, "Marisa Cantú is a figment of my imagination—let's say the writer I wanted to be in the metropolis."[29] During this time, Alarcón was living in Indiana, but her letters often express the wish to live closer to her friends in Chicago. The invention of Cantú thus underscores the isolated writer's longing for escape to the metropolis. The two magazines in the biographical note are also somewhat fanciful. While *Odds and Ends* does not exist, *Un Verano* was the title of the student magazine that Cisneros put together with her student mentees at Latino Youth Alternative High School in 1978–1980. The fictionalization of Cantú's work in *Verano* suggests the deep kinship between Alarcón and Cisneros, as it expresses Alarcón's desire not only to have worked with Cisneros earlier in their careers but more significantly perhaps to have been guided as a mentee by Cisneros.

Similarly, Cisneros reinvented herself as "Katarina Kremidis," positively reviewing Badikian's poetry chapbook *Akewa Is a Woman* in *Third Woman*.[30] In a letter accompanying her book review, Cisneros writes to Alarcón,

> Please sign with pseudonym Katerina Kremidis which Beatriz [Badikian] tells me means Katerina Onions in Greek. Actually a Katerina Kremidis does exist in Athens. I met her. A mad woman who was quickly losing what little shred of sanity she had left. Something about this emotional sad woman who was looking desperately for a man to save her instead of realizing they were only plunging her deeper into her madness, touched me.[31]

Unfortunately, there is no biographical note for Kremidis in the issue's list of contributors. However, the necessity for Cisneros's invention of the pseudonym Kremidis illuminates the sexist, racist, and ethnocentric publishing culture in which they were working. In the same issue, Cisneros used her own name to review two other books, both of them written by Latinas with whom she, according to a culture that homogenizes Latina writers, is not supposed to be acquainted. Cisneros's decision to use a pseudonym for her review of Badikian's chapbook but not the Latinas' writings suggests an effort to thwart the misguided notion that a Latina could not review the work of someone with the Greek last name Badikian—even though the Badikian in question is an Argentine of Armenian and Greek descent and considers herself a Latina. Cisneros's choice of the specifically Greek-language pseudonym Kremidis to evaluate Badikian's *presumably* Greek work suggests that a reviewer of Greek descent would be taken more seriously than a Latina. To reiterate, an ethnocentric literary publishing and promotion culture tolerates non-Anglo people's reviews of writers from their own ethnic group. However, non-Anglo people cannot review acquaintances (because objectivity is at stake) or writers of a different ethnicity from their own (because non-Anglo people supposedly know only their own ethnic culture). Conversely, the mostly male reviewers of Anglo descent, especially in the 1980s United States, operate from an "objective" standpoint that does not recognize the construction of their own ethnicity, race, or gender. Their alleged objectivity entitles them to review anyone's work, no matter the author's ethnicity.

The invention of Kremidis suggests Cisneros's and Alarcón's awareness of the literary world's negation of intersectional identities, especially during this time period. As Third World women who experienced racism and sexism simultaneously, Cisneros and Alarcón were acutely aware of how the Anglo and male literary world positioned the Other as either an ethnicized subject or a gendered subject, but never a subject who was both ethnicized and gendered simultaneously, as in the case of non-Anglo women. Alarcón's scholarship, as I explain later in this chapter, indeed focuses on the subject position of women of color. Cisneros's fictionalization of Kremidis encourages us to think about the mainstream literary world's expectations for "ethnic" (non-Anglo) women writers to write about only "ethnic" issues—if they are to write at all.[32] Badikian's awareness of the pervasiveness of colonization/imperialism throughout the world, her experience of site-specific patriarchal oppression in the United States, and her identity as a Latina all link her more to Cisneros than to the woman named Katerina Kremidis who lives under another face of patriarchy, in Athens, where Badikian was born. As a good friend of Badikian's, Cisneros is aware of this connection. Her acquiescence to ethnocentric literary norms becomes a strategy to promote Badikian's work. Overall, Alarcón and Cisneros's shared commitment to self-invention has been integral to their respective professional successes, the success of other Latina writers, and the field of Chicana/Latina feminist literature as a whole.

MAKING FACE, MAKING SOUL THROUGH *TONANTZÍN* AND *THIRD WOMAN*

The two Chicana feminists' love for each other extended outward as they shared a commitment to Third World women writers.[33] For both Cisneros and Alarcón, Chicana/Latina feminist letters mapped and became the escape route from patriarchy. In her introduction to the first issue of *Third Woman*, Alarcón remarks on the motivation to create a new intellectual and creative space: "We all agreed that we needed a journal that promised continuity, and offered encouragement to the creative work of Latinas and other Third World Women, and we also wanted to overcome the dependency on the 'special-issue syndrome' that has beset the work of minority women for years."[34] According to Alarcón, "It was [Cisneros's] enthusiasm and creative energy that compelled me to become a publisher and editor of Third Woman Press."[35] As the duo invented themselves, they nurtured a relationship that supported up-and-coming writers.

Alarcón served as editor of *Third Woman*, while Cisneros's role shifted from editorial board member for the first two issues to associate editor for the remaining issues. In "Haciendo Caras, Una Entrada" (Making Faces, An Entrance), Anzaldúa, like Alarcón and Cisneros, takes direction from Rosario Castellanos, who observes, "Usted es el modeador de su carne tanto como el su alma."[36] Anzaldúa translates and clarifies, "You are the shaper of your flesh as well as of your soul. According to the ancient *nahuas*, one was put on earth to create one's 'face' (body) and 'heart' (soul). To them, the soul was a speaker of words and the body a doer of deeds."[37] Through their individual writings, Cisneros and Alarcón shaped their own faces/bodies. Their joint activist efforts in *Third Woman* and Third Woman Press shaped the heart/soul of the field of Latina arts and letters.

On January 13, 1983, Alarcón wrote to Cisneros: "THIRD WOMAN is the only way we can challenge others to pay more attention to women writers and also to provide the continuity of that writing and that vision and that existence."[38] As she explained in an interview with the *Berkeleyan* in 1999, Alarcón saw Third Woman Press as "an activist vehicle" that would shed light on the work of women writers.[39] Both Cisneros and Alarcón strongly believed that they needed not only to cultivate these writers' craft but also to promote the longevity of their writing careers.[40]

Their work with *Third Woman* interplayed with their work in other more localized channels. For example, Cisneros had a variety of responsibilities as literature director at the Guadalupe Cultural Arts Center. She organized a reading series with local and guest writers, coordinated Chicana/o writer residencies, led creative writing workshops, and edited and prepared the

"HAY QUE INVENTARNOS / WE MUST INVENT OURSELVES"

Guadalupe's journal, *Tonantzín*, for publication. She also coordinated the first annual Texas Small Press Book Fair. No matter the event, however, Cisneros found ways to collaborate with Alarcón and Third Woman, especially because the Guadalupe served San Antonio and its visitors while *Third Woman* served a national and international audience.[41]

In her earliest work with the Guadalupe, Cisneros highlighted feminist poets and writers in *Tonantzín*. In the June/July 1984 issue, Cisneros featured poetry by Angela de Hoyos, Rosemary Catacalos, and Beatriz Badikian. She also drew attention to feminist publications in the recommended reading section of this issue.[42] The issue even included a call for submissions for *Third Woman*'s next publication, which was to center Texas women's arts and letters. With few exceptions, all the feminist writers promoted in *Tonantzín* eventually had their work published in *Third Woman*, which demonstrates Cisneros's and Alarcón's shared sensibilities as well as their commitment to promoting feminist writers' careers. This detail serves as evidence of how together they strategized to carve out a literary cultural space for Chicana/Latina feminist writers and, in doing so, helped shape the field of Chicana/Latina feminist letters.

Cisneros also organized the Guadalupe's literature program's monthly reading series and writer residencies. In 1984, the March event included Alarcón, Badikian, Ana Castillo, Angela de Hoyos, and Silvia Peña. The April event featured poets José Montoya and Evangelina Vigil. The series event in May highlighted the work of Art Muñoz and Luis Omar Salinas. June's event spotlighted Pat Mora and Jose Flores. Cherríe Moraga and Rolando Hinojosa read in July, and Helena María Viramontes and John Phillip Santos shared their work in August.[43] While the March event included only women, the rest of the reading series lineup suggests an attempt by Cisneros to balance men and women writers. Significantly, the summer events coincided with Alarcón's position as writer in residence for the Guadalupe. Described in *Tonantzín* as a "Ph.D., poet, critic, and editor," Alarcón conducted a ten-week poetry workshop focused on "the woman writer."[44] Due to Cisneros's position at the Guadalupe, the year 1984 brought together some future greats of Chicana feminist literature (see figure 10.3). Like the women whose names appeared in *Tonantzín*, all the women who participated in the reading series were eventually published in or promoted by *Third Woman*.

Cisneros shared Alarcón's belief that *Third Woman* was an important way to encourage people to pay attention to Latinas in arts and letters. For example, in a letter dated February 5, 1985, Cisneros wrote to Alarcón, explained that she was "building a wonderful collection of photographs of Latina writers," and asked whether *Third Woman* had the funds to print them.[45] Among the photographs were images of Alarcón, Badikian, Xelina, Helena María Viramontes, Cherríe Moraga, Mary Sue Galindo, and Margarita Lopez Perez.[46]

Figure 10.3. Sandra Cisneros with Chicana/Latina writers and artists outside Guadalupe Cultural Arts Center, San Antonio, Texas, summer 1984. *Left to right:* Norma Alarcón, Sandra Cisneros, Cherríe Moraga, Mary Sue Galindo, Marsha Gomez, and Carmen Rodriguez. Image courtesy of the Sandra Cisneros Papers, Wittliff Collections, Texas State University.

Cisneros was aware of the potential of such photographs, as these images had the power not only to represent the body of a woman writer of color and to capture a moment in literary history but also to communicate to the viewer the writers' inarticulable innermost being. Cisneros's faith in *Third Woman* was staunch, and she made sure that the journal was represented at the first annual Texas Small Press Book Fair, which she co-organized with Bryce Milligan. Because Alarcón was unable to attend, Cisneros asked friends including Galindo, who was both an intern with the Guadalupe and a poet published in *Tonantzín* and *Third Woman*, to "woman" the table. "If not," said Cisneros, "I'll have to do the best I can."[47]

Cisneros conducted creative writing workshops in her role at the Guadalupe, too. A letter to Alarcón expresses glee that one of the writing workshops is not a "teen workshop" as she thought it would be, but instead "has evolved into a [drawn Venus symbol]'s workshop! 8 feisty Texas women my age for the most part.... I'm holding the Latina women's workshop I always dreamed of. I've plugged your mag + I think I have a few talented writers you might consider for that Texas issue."[48] Her desire to foster Latina writers made possible serendipitous moments such as this women's workshop. With good reason, she was surprised that the workshop was attracting women in their late twenties or early thirties because, especially during this time period, women were too busy with children and work to cultivate gifts such as writing. It appears that in all her roles at the Guadalupe, Cisneros was dedicated to furthering the work of Latina writers and facilitating career opportunities for them locally, through *Tonantzín*, but also nationally, via *Third Woman*.

Ellie D. Hernández argues that Chicana activist grassroots publications such as *Third Woman* helped give rise to Chicana studies as a field within academia.[49] While Hernández suggests that the *Third Woman* journal—and, later, Third Woman Press—functioned as a bridge between grassroots literary activism and the academic world, she does not fully capture the significance of Alarcón's and Cisneros's labors. Both women were motivated to solicit art, poetry, and short stories for the publication. However, it was Alarcón's willingness to learn the nuances of the publishing industry, including how to set type and how to process financial numbers, that helped launch the career of many well-known Latina creative writers and scholars, including Castillo, Moraga, Julia Alvarez, Achy Obejas, Tey Diana Rebolledo, and Yvonne Yarbro-Bejarano.[50] Cisneros, too, recognizes the impact of Alarcón's labor on her career:

> Thanks to her press, her critical writing, and her wholehearted support and encouragement, I can call myself an author today.
>
> When no one else would publish, acknowledge, or take our work seriously, Norma Alarcón did so, often carrying the brunt of the criticism from other scholars, especially by Chicano scholars who were often the most hostile to the work of Chicana feminists. Because there was no central zone for writers like myself to gather, Norma Alarcón created that space at great personal expense and time.[51]

Unlike Cisneros's archive, the Norma Alarcón Papers, held at the University of California, Santa Barbara, do not offer details about her tasks or responsibilities with Third Woman. However, the six issues of *Third Woman* for which she served as editor (1981–1989) and the twenty-five books that she published through her press (including Cisneros's *My Wicked Wicked Ways*, 1987) prove that she shared with Cisneros a great commitment to the careers of creative writers and scholars. Because of her position as both Chicana poet and feminist philosopher with a PhD, Alarcón has been uniquely able to bring critical attention to these women writers and to cultivate an academic field of Latina arts and letters.

Theorizing the subjectivity of women of color, Alarcón was one of the first scholars to bring academic attention to what the Combahee River Collective described as the "interlocking" of "major systems of oppression" in 1977 and legal scholar Kimberlé Crenshaw would identify as "intersectionality" in 1989.[52] One of her earliest academic essays on Chicana feminist literature, dispelling the Chicano patriarchal myth of La Malinche, was included in the foundational, grassroots anthology *This Bridge Called My Back* in 1981.[53] In a 1984 interview with Cisneros, Alarcón commented on the attention that the essay had garnered. Positive attention had come from women, while men had deemed it "controversial" for breaking down Chicano nationalist (and patriarchal) "solidarity" by turning its intersectional lens to Chicana nationalism specifically.[54]

Alarcón's particular influence on Cisneros becomes most apparent in Cisneros's 1991 collection *Woman Hollering Creek and Other Stories* and her 1996 essay "Guadalupe the Sex Goddess."[55] These two texts consider the relationships and differences between men and women of Mexican descent by rewriting several Chicano patriarchal myths about women, including La Llorona, La Malinche, La Lechuza, La Virgen de Guadalupe, and Prince Popo and Princess Izta.

In recognition of Alarcón's influence on herself and other Chicana/Latina feminist writers, Cisneros refers to her as "our Sor Juana Inés de la Cruz, the genius nun who was one of the great thinkers of the Americas." Cisneros explains, "For us, she has been our crusader in the academy. . . . For many of us, she was the only source of intellectual support."[56] Alarcón's intellectual and publishing support facilitated a focus on many of the themes and issues that Chicana/Latina feminist literature would be known for, including the intersectionality of gender, race, class, and sexuality; girls and women as subjects in process; the critical inquiry into family and *familismo*; and questions of sociopolitical justice. In these ways, she created the face and heart of the field of Chicana/Latina literature.

DEEPLY CONNECTED KIN: A LITERARY MOTHER AND *HIJA*

Cisneros's archive includes her collection of writings by others, including a draft of one scholarly essay by Norma Alarcón titled, "What Kind of Lover Have You Made Me, Mother? Towards a Theory of Chicanas' Feminism and Cultural Identity through Poetry."[57] The typed draft has a handwritten note from Alarcón to Cisneros: "Para Sandra con Amor," with "Norma" written under it. In the essay, Alarcón theorizes the subjectivity and multiple concerns of the contemporary Chicana poet-protagonist circa 1985. The essay provides a literary analysis of the mother-daughter relationship from the poet-protagonist's perspective, arguing that the mother symbolizes historical and creative continuity for the daughter. The title of the essay refers to Cherríe Moraga's question

"HAY QUE INVENTARNOS / WE MUST INVENT OURSELVES"

in the poem "La Dulce Culpa," in which, according to Alarcón, the speaker internalizes her mother's rage and disappointment. Alarcón posits, "In considering these poets, it is clear that the intimate relations with mothers and lovers are interconnected in ways that help define the daughter."[58] I am drawn to the fact that Cisneros kept and archived this and no other scholarly essay by Alarcón. How might this essay have affected Cisneros's understanding of herself as a daughter and a lover or, to borrow from Lorde, an erotic being?

A 2017 letter from Alarcón to Cisneros seems to point to an answer. Alarcón writes:

> Querida Sandra:
> Did your mother ever say to you upon greeting "hija de mi vida," as a sign of love and affection? I hope you enjoyed it as you heard it. In recent times you have said to me that I was your "literary mother." There are so many ways I can play with that "bon mot," and I recall my own wish once upon a time, but I did not find a literary mother or father. In a sense, I had to become my own.[59]

In the spirit of Castellanos's "third way," Alarcón had to reinvent herself and become her own mother. Still, she accepts Cisneros's title for her, "literary mother," and bestows her own title on Cisneros, "hija de mi vida," or daughter of my life. This relationship incites me to imagine Cisneros asking of Alarcón, "What kind of lover have you made me, [literary] mother?" The relationship with her literary mother enables the poet-artist to grasp the complexity of herself as more than a "lover"; the poet-artist understands that she is an erotic being, "a well of replenishing and provocative force."[60] But the Chicana feminist friends have had a reciprocal influence on each other; they have shaped *each other* as "lovers" of Latina arts and letters. Given their mutual recognition as deeply connected kin, Cisneros's use of "mother" and Alarcón's use of "hija" are not aligned with the heteropatriarchal mother-daughter paradigm. On the contrary, they use these labels to underscore their deep, *generative* connection.[61] Their connection positions them as the women whom Lorde describes as "brave enough to risk sharing the erotic's electrical charge without having to look away, and without distorting the enormously powerful and creative nature of that exchange."[62] After all, Cisneros's support of Alarcón's publishing and academic endeavors also shaped Alarcón as a person, an erotic being, who was willing to come into her own power.

My aim in this chapter has been not only to restore and document a Chicana feminist literary friendship but also to illuminate why Alarcón may remember 1979 as "a good year." The year 1979 marked the beginning of a friendship based on a commitment to embodying the *third woman*, the one who rejects her preordained sociopolitical condition, as envisioned by Castellanos. Together, the third women—literary mother and daughter—engendered a love that offered generous and reciprocal support, as they invented themselves as part of their commitment to Latina arts and letters. The effect of this love has been an entire academic and popular field of Chicana/Latina feminist literature and art.

NOTES

Thank you to Norma Alarcón, Diana Solís, Margarita Lopez Perez, Irene Campos Carr, Mary Sue Galindo, and Marjorie Agosín for digging into their memories and providing me with additional details for this essay. Thank you to the Sinvergüenza Collective, especially Geneva M. Gano, Linda Greenberg, and Belinda Linn Rincón, for their comments and suggestions on this chapter.

1. See Richard Jean So, *Redlining Culture: A Data History of Racial Inequality and Postwar Fiction* (New York: Columbia University Press, 2021).

2. More than 130 Chicano-led journals and periodicals appeared during the 1970s alone. For details about Chicana-led journals and issues during this period, see Luis Leal, "Journals," in *A Decade of Chicano Literature, 1970–1979: Critical Essays and Bibliography*, ed. Luis Leal et al. (Santa Barbara, CA: Editorial La Causa, 1982), 83–93.

3. Solís, a poet and photographer, organized the meeting because she and her friends had a hard time finding the works of published Latina writers. Solís recognized that there was a need for Latina-led presses and submitted an application for the conference in order to see who could be convened in one space. Diana Solís, pers. comm., March 23, 2022.

4. Norma Alarcón, pers. comm., May 8, 2022.

5. Alarcón, pers. comm.

6. Norma Alarcón to Sandra Cisneros, October 17, 1979, box 7, folder 7, Norma Alarcón Papers, Department of Special Research Collections, University of California, Santa Barbara, Library.

7. Sandra Cisneros to Norma Alarcón, October 26, 1979, box 7, folder 7, Norma Alarcón Papers.

8. Sandra Cisneros to Norma Alarcón, January 30, 1980, box 7, folder 7, Norma Alarcón Papers. While Alarcón is mostly known for her publishing and philosophical writings, she is indeed a published poet.

9. Norma Alarcón to Sandra Cisneros, February 1, 1985, box 98, folder 9, Sandra Cisneros Papers, Wittliff Collections, Texas State University.

10. Sandra Cisneros, *My Wicked Wicked Ways* (Berkeley, CA: Third Woman Press, 1987), 65.

11. Alarcón to Cisneros, February 1, 1985. Cisneros has since restored her relationship with the Guadalupe Cultural Arts Center.

12. Alarcón to Cisneros, February 1, 1985. Alarcón's closing words, "whatever that is," however, are cautionary, as they call into question the fixedness of the center; the

ideology of the center tends to infiltrate all spaces.

13. Norma Alarcón to Sandra Cisneros, April 15, 1982, box 7, folder 7, Norma Alarcón Papers.

14. The Third Woman Collective was never formalized as a group. I have found only a couple of mentions of it in the archive. Its members changed throughout the years due to life circumstances, but Alarcón and Cisneros remained core members.

15. This sharing of themselves appears also to apply to the letters between Alarcón and Cisneros.

16. Sandra Cisneros to Norma Alarcón, May 18, 1982, box 7, folder 7, Norma Alarcón Papers.

17. Audre Lorde, "Uses of the Erotic: The Erotic as Power," in *Sister Outsider* (1984; New York: Penguin Books, 2020), 43.

18. We might examine these particular comments about men through Eve Kosofsky Sedgwick's theorization of "male homosocial desire." See Sedgwick, *Between Men: English Literature and Male Homosocial Desire* (New York: Columbia University Press, 1992).

19. Lorde, "Uses of the Erotic," 42–43.

20. Sedgwick underscores the intelligibility of such bonds between women, which Adrienne Rich conceptualizes as part of a "lesbian continuum." See Sedgwick, *Between Men*; Rich, "Compulsory Heterosexuality and Lesbian Experience," *Signs: Journal of Women in Culture and Society* 5, no. 4 (1980): 631–660.

21. Cisneros to Alarcón, May 18, 1982.

22. Norma Alarcón to Sandra Cisneros, April 15, 1982, box 7, folder 7, Norma Alarcón Papers.

23. Gloria Anzaldúa, *Borderlands/La Frontera: The New Mestiza* (San Francisco: Aunt Lute Books, 1987), 104.

24. Norma Alarcón, "Hay Que Inventarnos / We Must Invent Ourselves," *Third Woman* 1, no. 1 (1981): 4–6.

25. Sandra Cisneros, *A House of My Own: Stories from My Life* (New York: Alfred A. Knopf, 2015), 167.

26. "Sandra Cisneros Receives the Fuller Award for Lifetime Achievement," YouTube video, uploaded by American Writers Museum, March 14, 2021, 1:34:16.

27. Catherine S. Ramírez, "Alternative Cartographies: The Impact of Third Woman on Chicana Feminist Literature, 1981–1986," Third Woman Press (archived website), January 2001.

28. Book reviews, *Third Woman* 1, no. 1 (1981): 52.

29. Norma Alarcón, pers. comm., May 8, 2022.

30. Book reviews, *Third Woman* 2, no. 1 (1984): 118–119. The archives reveal that Badikian was a good friend of Alarcón and Cisneros and was part of the Third Woman Collective.

31. Sandra Cisneros to Norma Alarcón, October 23, 1983, box 7, folder 7, Norma Alarcón Papers. Cisneros's travels through Europe were the result of a grant from the National Endowment for the Humanities to write *The House on Mango Street*. Between the fall of 1982 and the fall of 1983, the writer lived in Greece, France, and Yugoslavia and traveled throughout Europe.

32. Cisneros/Kremidis explains in her review that Badikian's poetry offers "a

collective voice more akin to the poets of the Third World." Book reviews, *Third Woman* 2, no. 1 (1984): 118–119.

33. Between the 1960s and 1980s, women of color identified as US Third World feminists and practiced solidarity with anticolonial feminists in developing countries that were identified as the Third World. Third World feminism recognized the dismantling of colonialism and imperialism as integral to the fight against sexism, racism, and capitalism.

34. Alarcón, "Hay Que Inventarnos," 5.

35. "Sandra Cisneros Receives the Fuller Award for Lifetime Achievement," YouTube video.

36. Rosario Castellanos, "El Mar" (1975), quoted in Gloria Anzaldúa, "Haciendo Caras, Una Entrada: An Introduction," in *Making Face, Making Soul: Haciendo Caras*, ed. Gloria Anzaldúa (San Francisco: Aunt Lute Books, 1990), xvi.

37. Anzaldúa, "Haciendo Caras," xvi.

38. Norma Alarcón to Sandra Cisneros, January 13, 1983, box 98, folder 9, Sandra Cisneros Papers.

39. Cathy Cockrell, "A Labor of Love, a Publishing Marathon: Professor Norma Alarcón's Berkeley-Based Third Woman Press Turns 20," *Berkeleyan*, May 12, 1999.

40. *Third Woman*'s commitment to non-Latina Third World women is evident in each issue's promotional list of publications by Third World women. Once the press was established, its effort to promote non-Latina Third World women became more apparent through publications such as the second edition of Theresa Hak Kyung Cha's out-of-print *Dictée* (1982; 2nd ed., 1994), Elaine H. Kim and Alarcón's edited volume *Writing Self, Writing Nation: Essays on Theresa Hak Cha's "Dictée"* (1994), and the third edition of Cherríe Moraga and Gloria Anzaldúa's *This Bridge Called My Back: Writings by Radical Women of Color* (1981; 3rd ed., 2002).

41. Aída Hurtado writes about collaboration as a Chicana feminist method; see Hurtado, *Intersectional Chicana Feminisms: Sitios y Lenguas* (Tucson: University of Arizona Press, 2020).

42. These recommendations include an issue of the Mexican feminist journal *FEM* focused on "Las Chicanas" (1984); Alma Gomez, Cherríe Moraga, and Mariana Romo-Carmona's edited volume *Cuentos: Stories by Latinas* (1983); Evangelina Vigil's editorial work in *Revista Chicano-Riqueña* 2, no. 3–4 (1983); Claribel Alegría's *Flowers from the Volcano* (1982); Enedina Cásarez Vásquez's *Recuerdos de Una Niña* (1979); Jo Cochran, J. T. Stewart, and Mayumi Tsutakawa's edited volume *Gathering Ground: New Writing and Art by Northwest Women of Color* (1984); and *Bearing Witness/Sobreviviendo: An Anthology of Writing and Art by Native American/Latina Women* (1984).

43. See "Literature Program's Monthly Reading Series Underway" and "Writers-in-Residence to Teach Summer Writing Workshops," both in *Tonantzín* 1, no. 3 (1984): 12.

44. "Writers-in-Residence to Teach Summer Writing Workshops," *Tonantzín*.

45. Sandra Cisneros to Norma Alarcón, February 5, 1985, box 7, folder 7, Norma Alarcón Papers. The archives demonstrate Cisneros's great interest in photography. While in high school, she worked with photograph negatives at La Salle Photo Service in Chicago. Hiroko Warshauer, pers. comm., June 22, 2022. Her photography was also accepted into a 1985 photographic exhibition and competition titled *Enfoque Femenil: Visions of Chicana/Latina Women*, curated by visual artist Kathy Vargas in

San Antonio, Texas. Pedro A. Rodriguez to Sandra Cisneros, February 18, 1985, box 29, folder 10, Sandra Cisneros Papers.

46. These photographs did not appear in Third Woman publications, but they are housed in the Sandra Cisneros Papers.

47. Sandra Cisneros to Norma Alarcón, February 12, 1985, box 7, folder 7, Norma Alarcón Papers.

48. Sandra Cisneros to Norma Alarcón, February 5, 1985, box 7, folder 7, Norma Alarcón Papers.

49. Ellie D. Hernández, *Postnationalism in Chicana/o Literature and Culture* (Austin: University of Texas Press, 2009), 60.

50. Catherine S. Ramírez, "Alternative Cartographies: The Impact of *Third Woman* on Chicana Feminist Literature, 1981–1986," *Midwestern Miscellany* 30 (2002): 54.

51. Sandra Cisneros to Fania E. Davis, August 8, 2005, box 98, folder 9, Sandra Cisneros Papers.

52. See Combahee River Collective, "A Black Feminist Statement," in *This Bridge Called My Back: Writings by Radical Women of Color*, ed. Cherríe Moraga and Gloria Anzaldúa (Watertown, MA: Kitchen Table Press, 1983), 210–218; Kimberlé Crenshaw, "Demarginalizing the Intersection of Race and Sex: A Black Feminist Critique of Anti-Discrimination Doctrine, Feminist Theory, and Anti-Racist Politics," *University of Chicago Legal Forum* 1 (1989): 139–167.

53. See Norma Alarcón, "Chicana's Feminist Literature: A Re-Vision through Malintzin / or Malintzin: Putting Flesh Back on the Object," in Moraga and Anzaldúa, *This Bridge Called My Back* (1983), 182–189.

54. Norma Alarcón, "A Radical Woman of Letters," interview by Sandra Cisneros, 1984, box 41, folder 11, Sandra Cisneros Papers.

55. See Sandra Cisneros, *Woman Hollering Creek and Other Stories* (New York: Random House, 1991); Sandra Cisneros, "Guadalupe the Sex Goddess," in *Goddess of the Americas / La Diosa de las Américas: Writings on the Virgin of Guadalupe*, ed. Ana Castillo (New York: Riverhead Books, 1996), 46–51.

56. Sandra Cisneros to Fania E. Davis, August 8, 2005, box 98, folder 9, Sandra Cisneros Papers.

57. Norma Alarcón, "What Kind of Lover Have You Made Me, Mother? Towards a Theory of Chicanas' Feminism and Cultural Identity through Poetry," draft, box 90, folder 4, Sandra Cisneros Papers. This essay was published with the same title in Audrey T. McCluskey, ed., *Women of Color: Perspectives on Feminism and Identity* (Bloomington: Indiana University Press, 1985), 85–110.

58. Alarcón, "What Kind of Lover Have You Made Me, Mother?," draft, 20.

59. Norma Alarcón to Sandra Cisneros, unpublished and unarchived public letter, April 28, 2017, cited with permission.

60. Lorde, "Uses of the Erotic," 42.

61. Alarcón's invention of Marisa Cantú's biographical note emphasizes this point, as she illuminates a desire to have been mentored by Cisneros.

62. Lorde, "Uses of the Erotic," 47.

CHAPTER 11

FAXES, FRIENDSHIP, AND THE RISE OF CHICANA LITERATURE
Examining the Archive of Letters between Sandra Cisneros and Helena María Viramontes

Linda Margarita Greenberg

Over the course of the 1980s and early 1990s, Sandra Cisneros and Helena María Viramontes exchanged a long series of letters and faxes with each other and with other emerging Chicana writers. These letters reveal the interior struggles and empathetic crosscurrents within the Chicana feminist literary community through its journey from newly established ethnic and feminist presses and homegrown journals until its emergence as the Latin boom in publishing of the mid- to late 1990s. This essay examines how, before email or the internet was widely available, the fax machine, a newly popular technology, helped connect a tight-knit circle of women who would become the rising stars of Chicana feminist literature. The fax offered a quick means for sharing ideas, aesthetics, and emotional support across geographic distance. In particular, Viramontes and Cisneros used their faxes to nurture and validate each other and other Chicana authors, insisting on writerly self-care, exorcising inner doubts, and building Chicana literary networks.

In the 1970s and 1980s, many Chicana writers were creating new work, despite widespread messaging that writing about Chicanas and writing about Mexican American communities was not truly literary—messages received explicitly from faculty mentors in MFA programs (as in Viramontes's case) but also implicitly from a literary landscape in which mainstream publishers and reviewers ignored Chicana-authored work. Given the devaluation of Chicana voices and creative work, achieving success required creating a self-sustaining Chicana literary community. Being a writer couldn't simply be about aesthetics, art, and creativity; being a writer also meant being a literary activist. In the 1980s, literary activism and Chicana literary networks developed through the creation of writerly and creative associations, presses, and literary journals.

These were largely local activities that required intensive face-to-face coordination and development.

In the 1990s, as Cisneros, Viramontes, and other Chicana writers developed national audiences, began working with mainstream publishing houses, and coalesced into a recognizable canon of Chicana authors, these locally situated endeavors remained necessary but also became insufficient. During this period, the fax machine—with its ability to instantaneously transmit feedback, edits, contracts, and so forth—became an indispensable tool for sustaining Chicana literary networks across geographic locations. Moreover, as a technology that automatically duplicated each fax sent—returning the sender's original while producing a copy for the receiver—the fax machine resulted in an unusually thorough archive of communications during a critical transition period for Chicana writers, as they were entering the national (and international) stage.

This essay lightly touches on the letters Cisneros and Viramontes exchanged through the postal system, but primarily focuses on a series of faxes between the two women sent in the early to mid-1990s. The fax exchanges of this time—a period during which Viramontes was finishing her novel *Under the Feet of Jesus* and developing the novel that would become *Their Dogs Came with Them*, and Cisneros was working on her novel *Caramelo*—illuminate a pivotal moment in the rise of Chicana literature.

PUBLIC WORKS: WRITING INTO THE LATINO/A BOOM

As readers, we know Viramontes and Cisneros largely through their published works. The archives allow us windows into their private writings. Yet these two bodies of work, the public and private, are linked and layered together. Through their private writings, Viramontes and Cisneros encouraged each other in the revision and publication processes as they transitioned from small presses to major publishing houses. This transition and the emergence of US Latino/a writers onto the national stage would form a US Latino/a boom.[1]

The publishing industry in the United States is primarily white, both historically and continuing into the present day, from agents to publishing executives to authors to book reviewers to prizewinners.[2] While Latinx authors, and other US ethnic authors, are regularly published in mainstream presses today (even if still in disproportionately small numbers), in the 1980s, Sandra Cisneros and Helena María Viramontes were establishing themselves as Chicana authors in an industry that had no Chicana precedents in the major New York–based presses, the dominant forces in mainstream publishing.[3]

Instead, small Chicano/a and women of color presses founded in the mid-to late 1970s published narratives and voices otherwise marginalized by mainstream presses. California-based Mango Publications, founded in 1976 by the Chicana poet Lorna Dee Cervantes, published Cisneros's first poetry chapbook, *Bad Boys*, in 1980. Arte Público, founded in 1979 by Nicolás Kanellos in Houston, Texas, as a press for Hispanic literature, published Cisneros's *The House on Mango Street* in 1984 and Viramontes's *The Moths and Other Stories* in 1985. Arte Público published critical works in addition to literary works, fostering an academic legacy and legitimacy for Chicana/o writing as a field; these more academic contributions included Viramontes and María Herrera-Sobek's 1988 coedited anthology *Chicana Creativity and Criticism: Creative Frontiers in American Literature*. Third Woman Press, founded in 1981 by groundbreaking Chicana academic Norma Alarcón, published Cisneros's poetry collection *My Wicked Wicked Ways* in 1987.[4] Like Arte Público, Third Woman Press was dually invested in creative and critical cultures, and it published Viramontes and Herrera-Sobek's second coedited critical anthology in 1995, *Chicana (W)Rites: On Word and Film*.

The late 1980s marked a turning point for Cisneros as mainstream presses with larger marketing budgets picked up her work. In 1989, Vintage published the second edition of *The House on Mango Street*, and, in 1991, Random House published Cisneros's *Woman Hollering Creek and Other Stories*. Her subsequent major works, including her novel *Caramelo*, were published by the New York press Knopf. Mainstream presses also picked up Viramontes's works in the 1990s, with Dutton publishing *Under the Feet of Jesus* in 1995 and Atria Books publishing *Their Dogs Came with Them* in 2007.

These authors' published and private writings—including the personal letters they shared during this pivotal turn from small presses to national presses—are held in the Helena María Viramontes Papers at the California Ethnic and Multicultural Archives, University of California, Santa Barbara, and the Sandra Cisneros Papers, Wittliff Collections, Texas State University.

PRIVATE WRITINGS: INTIMACY IN THE ARCHIVE

One difficulty of conducting archival work on living writers, and especially on close correspondents like Viramontes and Cisneros, is that their letter exchanges are often intimate and personal. Letters are, after all, written and sent to a particular person in a particular moment. Expanding the audience beyond a sole intended recipient, and expanding the purpose beyond one-to-one connection with a confidant, changes readers' relationship to the letters in sometimes uncomfortable ways. As an archival researcher, I have been troubled as to my responsibility, not only to the authors who donated their materials to the archive, but also to those mentioned in personal letters who did not choose to have their lives or names publicly disclosed. To some degree, one can assume an awareness and willingness on the part of the author to disclose personal material via their act of archival donation. But even so, it is hard as a researcher to determine when to share material because it could be useful for understanding authorial work or because it is representative of archival materials, versus because it fulfills the too-human desire to peek into others' lives and see what lies hidden under the covers and in closet corners.

There are, for instance, moments in Viramontes's and Cisneros's archives that touch on professional jealousies and frustrations among a generally close-knit circle of Chicana writers. In highlighting those aspects of the archive, would I be needlessly bringing up old hurts or aggrandizing trivial and passing feelings that are titillating but not representative? In omitting that part of the archive, would I be glossing over breaks in the Chicana sisterhood that I am presenting, therefore fashioning a glossier and more perfect version of my argument than reality would allow? In the end, I chose to focus this essay on the archive's dominant narrative of solidarity and support rather than allow small disagreements to take a disproportionately larger place in the narrative.

Similarly, there are moments in the archive that make clear that what is being shared is personal, even private, and not meant for public or family consumption. Sometimes the archive explicitly names sexual encounters or desires, whether in Viramontes's love letters to her husband or in Cisneros's recounting of her romantic encounters. Here, again, I had to consider what should be shared for better understanding of Cisneros's and Viramontes's lives and work, and what could be omitted because it might titillate but not lend better understanding. Ultimately, I decided that erring in the direction of prudishness and omitting sexual content went against the very nature of Viramontes's and Cisneros's work—work that voices Chicana girls growing into their sexuality, and women whose sexual lives have worth well beyond the extent to which they appeal to men or enable children. Sex and desire matter in Cisneros's and Viramontes's work, and they matter in the archive as well. While I do not focus on or draw out sexual content in itself, it would be wrong to exclude this content from the archival material under discussion.

Finally, one aspect of the archive I most love is the texture of the language, the things written over, the typos, the missed words, the delicious unpolishedness of letters from one friend to another. When we read fiction, the works have been pored over, revised, edited, and re-edited to provide a seamless window into the story being told, uninterrupted by spelling errors or mixed-up words. While I could not reproduce the material intimacy of holding paper held by Cisneros and Viramontes, I did reproduce their sentences as written, and I find the intimacy of reading their language a treasure and a gift.

CISNEROS AND VIRAMONTES: LETTERS, FAXES, EMAILS, AND FRIENDSHIP

Sandra Cisneros and Helena María Viramontes met in 1984, after Cisneros read one of Viramontes's short stories and invited her to Texas to do a reading at the Guadalupe Cultural Arts Center in San Antonio.[5] This was a pivotal time in both their careers, being the year of Cisneros's publication of *The House on Mango Street* and a year before Viramontes's publication of *The Moths and Other Stories*, both of which would become foundational in Chicana literature.

Cisneros and Viramontes's growing friendship was sustained through a regular exchange of letters, faxes, and emails. In their exchanges, they shared drafts, poems of their own and by others, newspaper clippings, personal details of their intimate and daily lives, appreciation and hurts, professional advice, and, always, encouragement. The letters sent by post are personal and profound, but they were more sporadic than the faxes, with longer gaps between letter exchanges, given the time required to send letters through the postal system. In addition, it is harder to trace these letters in the archive, since dual copies were not saved (unlike with faxed exchanges). Faxed and emailed letters sped up conversations and textual relationships. They were sometimes simple and quick missives and at other times outpourings of emotion, with the urgency and immediacy that conversations with a close friend provide.

Viramontes and Cisneros began exchanging mailed letters in the mid-1980s, after Viramontes's visit to San Antonio; the letters were usually handwritten, but sometimes they were typed. These letters, sent through mail, create a gap in time from the moment written and the moment read, and reveal Viramontes and Cisneros as deepening confidants, supporting each other's personal and professional accomplishments and sharing in each other's pains.

In the early 1990s, Viramontes and Cisneros largely shifted to writing letters by fax instead of mailing letters through the post. Although the fax was not new technology—it was invented in the 1840s—fax technology only became cheap and standardized enough to gain widespread popularity in the 1980s. When the fax finally took off, it seemed incredible to the new users who jumped on board: according to technology historian Jonathan Coopersmith, "it is hard to appreciate . . . the excitement in the 1980s of watching an exact copy of a letter emerge line by line from a machine connected to the telephone network."[6] For Chicana writers entering what would become the 1990s Latin boom, the fax machine offered a way to consolidate their networks and speedily communicate with one another on a more regular basis.

The fax exchanges between Viramontes and Cisneros at this time enabled more consistent communication and allowed them to share the minutiae of their lives alongside larger concerns. Letters from Cisneros to Viramontes, for example, comment on late drafts of *Under the Feet of Jesus* alongside recountings of trying to order groceries by fax. Faxing made casual exchanges easier and simplified the process of sharing drafts or drawings, which no longer needed to be photocopied before being put in the mail. For instance, Viramontes sometimes sent pictures drawn by her children along with her letters, offering a personal connection to her family life; this easy sharing of personal asides built friendship that exceeded professional interest.

The fax cover sheets allowed for playful branding of their missives, such as with Viramontes's cover sheets titled "Fax or Fiction" and Cisneros's cover sheets titled "The House on Guenther Street / Fax from the Left Bank of the San Antonio River." While there were still plenty of longer letters, it became possible to have more rapid, short messages in response, with faxes going back and forth sometimes within a day rather than a couple weeks or longer.

Some messages between Cisneros and Viramontes were more businesslike, coordinating details of visits and events, but other messages were akin to everyday poetry, like the following fax from Viramontes to Cisneros:

1:30 a.m.
~~TUE~~ WEDNESDAY morning

Dearest Sandra,
The Santa Ana winds are rising in So. Calif. It was said that these warm winds against the coming of winter inspires the edge of madness among those on the verge.
    Saturday, Nov 6 sounds perfect for a meeting with one of my favorite writers. I look forward 2 beer, 2 food 2 friends, to you, just us 2.
Love always—
The Viramontes[7]

There is something so sweet and poignant about this small message for a friend remembered in the middle of the night. This is not a letter that would be mailed with well-fleshed-out thoughts and longer reminiscences; this is not a phone call during the day amid all the busy chores. This is a bit of midnight friendship, a small thread of connection woven into the windy night.

AN EPISTOLARY SISTERHOOD

For Viramontes and Cisneros, the bond with each other and with other Chicana writers filled a crucial gap. While Viramontes's family was large and she was one of eight children, she was often outside the gender expectations of her family, which held that the women would grow up to become housewives and mothers, cooking and cleaning while their husbands provided for the family. Viramontes was the first in her family to go to college—she was allowed to attend because her family thought she might find a husband with better prospects there—and it took some time for her family to see writing as a viable means of self-support. Cisneros, who was "the only daughter and *only* a daughter" alongside six brothers, followed a similar trajectory: like Viramontes, Cisneros went to college with her father's support under the assumption that going to college would help her find a husband, and her writing career was largely separate from her family life for many years.[8] In Cisneros's 2015 memoir *A House of My Own: Stories from My Life*, she recounts a time that she invited a relative to one of her public readings and her relative "looked at [her], exasperated, and said, 'Sandra, I'm your family, I'm not your fan.'"[9]

While not diminishing the importance of her family bonds, Cisneros emphasizes that as a writer, she has developed additional familial ties through words and narrative: "Instead, I look for my kin in my fellow writers. Those I know in person and those I know on the page. I feel fortunate at least to open books and be invited to step in. If that book shelters me and keeps me warm, I know I've come home."[10] With each other and with other Chicana writers, Cisneros and Viramontes created a Chicana literary network that was not just professional, but also personal and sisterly. These bonds nurtured them as writers and formed the connections through which they could nurture others.

Cisneros and Viramontes's faxed letter exchanges demonstrate this writerly fellowship, enabling a close epistolary sisterhood. Typically addressed "Dearest Amiga" or "Dearest Sandra," Viramontes's letters reflect her close connection to Cisneros, and these sisterly affections are returned by Cisneros, who refers to Viramontes as her "diaphragm-sister."[11] In a 1994 faxed letter from Cisneros to Viramontes, Cisneros writes: "I need to be fed. You need to be fed. Gustave had his Louise. Who do we have? Honey, we have each other." The letter ends with, "You're tired, Helena. Sleep. Your body and spirit are demanding you look after them, and I do so worry no one is taking care of you. Feed the spirit and it will feed you."[12] Through their letters—a significant part of their relationship, since Cisneros and Viramontes never lived in the same state—they nurtured each other's spirits, engaged in mutual self-care, and honed their artistic craft.

The following two-page typed and faxed letter to Viramontes is from the beginning of the nine-year period in which Cisneros was working on her novel *Caramelo*. It includes typical themes in their letter exchanges—some work, some mundanities, some writing talk, some thanks, and some planning for future collaboration:

1.16.94[13]

Querida Helena,
It's taken a long time to find anything these days—the holidays were a big interruption starting with my birthday December 20th right on until this weekend. I know an awful lot of Sagittarians and Capricorns. It seems as if too many people have been around me, and as fun as that was, it's also been upsetting to the work. I've become so delicate of late. Maybe I just need an excuse to blame my lack of focus. Been trying since last week to get back to novel, but all I've produced are letters, a piece of sculpture for a St. Valentine's Day auction, and some book blurbs (2 more to go this week). And, I'm trying to pay my bills, balance the checkbook, order groceries by fax no less!, and get back to you and Andrea Otañez.[14]

Seeing as how I frittered away today—which was supposed to go to the novel—thought I'd write and salvage something of the workday. And perhaps it's a way to explain to myself why I can't seem to get a grip of my novel. I am slightly baffled, depressed, frightened by it today. But that's today, and in my own research I'm discovering ancestors I didn't even know I had. Vicente Cisneros and Josefa Durán y Sotomayor, Tomás Guillén y Maria del Rosario Montero, my great-great-great-great grandparents from Seville. So how come I dance a sevillana like a horse? Anyway knowing their names gives me power. I say their names, invoke their memories, ask them to help me in this Herculean task of writing a novel. And who the hell said I was a novelist anyway!!!?

Oh, I'm terrified tonight, as you can see. I can't see the forest for the trees. But let's get off the subject of me and my typical neurosis of terror. You—congrats on your Newsweek photo—ay, que bonita! Terry Y. and I were so excited for you.[15] Who took that photo and where. Y mira que seria te pusiste, mujer. You mean business, I guess. Felicidades on becoming a legal alien.

Can you explain to me again what is this Sandra Cisneros Scholarship Fund over in Montebello and where is Montebello? Nobody's written me from there, but I believe I have you to thank regarding donations in my name for a scholarship for writers, is that right? Why name it after me? Aint dead yet!!! Ay, pero thank you—it gave me a Frida Kahlo up and down my spine.[16]

In answer to your question re: Bookfair—October 19th–22nd, 1995. I'll be in Boston at the end of this March, en route to NYC afterwards. Seems I'll be everywhere this spring. Santa Fe, L.A., Dallas, NY,

Boston, El Paso, Laredo, D.C. Corpus, NYC, San Francisco, Santa Cruz. And I'm not even on a book tour!!! Lots of commitments, and then the others just piggy-back, and before you know it, well, look.

The day you faxed and asked how I felt being forty I had the worst hangover. I mean the worst. Amnesia even. I haven't been that bad since grad school when I used to get drunk at the post reading parties and take someone home, anyone available and left over. What a mess I was. I realized I was terribly sad and tried to forget with drinking in sex, but at the time I couldn't see that's what I was doing.

New Year's resolution—no sex unless it's with someone who adores me. And preceding that—no sex unless I get to know a man first. That's a new one! I realize I've always used sex as a way to become automatically intimate. Except when I've slept with my friends. But when I sleep with my friends it never turns out being passionate and usually I wind up giving up the sex, purely intellectual attraction anyway, and just remain friends. Two papers faxed inquiring my resolutions, but one was the Chicago paper, and I couldn't print my resolutions there, what with my family and all. The other was a local paper, but fortunately they asked me after I'd left town and I didn't get the fax till after the fact.

Luis Rodriguez and I met over the holidays and he's kicking this idea about organizing an association of Latino writers and thinkers, something like P.E.N., but our purpose would be to have a national directory and instant communication to each other; intent—to respond publicly to issues like Prop. 187 and the Harold Bloom's of the world. We need to unite like the Jewish writers did in the 50's, says Luis, and have a united network, something that would umbrella us in all our diversities, something regardless of our diverse politics. I said I would pass the word around to others. I think it's a good idea, but let's see if we can't get together and form a directory, a E-mail, a fax line, something to communicate rapidly and organize in numbers. Luis's fax # is [redacted], phone is [redacted]. Tell him what you think and pass the word.

Bueno, that's all the chit chat I'm allowed. Supposed to be writing. I think of you often, and am thrilled for you regarding your recent success. Abrazos,

♡. xxx
Sandra[17]

Viramontes's wide-ranging reply likewise offers a window into the burgeoning production and canonization of Chicana literature. Following two days after Sandra's fax, Viramontes opens by commenting on a phone call with Sonia Saldívar-Hull, a close mutual friend and a foundational figure in Chicana feminist thought and literary criticism, on the new genres emerging from Cisneros's work.[18] This faxed letter also responds to Cisneros's mentions of Viramontes's photo shoot for a *Newsweek* feature and her anticipated community work with Luis J. Rodríguez, author of the acclaimed 1993 autobiography *Always Running: La Vida Loca, Gang Days in L.A.* and founder of Tia Chucha Press.[19] All these events and conversations form part of the growing cultural understanding and critical framing of Chicana literature in the 1990s.

Dearest Sandra,

Whew! It was good to hear from you. I had just gotten a call from Sonia on Sunday. She's been in hiding in L.A. trying to prepare for her classes, etc. and asked about you. Let me give you her new fax/phone number: [redacted]. We talked about how your novel is developing into a sorta distinct genre in and of itself. It is a new type of narration that begins almost as a parable but leaves room for folly, breathe, unforgettable imagery that spirals onto itself. The reason I'm going on this way, is because, that's why the writing of the novel is such a challenge: you are not only creating a story, a history but a new way of telling this story and history. See what I mean? Of course its terrifying—because your writing is unlike anything else. Here, you have to design the tools before you begin building the house. It's just you against the challenge on those nights in absolute solitude. On those nights, I know its hard to remember those who love and respect you, those who have faith in you. But remember us. You are not alone.

To de-stress myself, after a particularly bad day of nothing, I had a mantra and it went like this "If not today, tomorrow. If not tomorrow, tomorrow." This reminded me that stamina and patience are essential. Sooner or later, something would break. Sooner or later, the novel would get done.

Traveling can be distracting. I only hope I don't impose on your time when we bring you to Ithaca in October. Thanks for the dates. With this, we can have a better idea on dates to reserve rooms etc. It's beautiful then. The leaves become a brilliant red or gold and flutter down like rain. Hopefully, you can sleep late. And we'll have time to do some shopping.

The photograph in Newsweek was a comedy of errors. The more I put them off, the more they came after me. Since I was in L.A., I was staying in different places, visiting here, babysitting there. They couldn't track me down. When they wanted a photograph of me (just in case, they said, but no promises), I couldn't find the time because of a commitment to my brother [redacted]. I agreed to meet with them at my parent's house at the end of the week. A few days after, they tracked me down for an interview (just in case, they said, but no promises). I was babysitting and the phone ring woke my nephew who began a piercing wail. They had to call back.

The cross I'm on in the photo was built by my father. It sits in front of our house (see attached). The story goes on the day that I was born, my father finished the cross. However, my mother said he was "detained" (re: in jail. He was trying to get a cousin across the border and got caught), on the day of my birth, and she doesn't know why he comes up with these stories. The photo's okay, my father's cross beautiful, but I look as if I'm frowning. (Maria says I look sorta fat) Of course, this is the one they picked. But then again, I do have a perchance for looking dramatically serious.

Mayra Fernandez is the founder of Wings/Allas. A writer of children's books, a parent and foster parent of 15 children, a Phd. in Education, and a lesbian, shes always wanted to organize a writer's retreat strictly for Latinas. She's an amazing, gifted woman who I love dearly. In any event, I participated in the first retreat. You can imagine how wonderful it was for these mujeres! I donated my honorarium to establish a Sandra Cisneros Scholarship to be given to a Chicana writer of promise. I couldn't think of a better way to thank you, from all of us Chicanas. Montebello is a suburb right outside of E.L.A. In fact, it was where I lived when I was first married to Richard another life ago.

We definitely need to network. I'll keep in touch with Luis. Maybe we can donate some monies to pay his Tia Chucha Press to print the directory.

I've started to re-train the old body for early morning wake up again. Since I finished the novel, back in November, I've been a glutton for sleep, sometimes getting up at 11 am on weekends. Today I got up right before the alarm went off. Eloy had just come in from the lab. He's noisy and wants attention when he gets into bed. Since I had gotten such a good deep sleep, I wasn't resentful. Honestly, I sometimes feel my sleep is more important than sex. Francisco came to our bed awhile after because of a nightmare. By this time, I just decided to get up. I put a pot of beans on (I literally have to soak the beans that they sell here for a good 24 hours before cooking), and tend to this letter.

School is starting next week. I'm definitely nervous and really, very frightened. Remember this is a mostly an all white school. I spent last week working on our house files and doing the 1993 taxes AND preparing the 1994 taxes. Its been crazy, but I'm finally getting all the files (including my own) in order. I still have to set up my school office, buy my computer, prepare a syllabus etc etc etc.

Anyway, wish me luck. I really hope you enjoy "Under The Feet Of Jesus." Its a good story. I miss you very much, but "If not today, tomorrow . . ." Give my love to Terry Y.

[handwritten] Helena[20]

In Cisneros's reply, she reminds Viramontes to reserve her time and find others for tasks like taxes—and even to just respond with a one-paragraph letter instead of pages. She also offers advice on reframing the classroom as a Chicana writer space rather than a conventionally academic one:

Re: teaching your class. Don't panic. I remember the deep depression that my first semester teaching drove me to, a near death in Chico if you recall. Remember what the writing has taught you. Teach from that place that makes you different from any one else in that school. What can you bring to the classroom as a writer, as a writer of color, as a writer from East L.A., as a woman of Mexican descent, as a working class person, that no one else in the history of the department can bring? This point of departure is your gift to your students. Remember this! Remember this. That means your syllabus will not look like Sonia's. That means the way you teach will not be like your colleagues. That means the way you design the course will not be like me. But use your intuition and your unique points of difference and you will be powerful and make a difference. If you are afraid of being yourself, and imitate your colleagues, you will fail. But if you teach from a place no one else can imitate, then your teaching will come from your center of power. This I learned while almost killing myself. The same lesson as the writing that I had learned in Iowa.[21]

These letters combine the familial and the literary, the personal and the professional, weaving them together during a period of time that sees Cisneros and Viramontes emerge as national literary figures.

CHICANA SOLIDARITY AND THE RISE OF CHICANA LITERATURE

Cisneros and Viramontes shared feedback on each other's drafts, sometimes general comments on parts they found great or jarring, and sometimes specific edits on word choice, word order, and so forth on many pages of manuscript (such as Cisneros's comments on late drafts of Viramontes's *Under the Feet of Jesus*).[22] These messages foster a tight-knit and mutually supportive relationship, laying the groundwork for their mutual success.

Interspersed with recountings of everyday life and life-affirming advice are statements of support of each other's work as well as of a larger circle of Chicana writers. In one fax, Viramontes reflects on a character's motivation in Cisneros's chapter draft, offers praise of Cisneros's "utterly masterful" hallucinatory tone, shares excitement about getting a copy of *Hairs/Pelitos* by Cisneros and their mutual friend Terry Ybáñez, and voices anger over a negative book review of *Face of an Angel* by Denise Chávez, another friend of theirs. In her critique of the negative book review, Viramontes writes: "I took particular offense to his statement—'Ms. Chavez hasn't established enough distance between herself and Soveida for the reader to trust her authorial objectivity fully,' WHAT??? I ask you, does he KNOW Denise that well, that he can't differentiate between the character and the author? That's an awful bold assumption."[23] Here Viramontes speaks to the bind of authenticity that plagues Chicana fiction and US ethnic literature more generally: the assumption that works are sociological in nature rather than literary, that the author is being not imaginative but merely descriptive or biographical.[24] As Viramontes's letter indicates, the assumption that authors' and characters' lives replicate each other operates in a limited cultural economy where Chicana lives follow singular narratives (the one told in the story); reviews built on this assumption compound the problem by mislocating the lack of imagination (or "authorial objectivity") in the Chicana author rather than in the reviewer (the one who cannot imagine an authorial life beyond the written narrative). In their letters to each other, and through supportive connections with other Chicana writers, Viramontes and Cisneros negotiated and resisted assumptions of biographical authenticity by reframing criticism of published Chicana writing as embedded in structures of sociologically driven reading practices of ethnic works.

Cisneros's letters, too, speak to meetings with other writers, though she sometimes feels torn between her desire to be with others and her fear of being drawn away from her own writing. As with Viramontes's letters, Cisneros's letters offer praise as well as editorial feedback. Their exchanges form a circle of necessary care, and Cisneros writes in one faxed letter: "Thank you for sending me pieces of your novel and for communicating with me. Notes in a bottle from one woman on a raft to another, no?" She closes her letter with a mantra for peace, saying, "I appreciate your being there for me, Helena. Write again or fax me when you can, and remember, take a deep breath—I am a mountain—exhale. Inhale—I am as still as a pond of clear water—exhale. Pay attention to your breathing and be careful what you say. Words are not to be wasted."[25] Life affirmations such as these, amid the sometimes-chaotic schedules of book readings, talks, publishing, and personal troubles, are as much a personal balm to Cisneros (torn between needing to publicize work already written and needing to write new work), as they are to Viramontes (negotiating writing, the publication process, academic work, and a family life with young children).

BEING CHICANA, BEING HUMAN

For Cisneros and Viramontes, the circle of Chicana writers that they belonged to and whose writing and careers they upheld was a key part of their work as writers, in their literary development, and in their lives. To be Chicana was also to be invested in the lives of humans facing oppression, poverty, and violence in the United States and internationally. From Viramontes's keen concerns about undocumented Mexicans and Central Americans in California to Cisneros's appeals to help those starving, hurt, and under threat of genocide in Sarajevo, their letters and published works reveal interrelated concerns about what it is to be Chicana and to be human in structural conditions of racism and violence.

In a long-ranging, typed fax discussing publishing offers and Viramontes's campus visit to Cornell University (where they were both being recruited for academic positions), Viramontes ends with her and her husband's ongoing frustration at issues like California Proposition 187:

> Eloy and I are angry at the powerlessness of our people. We are moving into the twenty first century, and we are still fighting against the abstractions as those who dim the light of literacy. Fighting against basic malnutrition. Fighting against propositions like the kind proposed here— Don't let the children of undocumented workers go to school. Remember Lorna's poem with the line "They are aiming at my children." How dare they think they can even say that!!!! Fighting and fighting and fighting. I have decided to direct my energies to my writing because the grass roots efforts don't seem to make a dent in the problems. The enemy doesn't have a clue at our reservoir of strength. They haven't a clue has to how deep and limitless it is. We may die, but we'll die fighting those immoral and stupid fools who are aiming at our children.[26]

Proposition 187, in 1994, aimed to deny access to medical care, social services, and education for undocumented people in California. For Viramontes, this issue was personal: while her mother's family had been in Los Angeles for four generations before she was born, Viramontes grew up in a household and community where stories of family and friends crossing the US-Mexico border, without documents, were a part of life—and her family lore recounts her father missing her birth because he had been jailed after being caught helping a friend in a crossing.[27] Viramontes's deep empathy for those fleeing US-supported civil wars in Central America is visible in the articles about undocumented immigration that she cut from newspapers. It is also the central issue of "The Cariboo Cafe," one of her most celebrated and anthologized short stories, which tells the interwoven narratives of undocumented Mexican children, a Salvadoran woman traumatized by death squads and disappearances in El Salvador, and the devastating losses wrought by the Vietnam War and by US police brutality, showing the interconnected pain of US racial structures and imperial violence. Viramontes's anger at the "powerlessness of our people" combines with an assertion of their "deep and limitless" "reservoir of strength," marking out the structural conditions of power and oppression that cause harm, even as she insists on the strength and assets that enable survival and success. This perspective and anger emerge from her Chicana experience as Viramontes invokes Chicana feminist poet Lorna Dee Cervantes's "Poem for the Young White Man Who Asked Me How I, an Intelligent, Well-Read Person, Could Believe in a War between Races."[28] But Viramontes's indignation is as much about Chicanas as it is about the plight of humans under conditions of poverty and violence, whether these humans are Chicana or Salvadoran or, as in "The Cariboo Cafe," impoverished white people who have clung to racist narratives of power even as those structures enable their own loss and devastation.

A month later, Cisneros replies with a letter that reinforces the shared pain of humanity under international conditions of violence and oppression and that continues their ongoing conversation about writing and the human. A portion of the letter focuses on Bosnia:

> Got your last two faxes. Sorry I haven't replied. I am besieged. I send you a copy of my poem that gives you an idea of my inner weather. I am also besieged by what is happening in Sarajevo and how others misunderstand my involvement in an issue they neither understand nor recognize. It is for me an issue where I recognize myself, because if we aren't victims of ethnic extermination as Chicanos, as mexicanos, well, then what are we? So I don't feel well today. Roiled and rolling. Hurt, saddened, overwhelmed by the lack of humanity of humanity. I don't want to be ashamed to call myself a human being.[29]

The war and siege in Sarajevo during the Bosnian War manifest in Cisneros's own besieged body and mind. Her human body hurts with the knowledge of the pain humans inflict on each other.

Viramontes picks up this thread in a two-page typed letter, excerpted here:

When I wrote The Cariboo Cafe, I felt, (and often feel), indignant and ashamed to be called a human being. In vulnerable periods of my life the violence of the world is too, too much and I walk from one to room trying to suppress my panic. I become so afraid for my children. I see Francisco run up the hill with his back pack on. He turns to me near the tetterball, and waves good bye before the morning school bell rings. Nothing seems safe now. The school yards, places of worship, homes. (A 18 year old pregnant Palestinian woman was cleaning a rug in her house when a Jewish settler truck driver was being pelleted with stones as he drove through the village. To scare the attackers off, he randomly opened fire and one of the bullets killed her. In Chicago, parents are keeping children home because the walk to school is just too dangerous.) Who is at fault? Who do we mourn for? How can fate be so damned mean?

To keep this panic repressed would kill me. To deal with it is another matter. [redacted]

One thing that I have never lost faith in is the power of the written word. It has transformed me, and I see it transforming others. It can bridge cultures, connect all people to the human condition, enlighten, repel, anger. Stories will never leave you the same. I try changing strategies. No longer talking to students (as much), but to whole groups of teachers about the power to transform lives with the written word. No longer playing the role model bit, but trying to be a "great" writer (by this I mean truly satisfied by my own work. Remember, as Chicanas, we are not allowed to be just good.). And when Francisco runs down that hill at the end of the day, I become so grateful that there are no bullets to dodge, no crazies to come into the playground and spray gunfire as the balls roll quietly across the school yard. I remember to thank all the great spirits that he will be safely in my arms in a matter of moments and he will fill me with his day's concern and somehow the day will take on a different form and I am not so frightened by it after all. I will be filled with such love, that to even compare this abundance to the skies would be useless.[30]

To be human is to carry the weight, blame, and shame of all the injustices, but it is also to suffer those injustices shared by other humans. It is to recognize, in the moment of safety when your child runs down the play yard, the many moments of precarity implied in each such moment of return of child to parent in war-torn places: Palestine, Sarajevo, El Salvador, and, even if it is war by other names, the United States. This is a devastation that overwhelms and that could stifle or freeze—it is a panic that could kill—but Viramontes draws power and transformative potential through writing. Writing releases dangerous repression for Viramontes, enabling her own continuation, but it is also transformative and unifying, reminding others in violent, isolated conditions of an underlying bridge that can "connect all people to the human condition." This is not a humanity that erases difference, but a humanity that insists on connection both despite and through difference. Viramontes relates to Palestinians *as a Chicana*, connecting to humans not in ethnic neutrality, but through related experiences of ethnic difference.

AN INVITATION

The greatest difficulty in writing this chapter was the attempt to condense and capture snapshots of the wealth of conversation between Cisneros and Viramontes in their archival holdings. As much as possible, I have tried to let the authors' letters speak for themselves, with only contextual glosses to frame their words. Until the fuller project of a collected edition of their letters can be developed, I hope this serves as a window into their writings and an invitation to pursue further research in the archives themselves.

NOTES

Thanks to Geneva M. Gano and Sara Ramírez for their careful and insightful reading and to all the contributors as a collective whose sharing of resources, experiences, and ideas was inspirational and healing; particular thanks to Geneva for being a sister of mind and spirit when I most needed the lift. Finally, my thanks to California State University, Los Angeles, for providing critical support that allowed me to accomplish the necessary archival research.

1. This US Latina/o boom is distinct from the Latin American boom of the 1960s and 1970s, which brought figures like Gabriel García Márquez, with whom Viramontes would later work, to international acclaim. While these are different moments in literary history, they are connected not only through the mentorship and relationships between the authors involved, but also through the way that the prestige and marketability of the Latin American boom helped open doors for US Latina/o writers. While the Latina/o boom is variously defined, it is referenced both in individual critical essays and in literary anthologies such as John S. Christie and José B. Gonzalez, eds., *Latino Boom: An Anthology of U.S. Latino Literature* (New York: Pearson, 2006).

2. Richard Jean So persuasively demonstrates the persistent whiteness of the publishing industry, despite the rise of multicultural narratives of literary history; see So, *Redlining Culture: A Data History of Racial Inequality and Postwar Fiction* (New York: Columbia University Press, 2021).

3. While Chicana authors were not being published by these major presses, there were Black women writers, including Alice Walker and Toni Morrison, whose works had recently come out through major presses and who thus established an opening, market, and audience for ethnic women's literature.

4. While 1979 is usually the founding year given for Third Woman Press, Sara A. Ramírez's chapter in this collection provides context on the actual founding year of 1981.

5. Sandra Cisneros to Jonathan Culler, September 29, 1998, box 143, folder 4, Sandra Cisneros Papers, Wittliff Collections, Texas State University. The reading at the Guadalupe Cultural Arts Center took place on August 7, 1984, and Viramontes read alongside John Phillip Santos; the event description indicates that Viramontes's *The Moths and Other Stories* would be published the following spring. *Tonantzín*, June/July 1984, 11.

6. Jonathan Coopersmith, *Faxed: The Rise and Fall of the Fax Machine* (Baltimore: Johns Hopkins University Press, 2015), 1.

7. Helena María Viramontes to Sandra Cisneros, fax, October 27, 1993, box 143, folder 3, Sandra Cisneros Papers.

8. Sandra Cisneros, "Only Daughter," in *Latina: Women's Voices from the Borderlands*, ed. Lillian Castillo-Speed (New York: Touchstone, 1995), 157–160.

9. Sandra Cisneros, *A House of My Own: Stories from My Life* (New York: Afred A. Knopf, 2015), 40.

10. Cisneros, *A House of My Own*, 40.

11. In response to Viramontes's news that she received the NEA award, Cisneros wrote back, saying: "Querida Helena, / Felicidades! I just wanted to tell you again how happy your good news makes me, makes us all! / When one of us does a good job, she does it for us all. Thank you for making all of us look good. / Te abrazo, / diaphragm-sister, / Sandra." The diaphragm—a major respiratory muscle supporting breath and voice as well as a method of contraception enabling female bodily autonomy—is a particularly apt metaphor for embodied sisterhood. Sandra Cisneros to Helena María Viramontes, January 22, 1989, box 8, folder 18, Helena María Viramontes Papers, California Ethnic and Multicultural Archives, University of California, Santa Barbara, Library.

12. Sandra Cisneros to Helena María Viramontes, fax, July 14, 1994, box 3, folder 10, Helena María Viramontes Papers.

13. This letter is dated 1994 by Cisneros, but it was followed by a fax on January 18 from Viramontes that is time-stamped 1995 by the fax machine, suggesting that Cisneros mistyped the year, as is common at the beginning of a new year.

14. Andrea Otáñez was then an editor at large at the University of New Mexico Press, working on Chicana/o literary acquisitions and editing.

15. San Antonio artist and educator Terry Ybañez was a friend and collaborator of Sandra Cisneros; a few years after this letter, they would publish their collaborative children's book *Hairs/Pelitos* (New York: Dragonfly Books, 1997), with Ybañez illustrating Cisneros's vignette from *The House on Mango Street*.

16. Cisneros's play on words—Frida Kahlo for *escalofrío* (a chill or goosebumps)—slips together the female artistic heritage and bodily response in a way both humorous and in keeping with a perspective through which Mexican and Chicana art resides in physical embodied connection, durable apart from time and space.

17. Sandra Cisneros to Helena María Viramontes, fax, January 16, 1995, box 143, folder 3, Sandra Cisneros Papers.

18. Then a professor of English at the University of California, Los Angeles, Sonia Saldívar-Hull published *Feminism on the Border: Chicana Politics and Literature* (Berkeley: University of California Press, 2000), a major force shaping literary criticism on Viramontes's and Cisneros's works.

19. Luis J. Rodríguez founded Tia Chucha Press in 1989 as one of the small independent presses publishing Chicana literature before it found a national audience. His work with Tia Chucha Press would grow into Tia Chucha's Centro Cultural, a bookstore and community center that opened its doors in 2001 and continues to play a vital cultural role in the Los Angeles region.

20. Helena María Viramontes to Sandra Cisneros, fax, January 18, 1995, box 143, folder 4, Sandra Cisneros Papers. Then living in Ithaca, New York, Viramontes was about to begin her first semester teaching at Cornell University as an assistant professor in the English department's Creative Writing Program.

21. Sandra Cisneros to Helena María Viramontes, fax, January 18, 1995, box 143, folder 4, Sandra Cisneros Papers.

22. This draft can be found in box 143, folder 3, Sandra Cisneros Papers. I found more evidence in the archives of feedback from Cisneros to Viramontes than the other way around (though feedback was bidirectional), but it is difficult to say whether this was due to the sorts of archival materials that were saved or to general feedback practices.

23. Helena María Viramontes to Sandra Cisneros, fax, September 26, 1994, box 143, folder 3, Sandra Cisneros Papers.

24. Equally destructive, though this is not the issue at play in this particular critique, is the assumption that Chicana literature is only good to the extent that it speaks to preconceived notions of authenticity. For more discussion on the problems of authenticity and sociological readings of literary texts, see Maxine Hong Kingston, "Cultural Mis-Readings by American Reviewers," in *Asian and Western Writers in Dialogue: New Cultural Identities*, ed. Guy Amirthanayagam (London: Macmillan, 1982), 55–65; Viet Thanh Nguyen, *Race and Resistance: Literature and Politics in Asian America* (Oxford: Oxford University Press, 2002); Marissa López, "Chicana/o Literature: Theoretically Speaking, Formally Reading Ana Castillo's *Sapogonia*," *Aztlán: Journal of Chicano Studies* 32, no. 2 (2007): 139–156; Stephen Hong Sohn, *Racial Asymmetries: Asian American Fictional Worlds* (New York: New York University Press, 2014); Linda Margarita Greenberg, "Epistolary Women: Navigating Ethnicity and Authenticity in Ana Castillo's *Mixquiahuala Letters* and Hualing Nieh's *Mulberry and Peach*," *Genre: Forms of Discourse and Culture* 49, no. 3 (2016): 273–302.

25. Sandra Cisneros to Helena María Viramontes, fax, October 6, 1994, box 143, folder 3, Sandra Cisneros Papers.

26. Helena María Viramontes to Sandra Cisneros, fax, March 14, 1994, box 143, folder 3, Sandra Cisneros Papers.

27. Helena María Viramontes to Sandra Cisneros, fax, January 18, 1995, box 143, folder 4, Sandra Cisneros Papers.

28. Helena María Viramontes to Sandra Cisneros, fax, March 14, 1994, box 143, folder 3, Sandra Cisneros Papers.

29. Sandra Cisneros to Helena María Viramontes, fax, April 13, 1994, box 143, folder 3, Sandra Cisneros Papers.

30. Helena María Viramontes to Sandra Cisneros, fax, April 14, 1994, box 143, folder 3, Sandra Cisneros Papers.

PART III

¡Adelante! Seeing and Listening with Cisneros

CHAPTER 12

LA SANDRA COMO ARTISTA
The Visual Cisneros
Tey Marianna Nunn

I knew as I wrote this story that it was helping to bring me back to myself. It's essential to create when the spirit is dying. It doesn't matter what. Sometimes it helps to draw. Sometimes to plant a garden. Sometimes to make a Valentine's Day card. Or to sing, or create an altar. Creating nourishes the spirit.
SANDRA CISNEROS, AFTERWORD, *HAVE YOU SEEN MARIE?*

Color is a Story.
SANDRA CISNEROS, "¡QUE VIVAN LOS COLORES!"

What in the world am I doing writing about famed Chicana author Sandra Cisneros? After all, I am a museum director and curator, not a literary critic.[1] I research visual artists, not literary masters. I organize art exhibitions in museum galleries that highlight the creations and lives of Latina and Latino artists. I have been doing it for years, and in doing so, I hear and read a lot of stories. I am a visual learner, and I visualize those stories. Could that be why I am writing this essay? Do Ms. Cisneros and I have that in common? Stories? Collecting stories? Perhaps this is the reason why I wanted to delve into the visual Cisneros, since I know it can't be my prose. Or is it something more—a different connection? Could it be the influence of museums? The significance of art? The impact of color and the Chicano and Latino visual vocabulary? Could it be the love of stuff and the thrill of collecting? Could it be a shared passion for *rasquache*, the beauty in the everyday, the joy in vernacular details? Or could it be that as a curator, I recognize the innate quality of visual art in the work of Sandra Cisneros? Perhaps all of the above? As I always say, art comes alive for me when I know the artist and their story.

When articles and interviews about Cisneros appear, the words used to describe her include *writer, novelist, poet,* and *storyteller*. I do not disagree that Cisneros is a master literary artist, but few realize she is a visual artist as well. Let me expound: I don't mean a visual literary artist, I mean a talented visual artist who not only creates worlds with words, but also draws, paints, and designs and creates assemblages and *ofrendas*. Why this aesthetic superpower of hers isn't more widely known is intriguing to me because there are significant clues throughout her written works. More than any other writer I delight in reading, Cisneros paints with words as a visual artist would use brushstrokes. I have always been transfixed by her prose and its relation to visual imagery. Whenever I read her poems and stories my visual brain reacts with elaborate and complex visions. Her narrative scenes engulf me and come alive in my imagination. They are magical and visually tangible, illustrative—sprinkled throughout her many publications like the beautiful hues of Mexican confetti you can purchase at real piñata shops. She is drawn to color (remember her famous purple house?) and imbues color in her descriptions of Mexico and Mexico America. Only a visual artist, someone who has a practiced eye for the colors, details, textures, and composition of elements of visual culture, can translate these details verbally for the reader to experience. Cisneros recently confirmed this observation, admitting, "I think before I knew how to hold a pencil, I was an artist."[2] This essay, the first to place Cisneros's visual production in an art historical context, explores the written clues Cisneros has left us as to her talents as a visual artist. It addresses the significance of color and artistic components throughout her many publications, and it details her collegial affinity for and support of other visual artists, as well as her belief in the importance of collecting their work. It highlights the impact of museums and finally examines her body of production as a visual artist by sharing images of and describing her portraits, drawings, and installations.

It is no coincidence that Cisneros utilizes the power of color. Her intentionality is a device to conjure up a sense of a lively world and revelry in place. She writes: "It's like a top, like all the colors in the world are spinning so fast they're not colors anymore and all that's left is a white hum."[3] The permeation of color seeps into all the master's prose. Cisneros shares: "Sometimes the sky is so big and I feel so little at night. That's the problem with being cloud. The sky is terribly big. Why is it worse at night, when I have such an urge to communicate and no language with which to form the words? Only colors. Pictures. And you know what I have to say isn't always pleasant."[4]

Even the titles of Cisneros's books convey the significance of color, most notably *The House on Mango Street*. Doesn't the word *mango* instill a luscious, juicy, beautiful, orange-colored vision in your imagination? It always has in mine. Some of the first clues we have of Cisneros's utilization of color and aesthetics are in *The House on Mango Street*, when a neighbor gives Esperanza and her friends a bag of shoes. Here, Cisneros uses color to convey the thrill of fancy shoes and the aspirations that come with them. "Everyone wants to trade. The lemon shoes for the red shoes, the red pair for the pair that were once white but are now pale blue, the pale blue for the lemon."[5] Elsewhere in the novel, in the chapter titled "No Speak English," another neighbor, who lives across the street, has saved money to bring his wife (Mamacita) and his infant son to the United States and is finally able to send for them. Cisneros describes their arrival:

> Then one day Mamacita and the baby boy arrived in a yellow taxi. The taxi door opened like a waiter's arm. Out stepped a tiny pink shoe, a foot soft as a rabbit's ear, then a thick ankle, a flutter of hips, fuschia roses and green perfume....
>
> All at once she bloomed. Huge, enormous to look at, from the salmon-pink feather on the tip of her hat down to the little rosebuds of her toes. I couldn't take my eyes off her tiny shoes. Up up the stairs she went with her baby boy in a blue blanket, the man carrying her suitcase, her lavender hat boxes, a dozen boxes of satin high heels.[6]

Although the character of Mamacita is rarely seen again in the story, the author's use of seven colors across these two short paragraphs emphasizes the character of Mamacita and also the significance of color in Mexico and the cultural difference to the United States, as her arrival is announced through the outward expression of numerous bright hues.

In her poem "Curtains," in *My Wicked Wicked Ways*, Cisneros writes about how curtains "hide bright walls. Turquoise, or lipstick pink. Good colors in another country. Here they can't make you forget."[7] In "Amé, Amo, Amaré," another poem in the same collection, Cisneros highlights a "green green dress" and even notes, "Funny I remember that detail, the green green dress."[8]

The poem "The Blue Dress," in the same collection, includes the passage:

> Blue as a pearl
> The blue dress approaches late
> You wait along the whale display
> A slower gait a thinner smile
> Swell of the belly
> Ridiculously blue
> The blue dress embraces you[9]

Throughout her collection *Loose Woman*, the author describes more colors, often tying them in with artists' names. In "You Bring Out the Mexican in Me," she mentions red ocher, yellow ocher, indigo, and cochineal.[10] In "A Little Grief like Gouache," she includes the mention of a "Van Gogh ocher." Her utilization of blue for water and white for purity is peppered throughout all her literary works—as are mangos. When describing ephemeral *papel picado* and delicate handheld Mexican tissue paper flags in "My Nemesis Arrives after a Long Hiatus," she chooses rose, tangerine, turquoise, jade, and "Ave Maria blue."

Cisneros turns to color at different times in her life. When her father was near the end of his life, she came home to her house in San Antonio, Texas, and "stared at the walls. The mango against the pink, the green against the yellow, a vase of magenta carnations besides an ocher painting, a wood sculpture against an Ave Maria Blue. The art soothed and comforted me."[11]

In "Salvador Late or Early" from *Woman Hollering Creek and Other Stories*, Cisneros describes Arturito, the younger brother of the main character, Salvador, as he drops his crayons, a "cigar box of crayons . . . the hundred little fingers of red, green, yellow, blue and nub of black sticks." The preciousness of a cigar box of crayons conjures up the beloved pastime of coloring as a child. Even though Arturito apparently only has a few basic colors, they are valued as they are kept in the cigar box.[12]

Cisneros's considerable attention to detail is not just conveyed through solitary colors, it is communicated in patterns as well. The author's eye for the color combinations in fabrics and textiles is another constant presence in her writing. Parasols and umbrellas unfolding throughout her books help illustrate this phenomenon:

They gather like dusty birds
beneath their paisley
and polk-a-dot
and plaid and blue-checked
and yellow and plum-colored
parasols[13]

And Cisneros writes: "These days we run from the sun. Cross the street quick, get under an awning. Carry an umbrella like tightrope walkers. Red-white-and-blue flowered nylon. Beige with green and red stripes. Faded maroon with an amber handle."[14]

Of course, I could go on and on. With these descriptions, one could argue that Cisneros is doing her job, a literary genius writing legendary prose. After all, she was awarded the National Medal of Arts by President Barack Obama in 2015. But as someone who works with visual artists every day, I have to say that

LA SANDRA COMO ARTISTA

Sandra Cisneros is more visual than most writers. Believe me, I have gone shopping and thrift-storing with her, and her aesthetic prowess—her ability to home in on visual beauty and detail—is off the charts. Creativity inspires creativity, and Cisneros is naturally and intuitively a visual artist.

Throughout Cisneros's writing and her life, houses are almost always painted a color. They can be red or pink and even situated on Mango Street. Cisneros writes: "Home. Home. Home. Home is a house in a photograph, a pink house, pink as hollyhocks with lots of startled life. The man paints the walls of the apartment pink, but it's not the same as you know. She still sighs for her pink house, and then I think she cries. I would."[15] In her 2002 novel *Caramelo*, when the family arrives in Mexico City from Chicago, Cisneros describes the transition to a place with "exquisite houses painted purple, electric blue, tiger orange, aquamarine, a yellow like a taxi cab, hibiscus red with a yellow and green fence, pink plastic brooms and bright green buckets—not to mention the churches the color of flan."[16] In her story "*Bien* Pretty," in *Woman Hollering Creek*, the protagonist sits in a turquoise-colored home while her friends are away on a Fulbright grant. That turquoise house is filled with classic forms of Mexican art: Oaxacan pottery, a signed Diego Rivera monotype, a papier-mâché skeleton figure by the famed Linares family, altars, weavings, ceramics, and seventeenth-century retablos, among many other cultural works.[17] All the art is displayed against tangerine-colored walls.

Many Cisneros fans may be familiar with perhaps the most famous *cuento* of Cisneros's stance on color, that of the color of her house on Guenther Street in the King William Historic District of San Antonio. In 1998, her house became the subject of local, national, and international newspaper headlines when Cisneros painted it Sherwin Williams Corsican Purple (she has an affinity for purple, even once having a dog named Violeta). In response, the San Antonio Historic and Design Review Commission ruled that the color was not a historical color, and that the house would have to be repainted. A legal battle ensued, and in the end, the idea of what is "historical" color in San Antonio was reframed, but not without consequences.[18] For Cisneros the color purple was a historical color for her community, but for the review commission, which many of Cisneros's supporters felt was ethnically biased, it was anything but. Cisneros recalls that its palette of appropriate "colonial colors included Surrey beige, Séveres blue, Hawthorne green, Frontier Days brown and Plymouth red, [which] were *colores tristes* and in my opinion ugly."[19] Later, the review commission suggested she paint the house a vibrant pink color that it deemed to be historical.

The use of color as symbol in the works of Cisneros not only dovetails with the use of color to mark space and place, but also fosters poignant memory. Take the case of the red sweater in the story "Eleven," in *Woman Hollering*

Creek. An ugly red sweater is forced on the child Rachel by her teacher, even though it isn't hers:

> But when the sick feeling goes away and I open my eyes, the red sweater's still sitting there like a big red mountain. I move the sweater to the corner of my desk with my ruler. . . . In my head I'm thinking how long till lunchtime, how long till I can take the red sweater and throw it over the schoolyard fence, or leave it hanging on a parking meter, or bunch it up into a little ball and toss it in the alley.[20]

On the eve of Rachel's eleventh birthday and her transition from child to young woman, the feelings the red sweater evoke in her are deep and help set the stage for her tween years and impending adulthood. Red is a punctuating color that can signify danger. Cisneros uses it here to convey helplessness and the inequity of Rachel being unable to voice her disapproval of the used and ratty red sweater.

For me personally, perhaps the most exquisite and symbolic visualization of color from Cisneros's word crafting comes from the first pages of *Caramelo*, as "Uncle Fat-Face's brand-new used white Cadillac, Uncle Baby's green Impala and Father's red Chevrolet station wagon are racing to the Little Grandfather's and Awful Grandmother's house in Mexico City," the three cars taking turns passing one another.[21] The visual energy created in this passage evokes the waving *colores nacionales* of Mexico's *bandera* (flag), as well as the colors of postindependence depictions of La Virgen de Guadalupe's gown and manta. Reading this passage is both visual and sensory as I recall the scenery and emotions of past visits with my own family in Mexico and my own Mexicanidad.

Colors come alive in *Caramelo*, perhaps more so than in any collection of Cisneros's prose. Cisneros takes special note to repeatedly mention the impact of the colors as symbols of Mexico. "Sweets sweeter, colors brighter, the bitter more bitter. A cage of parrots all the rainbow colors of Lulu's sodas." Elsewhere, she writes: "He bought pumpkin-seed-studded *obleas*—transparent pastel wafers, pink, white, yellow, pale green, Ave María blue."[22]

Cisneros utilizes the iconographic significance of the color blue in reference to La Virgen's cloak throughout her writing. It appears in numerous poems and short stories. She also often incorporates blue when referring to boyhood and maleness.

The color of *caramelo* (caramel) and other shades of earth and skin run through the writings of Cisneros and allude to identities. In *Caramelo*, the eponymous term represents, among other things, a type of fine rebozo, and a visual symbol of mestizaje: "it was an exquisite rebozo of five tiras, the cloth a beautiful beautiful blend of toffee, licorice, and vanilla stripes, flecked with black and white, which is why they call this design a caramelo."[23] As Cisneros weaves the theme and history of the rebozo into her novel, not only does she describe the significance of the *caramelo*, she shares the symbolism of other rebozo patterns and colors: "Watermelon, lantern, pearl. Rain, see not to be confused with drizzle. Snow, dove-gray *columbino*, colla *jamoncillo*. Brown trimmed with white *coyote*, the rainbow *tornasoles*, red *quemado*, and the golden-yellow *maravilla*."[24]

Finally, when it comes to symbolic color, Cisneros often references black as a descriptor for nighttime, ink, and death. She writes about the character Ambrosio Reyes, a master rebozo maker, in *Caramelo*. Reyes was famous for his black *rebozos de olor*. His fingernails were always stained a dark blue because of the dyeing process: "It was due to his expertise as a maker of black shawls, because black is the most difficult color to dye. The cloth must be soaked over and over in water where rusty skillets, pipes, nails, horseshoes, bed rails, chains, and wagon wheels have been left to dissolve." The rebozos are highly coveted, and Cisneros describes them "as black as Coyotepec pottery, as black as *huitlacoche*, the corn mushroom, as true black as an *olla* of fresh-cooked black beans."[25]

Cisneros often speaks about the power and influence of museums in her life. In a 2015 interview with *Chicago Magazine*, Cisneros was asked how she was first exposed to the art world. She replied:

> Growing up in Chicago was special because all the museums were free on Sunday. My mother used to take us [Cisneros has six brothers]. We'd run around the Field Museum looking at mummies. I pretended the museums were my house, and that all of Grant Park was my garden. At the Art Institute, we saw the van Goghs and Seurat, and the colors of those paintings come up in my novels. We absorbed so much.[26]

Along with the Chicago Field Museum of Natural History and the Art Institute, the Cisneros family often went to the Shedd Aquarium, the Adler Planetarium, and the Museum of Science and Industry. In spring 2021, Cisneros delivered a keynote address, titled "Musing on Museums," for the annual conference of the American Alliance of Museums. She described to listeners some of her favorite museum moments: viewing textiles, a jade cabbage, and Frida Kahlo exhibits in both Detroit, Michigan, and Kahlo's Casa Azul in Mexico City.[27]

Punctuating Cisneros's writings are references to masterpieces in world-renowned museums from Chicago to Italy. Throughout her collection *Loose Woman*, Frida Kahlo, Henri Matisse, Amedeo Modigliani, Francisco Goya, and Diego Rivera, as well as pre-conquest art, religious imagery, and *arte popular,* are included, revered, and elevated. Art exhibitions and images appear as prominent plot points in "Never Marry a Mexican," from *Woman Hollering Creek.*[28] Cisneros's poem "ASS (for David)," in *My Wicked Wicked Ways*, demonstrates her art historical knowledge gained from museum visits throughout her life:

> My Michelangelo!
> What Bernini could compare?
> Could the Borghese estate compete?
> Could the Medici's famed aesthete
> Produce an excellent and sweet
> As this famous derriere.[29]

Even the author's personal journals and notebooks in the Sandra Cisneros Papers, Wittliff Collections, Texas State University, highlight her attention to artists and all she learned and saw during those family museum trips and her subsequent travels around the word. Botticelli's *Birth of Venus*, Rivera's *Kneeling Child*, Édouard Manet's *Flowers in a Crystal Vase*, Claude Monet's *Women in the Garden*, Rosso Fiorentino's *Cherub Playing a Lute*, Goya's *The Clothed Maja*, and Andy Warhol's *Cambell's Soup Cans* grace the covers of these valuable collections of writings, drafts, and notes. Portraits of La Virgen de Guadalupe and women writers such as Virginia Woolf can be found, while others have bold-*colored* covers in purple, blue, yellow, red, and green.[30]

Throughout her writings, Cisneros treats all artworks, from Europe to the Americas, as masterpieces. Additionally, she sprinkles in mention of her father and upholstery. It is clear that her well-honed eye for detail, whether in her writing or in her visual work, comes from the visual training she received from paying attention to her father's artistry and craftmanship. Textures like velvet and satin often crop up in her stories. When she was invited to write about an artwork in the Isabella Stewart Gardner Museum in Boston, she told the curator that she wanted to write about the upholstery. Cisneros writes:

> I know I should have been impressed by the Botticellis and Vermeers but I'm looking at the furniture the same rude way my father checks out a chair before sitting down. Scrutinizing the seams, examining the fabric to see if the upholsterer knew enough to match the patterns, paying attention to the details that mean the custom, quality work, work done with pride.[31]

Elsewhere in this essay, Cisneros draws comparisons between the works at the museum and her family's experiences by juxtaposing an image of a painting that hung in her Aunt Margaret's house with *Gypsy Lady* (*La Gitana*) by Louis Kronberg.[32]

Cisneros's interest in the canvases of recorded artists is matched by her treatment of unrecorded artists. Popular Mexican calendars, iconic images of Popocatépetl and Iztaccíhuatl, and Mexican singers appear in narrative scenes. Framed and brightly colored (happy pink or turquoise!) religious pictures, made of strips of paper that allow the viewer to see a different image depending on the angle, also appear. Religious imagery hangs in interiors and sits in sanctuaries throughout Cisneros's prose, from bultos (statues) of El Santo Niño de Atocha to painted canvas backdrops of Recuerdo del Tepeyac, used for pilgrimage souvenirs at the Basílica de la Virgen de Guadalupe. She pays homage to vernacular painting traditions of the ex-voto, the little miracle paintings that are placed as devotional offerings in churches and that always feature a helpful saint or religious figure. Her story "Little Miracles, Kept Promises," in *Woman Hollering Creek*, includes many of these appreciations, both real and fictionalized, the miracles described in vivid narrative form.[33]

Cisneros is a connoisseur of art as a museum visitor, a collector, and a patron. She has supported numerous visual artists by buying their work and including it in her personal collection. She too has experienced life as a starving artist and understands the challenges faced by creatives. She installs these works alongside vintage and contemporary examples of *arte popular* from Mexico and her world travels, paintings by Chicano artists, and *altares* and assemblages of things everywhere, all with meaning and relational posture. Reflecting on her experience working with the Isabella Stewart Gardner Museum, Cisneros writes: "What strikes me is the similarity between the house of the wealthy art collector Isabella Stewart Gardner and my mother's, that supreme collector of anything found in thrift stores, garage sales, and liquidations, who planted the collector's seed in me. These cabinets filled with *tiliches*, trinkets, and the precious next to the not so precious."[34]

Textiles are among Cisneros's favorite articles to collect, perhaps inspired by the fabric remnants that her father brought home from his job. She wears her collections of textiles as an art form made by women. Cisneros began collecting *huipiles* on a trip to San Cristóbal de las Casas, Chiapas. She notes: "Then I found the used *huipiles* in shops all along the typing school street. As the daughter of an upholsterer, I know how to look at seams and at the reverse to measure quality. By pulling the garments inside out, I could read their history. . . . Some were finely woven with birds and animals in tight, perfect stitches."[35]

After Cisneros had purchased several *huipiles*, she showed them to a friend, who asked her what she was going to do with all of them:

"I thought I could wear them," I said without conviction. "Or maybe hang them on the walls."

Once I got back I *did* hang some on the walls. Then, *poco a poco*, little by little, I started to take them down and wear them.[36]

Today, Cisneros cares for her *huipiles* by keeping them in her collection of Mexican trunks. "I like to mix my Mexican garments in nontraditional ways, maybe a Tehuanahuipil with a Tahitian sarong, or a Oaxacan skirt with a man's Chiapaneco vest, to create something new, something no one in Mexico would do."[37]

The visual Cisneros started long ago. She remembers:

When I was young, when I first left home and rented that apartment with my sister and her kids right after her husband left, I thought it would be glamorous to be an artist. I wanted to be like Frida or Tina. I was ready to suffer with my camera and my paint brushes in that awful apartment we rented for $150 each because it had high ceilings and those wonderful glass skylights that convinced us we had to have it.[38]

When Cisneros completed graduate school, she went on to teach and organize community arts events. Then, as she does now, she gravitated toward her creative peers, many of whom were and still are visual artists. She writes about moving to San Antonio:

I found it a community still locked in its provinciality. . . . I was surprised it was the gay community that sheltered and nurtured me, specifically the Latino visual artists, and they are still, for the most part, the crowd I run with. I reason this is because they too understand about having to reinvent oneself, about taking from tradition that which nurtures and abandoning the elements that would mean self-destruction.[39]

Cisneros is drawn (pun intended) to other visual creatives, and references to these artist friends and other contemporary artists make their way into her articles and essays. The twentieth-century artist Martín Ramírez reminds her of Fresno poet Luis Omar Salinas. The sculptor José Luis Rivera-Barrera and painter and printmaker César Martínez are mentioned as well. In 2006, Cisneros was invited by the San Antonio Museum of Art to write about a work by local artist and friend Franco Mondini-Ruiz. She wrote of Mondini-Ruiz that he "is an artist who sees elegance in the rascuache, the gaudy, kitsch, funky. Franco's shop, Infinito Botánica, is a place filled with the extraordinary and the divine, as he puts it. He is a painter, art curator, sculptor, businessman."[40]

LA SANDRA COMO ARTISTA

Elsewhere, artist friends David Zamora Casas (performance artist, painter, and sculptor) and Ito Romo (poet and visual artist) are mentioned, as is Terry Ybáñez, who creates ceramic mosaics out of pottery shards. Another artist friend, Ángel Rodríguez-Díaz, painted a portrait of Cisneros titled *The Protagonist of an Endless Story*. It is now part of the permanent collection of the Smithsonian American Art Museum (SAAM) in Washington, DC. Another portrait of Cisneros, a photograph by San Antonio artist Al Rendon, resides in the collections of the National Portrait Gallery, a sister museum to SAAM.

Throughout her life, Cisneros has drawn images in her *cuadernos*. Among these notebook visualizations are renderings of Cisneros's own pets, pets that belong to friends, flowers, and even a wine glass. There are also several drawings of people, especially of her parents, Alfredo Cisneros Del Moral and Elvira Cordero Anguiano. An examination of the available body of Cisneros's drawings reveals, first, that the artist takes the time to render the things that matter most to her, and second, that she also renders things that matter most to those closest to her. Pets have always been a wonderful part of Cisneros's life and writings. Her papers in the Wittliff Collections contain numerous examples of pen and ink drawings that capture her emotional connections. A group of some twenty works show curled-up dogs (and even one cat!), content and happy. Across them all, the artist depicts tenderness, sweetness, and a love for the animals rendered. Cisneros gets the curves just right in the pictures of curled-up dogs. Her pen and pencil strokes allude to fur and tails. One work, "Dante and Barney," pays homage to two of the artist's beloved dogs. Another is captioned "Barnitos" (a pet name for Barney?), and still another, this one of a cat, is inscribed "Panfeli Palafox." Many of the finished drawings are signed "Sandra" in the bottom left corner, indicating that the author is aware of herself as a visual artist.[41] Recently, a drawing of a friend's dog has come to light. The work depicts the dog of fellow animal lover and Mexican photographer Flor Garduño and is a promised gift from Cisneros to the National Museum of Mexican Art (NMMA) in Chicago. It is signed "Sandra, 18 Mayo [20]16, Tepotzlán."[42]

Mixed in with the dog series in the Wittliff Collections is a sketch of a bouquet of flowers, which the artist titled "Birthday Flowers December 2010." These are not the only flowers Cisneros is known to have drawn; two brightly colored paintings of vases filled with flowers were included in Cisneros's 2011 installation *A Room of Her Own: My Mother's Altar*. Cisneros created the paintings for her mother's bedroom so that her mother could have some beauty of her own. She also drew small watercolors to decorate the home of her dear friend Jasna Karaula in Sarajevo.[43] Finally, Cisneros has also been known to draw her poems in colored ink on beautiful handmade papers. The special and personal artworks are gifted to friends.[44]

Extraordinary and deeply personal is a series of fifteen drawings of Cisneros's father as he was ill and nearing the end of his life in 1996 and 1997. The series features portraits drawn as he lay in bed, while Cisneros sat by his side. The artist is focused on the details of his face: the gentle curls of his hair, his eyelashes, the fold of his neck and chin as they lay against a pillow. Many of the portraits are accompanied with words in the notebook, as if Cisneros was verbally and visually recording her grief and the process of grieving. One sketch is accompanied by the words, "My father's face is hardly my father's face." A peaceful image is accompanied by the pronouncement, "My father dead 6:30 am 2/9/97." One decade later, the artist drew an image titled "My Mother's Crossing." This work of her mother in the hospital is accompanied by Cisneros's thoughts and dated October 31, 2007.[45]

In addition to taking pen and pencil to paper, Cisneros is also a painter, as is evident from the two still lives of flowers and vases included in the *ofrenda* installation to her mother. Hints of the artist's ease with and interest in painting appear often in her body of work. In "*Bien* Pretty," the protagonist-narrator is a painter. Cisneros writes:

> I'd always wanted to do an updated version of the Prince Popocatépetl/Princess Ixtaccíhuatl volcano myth, that tragic love story metamorphosized from classic to kitsch calendar art, like the ones you get at Carnicería Ximénez or Tortillería la Guadalupanita. Prince Popo, half-naked warrior built like Johnny Weissmuller, crouched in grief beside his sleeping princess Ixtaccíhuatl, buxom as an Indian Jayne Mansfield. And behind them, echoing their silhouettes, their namesake volcanoes.[46]

In the story, the artist asks cucaracha exterminator Flavio whether he would consider modeling for the project: "I mean I'm an artist. I need models. Sometimes. To model, you know. For a painting. I thought."[47] The modeling episode leads to a relationship, which becomes emotional and heartfelt. Later in the story, Flavio leaves the artist, and the protagonist becomes inspired:

> Got a good idea and redid the whole thing. Prince Popo and Princess Ixta trade places. After all, who's to say the sleeping mountain isn't the prince and the voyeur the princess, right? So, I've done it my way. With Prince Popocatépetl lying on his back instead of the Princess. Of course, I had to make some anatomical adjustments in order to simulate the geographical silhouettes. I think I'm going to call it *El Pipi del Popo*. I kind of like it.[48]

LA SANDRA COMO ARTISTA

In her introduction to the ten-year anniversary edition of *The House on Mango Street*, Cisneros addresses her creative process in writing the novel and the way she found her own voice by defying and reframing the restrictions of graduate school. She describes the multiple vignettes about Esperanza using a visual art term, *collage*.[49] I see her mastery of this medium not only in book publications and in her visual work, drawings, and installations. As evidenced, she is a master of color, detail, and the art of putting things together. A *rasquachera* like no other, she champions the *rasquache* methodology of putting bits and pieces together, whether in words or in a visual installation. In the afterword to *Have You Seen Marie?*, Cisneros's collaboration with famed Chicana artist Ester Hernández, Cisneros writes: "I wanted both the story and the art to capture the offbeat beauty of Rasquache, things made with materials ready at hand, funk architecture and funky gardens, creative ways of making do, because it seems to me that this is what is uniquely gorgeous about San Antonio."[50]

As evidenced by her notebooks and journals—each a collage of her experiences, filled with souvenirs, clippings, and memories, as well as phrases, ideas for essays, and poems—Cisneros is constantly acquiring elements for both her writing and her visual assemblages and installations. Bits and pieces are gathered to complete a whole. Cisneros uses this process of piecing together smaller parts (whether memories or actual objects) to create her literary and visual masterpieces.

Her largest installation to date is the ofrenda to her mother, *A Room of Her Own*. The work was first installed at the NMMA in Chicago. In 2011, Cisneros, along with project assistant Irma Carolina Rubio, came to the National Hispanic Cultural Center (NHCC) in Albuquerque, New Mexico, to install the incredible work (see figure 12.1). I was serving as director and chief curator of the NHCC Art Museum and Visual Arts Program at the time. Watching and helping, members of my staff and I were mesmerized. Of course, the author literally started by writing on the wall. I thought, ah hah! Of course, how could she not? Over the next three days she carefully placed and considered each object, memory, photo, and *chuchuluco* (little things or knickknacks). In her visual assemblages and collage installations, she carefully combines trinkets, curios, *arte popular*, sequins, *chuchulucos*, and *brillantes* and *chillantes* (bright, loud, intense colors) like she would nouns and verbs. She also treats words and fonts as art. They are necessary embellishments, like the gilding and foil of her compositions. In utilizing the design elements of letters and fonts to create her *ofrenda*, Cisneros adorned walls, mirrors, frames, and photos with her cursive painted and penned characters, thus directly and adeptly intertwining visuals and literature into her narrative.

Photos of her mother were placed in beautiful frames, and Cisneros wrote

Figure 12.1. Sandra Cisneros, *A Room of Her Own: My Mother's Altar*, National Hispanic Cultural Center Art Museum, Albuquerque, New Mexico, 2011. Photo by Tey Marianna Nunn.

LA SANDRA COMO ARTISTA

Figure 12.2. Detail during installation, Sandra Cisneros, *A Room of Her Own: My Mother's Altar*, National Hispanic Cultural Center Art Museum, Albuquerque, New Mexico, 2011. Photo by Tey Marianna Nunn.

over the glass to caption the images. One caption read, "Every weekend she went to the Chicago museums, parks, and library—all her life," and a photo of her mother holding a heart-shaped tomato was captioned, "From her garden." On many occasions, Cisneros wrote on the actual edges of the frames. The two most precious pieces included in the *ofrenda* were embroidered works of art by her mother, Elvira Cordero Anguiano, and by her grandmother (and Elvira's mother) María Romualdo Felipa Anguiano: a little embroidered burro with the initials EC embroidered above, and a delicately embroidered floral motif with the stitched words "Suspiro por tí." I realized that Cisneros's family members, like her, used a creative collaging process that joined imagery and words, and that this was one reason why these two artworks were so valued by Cisneros (see figure 12.2).

Sandra Cisneros taught me a lot about altar making. It is she who taught me to take a moment and pay attention—to relish the relationship of objects and words in order to complete the masterwork (see figure 12.3). As we

Figure 12.3. Detail of photos with writing, Sandra Cisneros, *A Room of Her Own: My Mother's Altar*, National Hispanic Cultural Center Art Museum, Albuquerque, New Mexico, 2011. Photo by Tey Marianna Nunn.

finished the installation right before the opening, Cisneros signed the adjacent wall with her acknowledgments. Next to her words, we hung the two floral still-life paintings that she had created for her mother. Cisneros's signature on the museum wall was kept up for years after the altar came down. "We can't paint over it!" I kept insisting, "It's the signature of a famous artist!"

After the installation moved to other museums and then back to its permanent home at the NMMA in Chicago, my colleague Cesáreo Moreno, director and chief curator of the Visual Arts Program at the NMMA, reflected on Cisneros's process:

> In subsequent years her ofrenda was installed at the National Hispanic Cultural Center, the Smithsonian National Museum of American History, and the Museum of Latin American Art, conforming to a new space at each venue. Like a literary work, it was edited and revised year after year and accordingly increased in size from 8' to 19' wide—assuming the feel of an actual room.[51]

Moreno's keen observation of the reinstallation and reconfiguration of each iteration of the Cisneros *ofrenda* as an ongoing editing process made total sense to me. This is the reason why the writing is on the wall for Cisneros, and on the picture frames, and on the mirrors.

In a personal letter written after the completion of the *ofrenda* installation at the NHCC Art Museum, Cisneros wrote to this author: "Thank you for the chance to create the altar ... and for elevating me to the status of 'Installation artist.' At 56 this is no small feat. Once I left visual arts as a young woman, I always lived with a desire to return."[52] To Moreno and the staff of the NMMA, she conveyed a similar message as a text panel for the exhibit. "I am a writer who was once an artist and who always longed to become an artist again. I've been granted this wish thanks to the many museums who have allowed me to create and recreate this altar in honor of my mother, Elvira Cordero Anguiano."[53]

In 2016, the NHCC hosted another Cisneros-related exhibit organized by the NMMA, *The House on Mango Street: Artists Interpret Community*. The exhibit, which was curated by Moreno, was filled with visual art inspired by the famed novel. Numerous portraits of Cisneros by inspired artist friends illustrated her close affinity and camaraderie with them. In the introductory area of the exhibition, above one of Cisneros's desks and typewriters, and amid shelving featuring some of her beloved and personal belongings, were two drawings. The portraits, by Cisneros, were of her father and mother as they were each close to death. In support of the exhibition, Cisneros came to Albuquerque to do a celebrity museum exhibition tour of the show based on her coming-of-age novel. Even though we had featured two of her paintings before (the florals on the thank-you wall in her *ofrenda* installation), this was the first time that many familiar with her writings realized that she was also a visual artist.

As I wrote this essay, I came to the realization that a museum curator can write about literary artists—and, in fact, should do so, often. A curator is trained in describing art, artists, and art movements, whether in a catalog essay, an exhibition text label, or an art historical lecture. Aesthetic storytelling is my job. As a writer, Cisneros tucks her visions away for another day, one when they might appear on the paper page. As an artist, Cisneros composes the visual and verbal together, as her writing and her visual production go hand in hand. I now see such an interwoven relationship between the two.

Moreno has described Cisneros's *ofrenda* to her mother as "a visual poem."[54] It is no wonder that when she was given the space for her *ofrenda* installation, the exhibition walls were painted a school bus (almost marigold) yellow and a deep, deep Guenther Street aubergine purple. As soon as they were dry, the first thing she did was write on them with chalk. She wrote about her mother, and about her hopes, dreams, and regrets. The central theme throughout so much of the *obra* of Sandra Cisneros highlights how brilliantly visual and verbal narratives are combined. Pen and prose must be interpreted differently when it comes to her work. More often than not, the author-artist intertwines the poetics of her words in order to highlight the beauty of aesthetics. The concept of a visual Cisneros is integral to understanding her process. In doing so we can see that she creates for her readers and her viewers an extensive body of masterpieces.

NOTES

Un million de gracias a Sandra, whose work I love so much, for her friendship, conversation, and support through all these years. Un abrazo fuerte to Cesáreo Moreno for his contributions to this essay. A big thank-you to Geneva M. Gano and Sonia Saldívar-Hull for the vision of this collection. Mucho amor to my family, friends, and colleagues who are always there.

1. Although I do know one personally: my mother, Tey Diana Rebolledo, a trailblazer in her own right/write (pun intended). She immersed me in the world of Chicana and Latina literature and gifted me with signed books by all her writer friends. This essay is dedicated with love to her.

2. Sandra Cisneros, "Musings on Museums" (keynote lecture, American Alliance of Museums annual conference, online, June 2021).

3. Sandra Cisneros, "One Holy Night," in *Woman Hollering Creek and Other Stories* (New York: Random House, 1991), 35.

4. Sandra Cisneros, "Never Marry a Mexican," in *Woman Hollering Creek and Other Stories*, 83.

5. Sandra Cisneros, *The House on Mango Street* (New York: Vintage Books, 1991), 40.

6. Cisneros, *The House on Mango Street*, 76–77.

7. Sandra Cisneros, *My Wicked Wicked Ways* (New York: Turtle Bay Books, 1992), 15.

LA SANDRA COMO ARTISTA

8. Cisneros, *My Wicked Wicked Ways*, 96.
9. Cisneros, *My Wicked Wicked Ways*, 36.
10. Sandra Cisneros, *Loose Woman* (New York: Alfred A. Knopf, 1994), 6.
11. Sandra Cisneros, "Tenemos Layaway, or How I Became an Art Collector," in *A House of My Own: Stories from My Life* (New York: Alfred P. Knopf, 2015), 181.
12. Sandra Cisneros, "Salvador Late or Early," in *Woman Hollering Creek and Other Stories*, 10.
13. Cisneros, *My Wicked Wicked Ways*, 42.
14. Sandra Cisneros, "*Bien* Pretty," in *Woman Hollering Creek and Other Stories*, 158.
15. Cisneros, *The House on Mango Street*, 76.
16. Sandra Cisneros, *Caramelo or Puro Cuento* (New York: Vintage Books, 2002), 18.
17. Cisneros, "*Bien* Pretty," 139–140.
18. For more on Cisneros's purple house, see Sandra Cisneros, "My Purple House—Color Is a Language and a History," Hispanic Link (online), August 31, 1997; "Beyond the Pale: A Novelist Defends the Vibrant Color of Her Historic San Antonio House," *House and Garden* 17, no. 4 (April 2002); Sandra Cisneros, "Our Tejano History Has Become Invisible," *San Antonio Express-News*, August 17, 1997; Kathy Lowry, "The Purple Passion of Sandra Cisneros," *Texas Monthly*, October 1997; Cisneros, "¡Que Vivan Los Colores!," in *A House of My Own*, 170–176.
19. Cisneros, "¡Que Vivan Los Colores!," 172.
20. Sandra Cisneros, "Eleven," in *Woman Hollering Creek and Other Stories*, 9.
21. Cisneros, *Caramelo*, 18.
22. Cisneros, *Caramelo*, 17, 201.
23. Cisneros, *Caramelo*, 94.
24. Cisneros, *Caramelo*, 93.
25. Cisneros, *Caramelo*, 92.
26. Sandra Cisneros, "Tapicero's Daughter," in *A House of My Own*, 143.
27. Cisneros, "Musings on Museums."
28. Cisneros, "Never Marry a Mexican," 68–83.
29. Cisneros, *My Wicked Wicked Ways*, 50.
30. Sandra Cisneros Papers, Wittliff Collections, Texas State University.
31. Cisneros, "Tapicero's Daughter," 147, 151.
32. Cisneros, "Tapicero's Daughter," 150.
33. Sandra Cisneros, "Little Miracles, Kept Promises," in *Woman Hollering Creek and Other Stories*, 116.
34. Cisneros, "Tapicero's Daughter," 147.
35. Sandra Cisneros, "Huipiles," in *A House of My Own*, 61.
36. Cisneros, "Huipiles," 60.
37. Cisneros, "Huipiles," 63.
38. Cisneros, "Never Marry a Mexican," 72.
39. Sandra Cisneros, "I Can Live Sola and I Love to Work," in *A House of My Own*, 137.
40. Cisneros, "Tapicero's Daughter," 157–158.
41. These drawings can be found in box 4, folder 7, Sandra Cisneros Papers.
42. Cesáreo Moreno, pers. comm., October 12, 2021.

43. Sandra Cisneros, "Who Wants Stories Now," in *A House of My Own*, 108.
44. The gifted art is in private collections; I have viewed some of these items.
45. These sketches are in box 15, folder 5, Sandra Cisneros Papers.
46. Cisneros, "*Bien* Pretty," 144.
47. Cisneros, "*Bien* Pretty," 144.
48. Cisneros, "*Bien* Pretty," 163.
49. Sandra Cisneros, *The House on Mango Street* (New York: Alfred A. Knopf, 1994), xviii.
50. Sandra Cisneros, *Have You Seen Marie?* (New York: Alfred A. Knopf, 2012), 93.
51. Cesáreo Moreno, pers. comm., October 28, 2021.
52. Sandra Cisneros, pers. comm., November 11, 2011.
53. Quoted in Cesáreo Moreno, pers. comm., October 28, 2021.
54. Moreno, pers. comm.

CHAPTER 13

SIN VERGÜENZA
A Plática with Sandra Cisneros
Macarena Hernández

I first met Sandra Cisneros in San Antonio, Texas, at the Liberty Bar. That was about two decades ago. Our mentor Norma Alarcón was visiting San Antonio, and she had invited a few friends to join her. Norma is not only a brilliant scholar and Chicana feminist pioneer who founded Third Woman Press, she is also one of Sandra's closest friends, her mentor, and one of her first publishers. Sandra calls Norma her literary *madrina*.

When we met, Sandra was copyediting galleys of *Caramelo* and I was a rookie reporter at the *San Antonio Express-News*. Over dinner, she and I bonded over our grief. Both of our fathers had recently died, a year apart. Hers in 1997. Mine in 1998. Over the years, she has become my literary *madrina* and *amiga del alma*.

This interview was edited for clarity and length from conversations that took place over two Zoom meetings during the spring and fall of 2021.

MACARENA: Sandra, you grew up in Chicago in a house full of men.
SANDRA: Yes, that's why I don't live with any.
MACARENA: Did you grow up in a house where you felt you had a say?
SANDRA: Well, you know, everybody talked at the same time, but my brother Kiki and I were the ones who were funny, and when you're funny, you get trained to be funny because that's how you get attention. And I think that's where I started honing my comedic skills.
MACARENA: You're number three, surrounded by boys—older and younger brothers. Do you think that affected your future relationships with men? Because I know, having grown up in the house I did, it certainly shaped my own future interactions.

SANDRA: I think it did negative and positive things. I had a sister who was born on December 16, right between me and my next brother, so I always wonder how our lives would have been different if she had lived—I think I would have liked her, cause she was Sagittarian. But I think, on the one hand, I felt very much that I could defend myself with men—very comfortable—but I also felt like I needed their approval and that kind of warped me, especially when I was very young. I felt safe among men and I felt comfortable and I didn't seek women. When I left high school, I had like one or two friends that continued on with me from my high school years, but generally, after my third year in college, I left my friends from high school behind and I deviated and felt more comfortable with artists rather than the people who just happened by chance to be my friends because we were in the same Spanish club or alphabetical order put us next to each other. You know how that is in high school. You make friends with people who walk home the same way you do. So I left those friends, and I never felt comfortable with my friends, but I felt comfortable within my family. And so I guess I felt like once I found the artistic community, I felt more at home with the men. I really didn't have close friendships with women after my third year in undergraduate. Even in graduate school, they were more distant—my women friends—they weren't confidants or close to me or like the sisters they are now. I had this idea of getting men's approval, which I remember feeling very invisible unless men noticed me.

MACARENA: I think that's the case for a lot of us, you know, because in whatever context—you were in Chicago, I was in the Rio Grande Valley—there is a high premium on a man's approval.

SANDRA: With my brothers, it wasn't anything with beauty because they made me feel ugly and, you know, they always cut me down. In fact, I've incorporated them as my evil editors—evil editors made up of my six brothers. And they don't realize that they still haunt everything that I do; every line I write, they're there which makes me self-edit and very self-critical. But on the other hand, I'm really critical about other people—their writing—everything. I have to just kinda stop myself. We always talk about that: the *chango* [the monkey] who doesn't see her *cola* [tail]. And I do that a lot, so I have to stop myself and say, "Okay, cut it out." It's like I've inherited the evil editor.

MACARENA: But it also seems to come from having grown up being hypercriticized, no?

SANDRA: Yeah that's it.

MACARENA: And that energy is probably worse toward yourself inward, no? I feel like I'm very hypercritical of myself.

SANDRA: Oh, I'm the worst! If you think I'm bad in workshops, you should hear me with my own self. I'm really, really hard. And I know that Iowa [the Iowa Writers' Workshop, where Sandra completed her MFA] was hard, too, but I also had this opposite thing: being very hypercritical with the six brothers and being elevated and treated like the best by my father. It may have been why the brothers were hypercritical, I think they were very jealous. My father made it very clear that I was his favorite child and that they should do anything for me and protect me and not complain and feel it was a pleasure. So of course, you know how that went over.

MACARENA: It's because your father was a caballero, right?

SANDRA: My father would say, "Go pick up your sister," and they'd [whine] and he goes, "It's a pleasure!"

MACARENA: That's incredible. I often think about your brothers and how they shaped you because I think about, in my own story, I take the same things from them. They were very hypercritical, they would say stuff like, "When you get married, we have to tell them there are no refunds! *¡No te pueden regresar!*"

SANDRA: When I was very young, my brothers would say, "You're not a real Cisneros because when you get married, you're going to give your name up." I was hypersensitive—was/am—and so that struck me as something that lodged itself in my heart and my memory. And when I started visualizing being an author, it was around that same time—middle school, fifth/sixth grade—had to be sixth grade because I moved to Campbell Street in sixth grade and that's when I visualized a book with my name on the spine and it wasn't with a husband's name, it was my name. So I guess maybe it was right around the time when I started writing poetry, which was the genre I began with.

MACARENA: You began with poetry in sixth grade. What were you writing about? What kinds of poems were you writing?

SANDRA: I wrote fixed verse, and by fixed verse I mean you're supposed to count the meters, but I wasn't counting them. I was just listening to them by ear and rhyming because those are the samples of poetry that I saw for the first time in my grade school textbook. And it all galloped to iambic tetrameter [demonstrates the rhythm of iambic tetrameter]. That's what I heard, and I composed things that were very emotional for me, like the sunsets, the wind, natural things that overwhelmed me. That's what I wrote about. I don't think I wrote very many, I don't remember but two.

MACARENA: Did you find a space or teachers who encouraged you?

SANDRA: I have a memory, very distinctly, of a late teacher who moved into the Humboldt Park neighborhood, into the house that became [the] house on Mango Street, and I can see her and her face and her hair, but I can't remember her name. And I'm going to try to do a meditation and see if it floats back. She was Mrs. Something, and she's the one who really changed my life. She didn't know I wrote, she noticed that I drew. And her approval was just—first time I got my teacher's approval since first grade—was so life changing for me. She just made me feel like I was worth something, that I was a remarkable child. I thought she was confused, but I felt sorry for her and her confusion and mistake, but because of her enthusiasm for my drawings, I worked harder. I never showed her the poems. But that was the year I started writing poetry. And my grades improved so you could see the mere difference from there, and then in seventh grade I went from being a mediocre and substandard student to a good student. Maybe not great in the sciences and math, but very good in humanities. By the time I was in high school, I was looked at as a smart student and I thought of myself as a smart student, and that wouldn't have happened without this teacher in the sixth grade. There's a difference when a teacher shines their light on you. Illumina, and it makes you value yourself when you have a teacher that believes in you. It's so important. So, I wrote bad fiction in seventh grade, and I wrote a children's story in eighth grade that I illustrated. And then in high school, I really wasn't as public of an artist until my sophomore year. I was known more as an interpreter of literature in my first year, and that was just a mistake. They just stumbled on that I could read and interpret literature well. I didn't think it was anything special, I thought everybody could hear how a piece of literature should be read. But it was in sophomore year when I had Elizabeth Lensick, who stumbled on me as a poet. She was a poet. She studied with Paul Carroll, the Chicago poet, and she brought Paul Carroll to our school to do a lecture, to do a class visit, and Lensick read her poems to us, and she made us write poems. So that's how she knew I could write, and that's when I got outed and forced—recruited—to be the literary magazine editor. I was very shy so the last thing I wanted was to have to be the [literary magazine editor]. It wasn't the editing that I objected to. The last thing I wanted was to have to go in front of every single class in school and invite them to submit drawings and poems. That's the part I hated. Then I became the writer.

MACARENA: How old were you then?

SANDRA: Sophomore . . . it was at fifteen.

MACARENA: About fifteen when you felt that you were a writer and classified yourself. Did you know then that you were going to pursue writing?

SANDRA: I knew it since fifth grade. Nobody else knew it. I knew it. But I didn't tell anyone that's what I wanted. I was always waiting to see if a guidance counselor or someone could recommend a route I could take; I was too embarrassed to say what I secretly saw in my future. I thought since sixth grade, when they said, "What [do you] wanna study?" I said, "Well, I guess I'm good at English?" That's what I would say. I wouldn't say, "I want to be a writer!" No, it was all, "Well, I guess I'm good at English?" I was hoping that they would give me something that wasn't on the menu, and the menu didn't look very appetizing. And I thought, "Oh, I guess I'll teach English?" You know how girls talk with a question mark at the end, because you're really not sure. But to myself, I said, "And I will write."

MACARENA: So when you went to college, you knew that you were still on your path to become a full-time . . .

SANDRA: I was very, very practical. Like my mother said, "Make sure you can earn your own living," and that has stayed with me with the advice I give young writers now. So I didn't expect to make any money from the writing. Not any at all! I just assumed, "Okay, I better take all the requirements to be a teacher in the Chicago public school system; I better take Spanish in case I have to teach ESL," and just a parachute—learn how to type. I was in the business classes with the B-level girls, not the A-level girls. I mean, I took classes with the A-level girls, but my friends were in the B level in school—the ones destined to work as secretaries. I took classes with them because I thought if I ever need to find a job, it'll help me if I know how to type. So I was in business classes with no intention of going into business. It was just that I had to have a very wide parachute if I was going to be an author.

MACARENA: Are you a poet because you were a sensitive child?

SANDRA: I'm lucky that I found that there was a medicine for my hypersensitivity. I mean, other people wind up stabbing or shooting people, but I was lucky that I had art to transform all of those emotions into lucidity. I feel like young people today don't, and that's why I really believe people wind up [with] severe depressions, violent outbursts as we've seen in the schools. They don't have any access to how to deal with depression or emotions that overwhelm them. People don't save them, and no one teaches them. All we have in movies and popular culture is violence. I don't know why we're surprised. It's not just guns, it's this whole mentality: violence and power and how we confront our demons—and we don't in the United States. I think that we don't have a practice. Maybe in some countries there's a dominant, maybe overdominant spiritual practice—but in our country, it's just running amok. It's really sad.

MACARENA: Homes figure so significantly in your life, in your work. Your homes are like your museums. When did you start craving and thinking about creating your own space, your own home? When did that *semillita* get planted that you were going to create a space of your own, regardless of whether a man came into your life?

SANDRA: I think around seventh grade. I started taking books on decorating and houses, and I didn't have but a little room that was big enough for a single bed and a dresser that was too big that the door wouldn't close. But I remember making little art corners in my room, having drawings with a little sign that said, "Sandra's Art Gallery." And it was mainly my drawings or maybe people had drawn a drawing and given it to me. I also had some ballerina prints of productions that they got in a plastic frame that I bought from the Woolworths, in my room. I was trying everything. I was visualizing it. I get a lot of books out about houses and decorating. And I started thinking, "Okay, I like this." Also my friend and I, Janis, a girl who lived in Libertyville but would come to visit her mom—a suburban girl who would come in—and she and I liked magazines. And we would buy *Seventeen* and tear out pictures of models and clothing and makeup and decor that we liked, and we had scrapbooks. So that started around seventh grade.

MACARENA: Well, and it continues today because you're a fabulous interior designer and you know how to dress people. You really are very stylish.

SANDRA: I like it! To me, it's the same thing as drawing or writing a poem. It's all the same, and it comes from the same place of balance, and beauty, and tranquility. It's just like writing, it comes from the same place. I like putting the colors together, or sometimes looking at what works for other people. And if I wasn't a writer, I would have liked to have done something with textiles or with furnishings or with curating fabric or something along that line that's still with the visual.

MACARENA: I'm curious—since this interview is going to appear in an academic anthology of conversations about your work—about how readers and scholars interpret your stories? How much or how often do scholars or students read too much or put their own spin on how they interpret your writing? And I guess, because probably, once you put it out in the world, people filter it through their own experiences.

SANDRA: I think it's valid that they filter it through their own experience, that's what art does. I have my own intention, but of course, there's lots of interpretations that when we write, we have no idea what we're writing. It takes the reader or critic to decipher it, the same way that an analyst would tell us what we dreamt and why we dreamt it and what it might mean. In other dreams, we're dreaming them and we often don't know what we mean. We might think we do, but it's fascinating to look at the interpretations and see what people have to say about our writing. I think everybody is valid as long as you can prove it. It may not be what I intended, but it's what I dreamt.

MACARENA: What are some of the books you keep going back to or poems or writers that keep nourishing you and your writing?

SANDRA: I come back a lot to the stories of Hans Christian Andersen. I come back to him a lot. I come back to Diana Athill, Harriet Doerr. I come back to Jean Rhys a lot. Also, these writers, I like reading memoirs and their creative writing and their biographies. I come back to van Gogh and his letters and his life. I come back to *Alice in Wonderland*; that's something that has always fascinated me, that book and how much it stays with me in my life. There's like the same book I can read over and over again. I love reading Mercè Rodoreda. I like reading Marguerite Duras. I don't like all her work, and I don't like all of Rodoreda's works. I go back to the same ones that I go back to and read. I love reading [Jorge Luis] Borges, or his lectures, especially. I have all of his collected works, which I have not read, but I like rereading his lectures. There's something very magical about them that I enjoy, and I always keep him on the bedside. I like poetry and I like essays and I like spiritual books on spiritual awareness. There's different books, but if I had to just read the same ones over and over again, I'd be really happy. I'd be just as happy. I feel fine. And, *One Thousand and One Nights.* Maybe I only got to thirty-three nights, so you know, I'd put it down when I'm tired of it and come back. I like books that open like that—that you never get tired of. Those are the kinds of books I like to read. That you can read them over and over throughout your life and you get something else out of them.

MACARENA: Now that you've been living in Mexico, how has that affected your work? I wonder if being in Mexico affected whether you also thought about publishing *Martita, I Remember You*, in the same book, in both Spanish and English.

SANDRA: Well, I don't think that was my idea. I think it's because it's such a short story that it makes sense to put it together. But I was certainly excited about it because I can give it to all my friends on this side of the border and they're excited because they have the English, and I can give it to my friends on the other side of the border and they're excited because they have the Spanish. It was practical, for practical reasons, so that we could have a book that was book length rather than a little booklet, since it's such a short story.

MACARENA: You have been writing books now for most of your life when you think about it. And I'm sure there's one book that's your favorite. Can you tell us how you feel about your babies? Do you still love all of them?

SANDRA: No, I don't love all of them. I don't, don't, don't. I don't really care for *My Wicked Wicked Ways*, because I think those are poems from when I had too many censors on my shoulders. I feel like I have outgrown that book except for the introductory poem for the new edition.

MACARENA: In what ways did those censors affect *Wicked Wicked Ways*?

SANDRA: It was to please my teachers and to finish my thesis and to please my publisher. I just feel embarrassed by it now. It's like my juvenilia. I don't like hearing those poems or seeing them performed. You know what? There's people that are young that need to hear those poems, but I outgrew them, so it's like looking at pictures of myself in my high school yearbook, thinking, "What were you thinking with that hairdo?" That's how I think when I see those poems. I'm very fond of *Have You Seen Marie?* I love that book, and I love *Caramelo*. And *House on Mango Street* has resurfaced in my appreciation because I've been working on the opera, of course. I like it now in ways I didn't five years ago.

MACARENA: How did you like it five years ago?

SANDRA: Oh, I was tired of talking about it! Now, it's because I've been working with people, going deeper into it, I feel more excited about it. But I'm always excited about my next book—the new poems that I'm putting together.

MACARENA: I was surprised to hear you mention recently at the San Antonio Public Library—and maybe you have before and I had just not heard you mention it publicly—your own #MeToo story and how you're going to write about that. And I wonder how the #MeToo movement brought that perspective or that story into focus for you.

SANDRA: No, the #MeToo movement didn't bring it into focus. I've always spoken about it. Maybe I didn't speak about it when I was living it and when I was younger. But it's always been there, and I've written about it in some of my work. But it wasn't the #MeToo movement; the #MeToo movement gave it a name. I think women like myself have those stories, and we sometimes discuss it with each other. I just feel like I haven't been able to be at some place where I can write about it where I wasn't angry or I wasn't ashamed. I can and should and will write about it now because I'm older and can see it clearly.

MACARENA: *Animalitos* factor in your life, drawing, writing in a big way, like in *Puro Amor*. Has that always been the case? What is it about *animalitos*?

SANDRA: Well, I would have more if I had more room. I don't have [much of a] yard. When I moved into my house on Guenther Street [in San Antonio's King William Historic District], it was the first time I could have pets besides cats. I had cats and moved them around; they didn't like that. I could finally have a dog, and I started with one. And then people gave me dogs or dumped them in my yard, or I found them in the river. It was just because I had a big yard! And then I had someone I lived with who was also an animal lover, so we wound up having a refuge center. You don't plan it, it just happens. Now that I live here, if I had more room, I would have a burro. If I had room, I would have more. . . . I like birds, but I don't like having them in cages like I did in Texas, so they're just free. I find they bring me a lot of *tranquilidad*. Especially since we create in solitude, they calm me down. They make me laugh. They make me mad. [Laughs] But even though they make you mad, they're so nonjudgmental. They remind me to be nonjudgmental and to be *puentes de amor* [bridges of love], to be just this . . . give unconditional love. And they also protect me and tell me when intruders are coming, so that's nice because I live a very private life now.

MACARENA: That is nice, and you never feel alone when you have *animalitos* around. And you're right, writing is such a solitary act. But you've collaborated with a lot of people. Do you wanna tell us a little about your collaborations? I know that you're working on an opera with composer Derek Bermel for *Mango Street*.

SANDRA: I don't know if I'm doing my best work because I've never done anything like this, and Derek is very accepting so sometimes I wonder, "Should he be harder with me and say, 'Oh, we need to do that line better'?" Because he doesn't do that, he likes what I give him, and I always think, "That's too easy!"

MACARENA: Maybe it's the inner critic in you.

SANDRA: It's fun being with somebody else because you know, we kind of riff off each other, and sometimes, I'll get into his area and say, "No! That music's too white! Can't you do something more like, Tejano here?" [Laughs] And he doesn't mind when I do that, and sometimes he'll detour into my area and say, "What about this line?" And I'll say, "Yeah, that's better than what I thought of!" So it really is a true collaboration. I don't think I can put my name completely on the libretto. I'd have to put his name, too, because he's very good with language and I'm not a musician so I'm not going to take any credit for the compositions. But I know when something's off, and I'll say, "Eh, this character's gotta be more like, you know, like this song. Listen to this. It's gotta be this." So a lot of times, I will come in and give him suggestions for what I'm hearing and what I'm not hearing, it's something that he'll create. He's been very, very open about that, and I'm happy that we're compatible in that sense. It's fun. I always have a lot of fun working with Derek.

MACARENA: That's interesting because collaborations, they do take a certain kind of synergy, right? It has to happen between both people in order for them to work, or they can be big headaches.

SANDRA: I guess I've never worked on anything like this before, so I had to have a collaboration. I couldn't have worked on it by myself because I'd never done anything like this. And I think that helps, when you have someone who's running alongside you—and you're on a bicycle with no training wheels and they're running alongside you holding you up. You know, that *confianza*, you get a little confidence there. Derek's doing that, he's allowing me to get on this two-wheel bicycle with no training wheels.

MACARENA: This next question is from Dr. Olga Herrera, who's a contributor to the book this interview is going to appear in. And she wanted to know why, in *The House on Mango Street*, the last line of the book in the first Arte Público Press edition differs from the Vintage/Random House edition.

SANDRA: The real line is, "For those who cannot out." That's what I wrote. But there are many interpolations in the small press edition because the editor added words thinking that I didn't know my grammar and did not get my approval and made editorial changes to my text. So by the time they made their money back—and, you know, a press has to make their money back from publishing the edition—Arte Público said they would correct it. But the first printings had those interpolations. And they did concede that they had made some changes without the author's approval and corrected it in later editions. So by the time it went to the large press, it was back to my original text.

MACARENA: You recently said that you have come to see *Martita, I Remember You*, your most recent novella, as perhaps your best work to date. I think some of your readers might find that an interesting declaration.

SANDRA: Well, why?

MACARENA: Because so many people love *The House on Mango Street*. For so many readers it was the first book they read and/or a definitive book. Perhaps it's like you say, "people come to books when it's time to take that medicine."

SANDRA: I think, for me, *House*, it did its work for a young writer, but I couldn't handle the complexity of drawing portraits of people in depth. It's a simple structure with one narrator who's making these observations, and it's not really complicated in its form. And that's because I wasn't that mastered at handling a lot of people. When I wrote *Caramelo*, I wanted to do the opposite. People dismissed *House* as being not a true novel, so I was working to do more experimental things. I was thinking of Manuel Puig, I was thinking of [Guillermo] Cabrera Infante, you know, writers who did experimental things with fiction. I hoped to make a big, messy story rather than succinct and tight. With *Martita*, which I don't even know what to call it because it's too complex to be called a story and it's very short. It's crossing borders in genre, again, something between a novel and a short story but not a short story because there's so much complexity in its characters. And its structure is more refined for me, more complex than anything, but succinct. I just feel like, working at the top of my creative powers, it may not be evident to a reader but to someone who writes and constructs things and is a writer, I'm very pleased. I think the writer I was trying to stretch myself to was closer to someone like a Mercè Rodoreda and her sensitivity to protagonists, and to detail, and to place, and to mood, that I think I accomplished.

MACARENA: I've heard you say that you feel like you have yet to write the book you want to write.

SANDRA: I don't feel like I have yet. Like the book that I would say, "Okay, now I can go!" I don't feel I've done that book yet.

MACARENA: And what is that book?

SANDRA: I don't know, you know? I want to write a book that is perfect, and you know, I love *Caramelo*, but it's a little bit uneven. It was a difficult book for me to write, it was very experimental. I don't know what that book is yet.

MACARENA: Why was *Caramelo* such a difficult book for you to write, and how long did it take you?

SANDRA: Well, nine years writing it and another year proofing the galleys.

It was very complicated because it was so much, too. I think it was complicated because you can't write when you're thinking about your reader, and a lot of it was with deadlines that were hard for me. I can't deal with deadlines. But once I had the MacArthur award, it gave me a reprieve from the deadlines and I could just work and that's what I needed. The MacArthur gave me the time to spend with my father when he was dying and to recover from his death by writing his story in *Caramelo,* so it was a very spiritual book for me.

MACARENA: I was thinking about your dad because I met you around the time you were editing *Caramelo*. Is there anything else you think readers should know about how you feel about any of your books? I hadn't heard you talk about *Wicked Wicked Ways,* but I know that there were some poems that you're like, "Oh, I hate it when people bring those poems up."

SANDRA: I've even outgrown *Loose Woman*. When I see those poems, I like them, but I've outgrown them.

MACARENA: Do you feel like someone else? Like you were at a different point in your life or something?

SANDRA: Yes, like when you look at pictures of yourself and you were twenty pounds thinner and had a different hairdo and you can say, "Oh, that's who I used to be." These are the concerns I had about lovers and love that are not interesting to me now. I don't care about them now. Some of my newer poems have to deal with love and lovers but they're boring to me now. I may publish them, I may not—I just kind of find them boring.

MACARENA: And if you were to write without any of those censors, what other stuff would you be writing? What is it that you feel? What are those censors?

SANDRA: I think those censors change for us, and I feel as if poetry, for me, is a way to uncensor myself. I had even considered calling the manuscripts "Cisneros sin Censura" [Cisneros without Censors], because I like the sound and also the idea of poetry being some place where we can come to our writing without *vergüenza* [shame]. To me, it's always about that *vergüenza*. [It] is there all the time for me, but it's different things in my life. Maybe it's love, or when I was younger and now it's about different *vergüenzas,* different forms of *vergüenza*. I don't want to be *escandalosa* or shameless or rude, but you know what? What's shameful for me is something that you might laugh and think, "Oh, well why is she ashamed about that?" For each of us, what's taboo for us is so personal. If I force myself, I can write a poem everyday. I'm trying to be in that place where even if it's a silly poem or a little poem, I feel like I want to be able to say things and they don't have to be so magnificent, heavy. They can be little, tiny poems, like a haiku, or funny. I want to be able to give myself *permiso*: they don't have to have such gravitas! They can be about the things that we notice when we're aging. A lot of that. Observations of things that people didn't tell me about growing older are some of the things I write about. Some of them are about language and being in Mexico. I'm asking everyday, "¿Cómo se dice?" My vocabulary is not where it should be as a writer. I'm still learning. I don't know anything when it comes to contemporary literature, contemporary politics, it's very hard for me to follow the news shows, let alone the newspapers in Spanish. So I'm always in some limbo, some little bubble. My own little bubble.

MACARENA: I always want to hear what books of their own writers still like or fell out of love with. It's always fascinating.

SANDRA: You know why? Because we're reading different books, and our standards keep changing as we get older. When we're younger, "Okay, I wanna write a book like Sylvia Plath." But then later on, you turn fifty, and say, "I don't wanna write Sylvia Plath poems. That's not my favorite writer anymore." You keep growing and changing and evolving. I'm just giving an example. I'm not a Sylvia Plath devotee or destroyer. I just feel neutral. I feel as if, *a estas alturas*, I'm aiming for something different because I'm searching. I feel like I'm searching, Macarena, for the book that's going to allow me to write the book I want to write. It's not a novel, it's not a poem, I don't know what it is. I'm always kind of hunting and thinking, "Will this get me there? How will I get there?" I'm always on a journey.

MACARENA: This last question is from Dr. Geneva Gano, who coedited this collection with Dr. Sonia Saldívar-Hull. Her question: what are some of the creative projects—writing or otherwise—that you wish you'd have the time, space, and energy to undertake and complete, but not been able to? Why have you had to abandon some?

SANDRA: Everything that I write has basically been abandoned one time or another because I feel like the publishing industry only wants you to write fiction. And every time you write something, they'll say, "It's been thirty years since she wrote," or "twenty years since she wrote this genre." They always put, like, [as] if I'm just sitting around scratching my ass, and I'm always working. I'm always working even if it's just going out there and speaking in communities because that, to me, is very important ministry. The fact that publishing and the press always put a number on how many years since the last time you wrote a novel, or the last time you published a book, it makes it look like you're just sitting on your behind. I feel as if publishers wish I would crank out novels. When you look at awards—the big, major, global awards—they're looking at novels. And I don't write to compete or for popularity; I write so I could live. And I'm not living to write, I'm writing so I could live my life, and sometimes something happens that I need poetry, and other times I need to finish a short story. I feel as if everything is market driven about, "What can you sell?" And I don't like that. I don't think about things, about what I can sell, or what's going to get me noticed, or what's going to get me a prize. I really feel like the prize is living this life and surviving it and coming out of the other end smarter and wiser and more lucid than when you began—a better human being. I want to be a better human being. That's better than any Nobel Prize.

ACKNOWLEDGMENTS

Many individuals and institutions have made this collection possible. At Texas State University, this project found many friends. Katie Salzmann and David Coleman, lead archivist and director of the Wittliff Collections, respectively, gave unflagging and unstinting support to this project. The Center for the Study of the Southwest, the College of Liberal Arts, and the Department of English likewise sustained our work on this from beginning to end. University of Texas Press editors Dawn Durante and Kerry Webb were advocates throughout the process of putting it all together. To my esteemed coeditor, mentor, teacher, and friend, Sonia Saldívar-Hull, it was a dream to undertake this with you! Thanks, of course, to las sinvergüenzas—those who show up big on these pages and everywhere. And finally, thanks to la incomparable Sandra, sin quien no puderia possible este colección (y la écstasis de lectura, claro).

—Geneva M. Gano

I would like to recognize the tireless work of Geneva M. Gano, who organized the original symposium on the work of Cisneros. She then organized the conference on Cisneros when the archive collection opened at the Wittliff Collections at Texas State University. As well, I want to acknowledge the arguably hundreds of students who have studied and furthered my understanding of the Cisneros texts over the years. And most importantly, I thank Sandra, who often sent me drafts of the stories to enjoy. She has been the inspiration for my tenure as a professor and literary critic.

—Sonia Saldívar-Hull

CONTRIBUTORS

Mary Pat Brady is professor of literatures in English and the director of the American Studies Program at Cornell University. She is the award-winning author of *Extinct Lands, Temporal Geographies: Chicana Literature and the Urgency of Space* and *Scales of Captivity: Racial Capitalism and the Latinx Child*.

Sandra Cisneros is internationally acclaimed for her poetry and fiction and has received numerous awards, including a MacArthur Fellowship, the National Medal of Arts, and the Ruth Lilly Poetry Prize. Her novel *The House on Mango Street* has sold nearly eight million copies. Cisneros is a dual citizen of the United States and Mexico and earns her living by her pen.

Adriana Estill teaches at Carleton College in Minnesota. She has authored several essays about Sandra Cisneros's poetry and prose, most recently an analysis of Mexican Chicago in *Caramelo*. Her work on affect and race includes a coauthored piece with Lee Bebout in *Aztlán* that examines the cinematic production of white lack emerging in response to Mexican affective fullness. Her current research project tracks how the telenovela genre circulates and creates racialized and gendered knowledge in the US public sphere.

Geneva M. Gano is professor of English at Texas State University. She is the author of *The Little Art Colony and US Modernism: Carmel, Provincetown, Taos* and a number of essays on hemispheric American literatures, modernism, and multiethnic women's literature. She is currently completing a manuscript on the impact of the Mexican Revolution on US writing in the early twentieth century.

CONTRIBUTORS

Audrey Goodman is the author of *A Planetary Lens: The Photo-Poetics of Western Women's Writing* and two other books on the history of literature and photography in the US Southwest and US-Mexico borderlands. The recipient of fellowships from the Georgia O'Keeffe Museum Research Center, the Huntington Library, and the Wittliff Collections at Texas State University, she has served as copresident of the Western Literature Association and is currently professor of English at Georgia State University.

Linda Margarita Greenberg is professor of English at California State University, Los Angeles. She is currently finishing a book project on the Chicana author Helena María Viramontes that situates Viramontes's fiction within the context of the Chicana/o movement, transnational feminism, ecocriticism, and cultural memory.

Georgina Guzmán is associate professor of English and faculty director of the Center for Community Engagement at California State University, Channel Islands. A daughter of Mexican immigrants, she teaches courses on Chicanx and Latinx literature and service learning. Her research and teaching interests center on exploring Latinx students' racial and class shame within educational systems as well as the development of their critical consciousness and anti-deficit thinking through their horizontal relationships to working-class laborers such as farmworkers, domestic workers, and campus custodians.

Macarena Hernández is a multimedia journalist and educator who has worked as a reporter, editorial columnist, producer, and editor. She has held two endowed chairs in her field, at the University of Houston–Victoria and Baylor University. She has lectured extensively on media literacy, the US-Mexico border, immigration, and education issues.

Teresa Hernández is a border scholar from the Rio Grande Valley in South Texas. Her research is situated within the intersections of border theory, women of color feminist theory, and Latine/x literary and cultural studies. She is assistant professor of English, ethnic studies, and women's and gender studies at Willamette University in Salem, Oregon.

Olga L. Herrera is associate professor of English at the University of Saint Thomas in Minnesota. Her research and teaching interests include Mexican Chicago literature, labor history and urban studies, and Latinx representation in media and culture. She has written about Sandra Cisneros's fiction, poetry, and essays for *MELUS*, *Chicago: A Literary History*, *The Oxford Encyclopedia of Latina and Latino Literature*, and *New Territory* magazine.

CONTRIBUTORS

Tey Marianna Nunn is the associate director for content and interpretation at the Smithsonian National Museum of the American Latino. She is an award-winning scholar, author, and curator who has served as director of the American Women's History Initiative of the Smithsonian Institution, director of the Art Museum at the National Hispanic Cultural Center in Albuquerque, New Mexico, and curator of contemporary Hispano and Latino collections at the Museum of International Folk Art in Santa Fe. In 2016, President Barack Obama appointed Dr. Nunn to the National Museum and Library Services Board.

Sara A. Ramírez earned her PhD at the University of California, Berkeley, in 2016. She is assistant professor of English at Texas State University, affiliated with Latina/o studies. She is the author of "Making (Sense of) Place: Sandra Cisneros's Literary Arts Activism in the Midwest" and co-author of "Publishing Work that Matters: Third Woman Press and Its Impact on Chicana and Latina Publishing."

Belinda Linn Rincón is associate professor of Latin American and Latinx studies and English at John Jay College of Criminal Justice, City University of New York. She specializes in Chicana/o/x and Latina/o/x literary and cultural studies, Latina feminisms, war and militarism, and Latinx Gothic and horror. She is the author of *Bodies at War: Genealogies of Militarism in Chicana Literature and Culture* and is currently working on a monograph about Latinx horror and Gothic in film and literature.

Richard T. Rodríguez is professor of English at the University of California, Riverside. He is the author of *Next of Kin: The Family in Chicano/a Cultural Politics* and *A Kiss across the Ocean: Transatlantic Intimacies of British Post-Punk and US Latinidad*.

Sonia Saldívar-Hull is professor emeritus of English at the University of Texas, San Antonio. She is the founding director of the Women's Studies Program and the Women's Studies Institute. She served as the inaugural associate dean of diversity, equity, inclusion, and justice in the College of Liberal and Fine Arts. Saldívar-Hull's publications include *Feminism on the Border: Chicana Gender Politics and Literature* and several journal articles and book chapters on such Chicana writers as Gloria Anzaldúa, Helena María Viramontes, and Sandra Cisneros.

Shanna M. Salinas is associate professor of English and cochair of the Department of Critical Ethnic Studies at Kalamazoo College, where she teaches nineteenth-, twentieth-, and twenty-first-century US literature with an emphasis on race and ethnicity and a specialization in Chicana/o/x literature. Her work can be read in *Transnational Chicanx Perspectives on Ana Castillo, Studies in American Fiction,* and *Critical Insights: Virginia Woolf and 20th Century Women Writers.* She is co–primary investigator of the Humanities Integrated Locational Learning (HILL) initiative, a Mellon Foundation Humanities for All Times grant recipient.

INDEX

Notes: Page numbers in *italics* refer to images.

Aarons, Leroy, 113
Aarseth, Espen J., 66
affect studies, 122–123
Alarcón, Norma, 3, 10, 110, 142, 173–190, *186*, 197, 237; archives, 187; editor of *Third Woman*, 184; founder of Third Woman Press, 173, 174, 197; on importance of Third Woman Press, 184; pseudonym "Marisa Cantú" used by, 182; "What Kind of Lover Have You Made Me, Mother?," 188–189
Alfredo Cisneros Del Moral Foundation, 6
Allison, Dorothy, 5
altars, 231–233
Alvarez, Julia, 187
Anderson, William, 2
anti-Blackness, 22, 35
Anzaldúa, Gloria, 9, 102, 122–123, 162, 168, 169, 180, 184
Arredondo, Gabriela F., 42
Arrieta, José Agustín, 15–17, *16*, 19, 28
Arte Público, 4, 197, 245–246
art installations. *See* visual art and installations

Bachelard, Gaston, 31, 33, 170n30
Bad Boys (Cisneros), 3, 197
Badikian, Beatriz, 3, 176, 178, 182–183, 185
Bailey, Steve, 5
Baker, Gertrude, 5
Bambara, Toni Cade, 162

Bell, Marvin, 2–3, 161
belonging: *casta* system and, 18–19; community, 134, 208; identity and, 44–45; institutional, 124; racial and ethnic, 32, 44–45; territorial and spatial, 81–82, 84, 87, 89. *See also* exclusion
Benamou, Catherine L., 51
Bergholz, Susan, 5
Bermel, Derek, 244–245
bildungsroman, 19, 27
bodies: borderlessness of, 105–106; boundaries of, 50; desire and, 9, 49, 101–114; duality and, 156–157; essentialisms, 51; gendered, 52, 57–60, 65, 77, 90, 183; male, 102; patriarchy and, 48; racialized, 65, 69, 77; of saints, 143; storytelling and, 76–77; telenovela feeling and, 48–60. *See also* body ignorance
body ignorance, 103–104
body knowledge, 102, 103–105
border culture, 47
border feminisms, 81–82, 90–93
borderlessness, 105–107
border narratives, 81–83, 89–90
borders and boundaries: bodies as boundaries, 50; *casta* art and, 16; metaphorical border crossings, 1, 11, 131, 138–139, 161, 246; neighborhood boundaries, 32, 34, 35–36, 48; physical border crossings, 138–139, 205, 209; racialized and segregated, 32, 35–36, 42; subjects and subjectivities boundaries, 94–95

INDEX

border studies, 81
Borges, Jorge Luis, 161, 167, 243
Bosnian War, 6, 113–114, 209–210
boundaries. *See* borders and boundaries
Brady, Mary Pat, 7, 8, 33–34, 84–85, 87, 92
Bravo Bruno! (Cisneros), 6
Briseño, Rolando, 5, 143–144
Brooks, Gwendolyn, 159, 167
Buddhism, 6
Butler, Judith, 105
Byrd, Gloria, 162

Cantú, Norma E., 121
capitalism, 33, 52, 59, 96n17, 101, 103, 174, 178
Caramelo (Cisneros), 6, 16–28, 63–77; *casta*/costumbrismo tradition and, 15–23, 25, 28; cataloging and lists in, 23–25; Cisneros on, 243, 246–247; Cisneros's audio performance of, 17; colors used in, 221, 222–223; *dichos* in, 20–21; "Disclaimer," 19–20; familial shame and, 70–73, 74, 77; footnote structure in, 17, 47, 65–69, 70, 71, 73, 78n23, 121, 130; maximalist aesthetics in, 130–133; mestizaje and, 18–19, 23, 25, 70, 127, 222; "Pilon" (coda), 76; racialized bodies and, 65, 69, 77; racialized gender identity and, 63, 65, 70, 73, 77; racialized imaginaries and, 19, 21–23, 28; racialized norms and, 73–74, 77; *rasquachismo* and, 130–133; recognition and misrecognition in, 18–19, 21, 26–27, 28; storytelling in, 63–71, 76–77; telenovelas and, 47; types and typicality in, 16–21, 23, 25, 27
Careri, Elisabetta, 33
Casas, David Zamora, 146, 147–149, 227
castagories, 17–19, 27, 28
casta system, 15, 16, 17–23, 25, 28
Castellanos, Rosario, 180–181, 184, 189, 190
Castillo, Ana, 4, 174, 182, 185, 187
Castillo, Debra A., 93
Catacalos, Rosemary, 185
catachresis, 105–108
cataloging and lists, 23–25, 105, 163
Catholicism, 23–24, 86, 104, 123–124, 131–132, 139–140
Cervantes, Lorna Dee, 3, 197
Chávez, Denise, 207
Chávez-Silverman, Suzanne, 51, 149
Chicago, Illinois: Black Belt neighborhood, 34; Humboldt Park, 32, 34, 35–36, 39, 41, 42, 239; King assassination riots of 1968, 36, 37–40; museums, 223; race riots of 1919, 32, 34–35, 41; racialized space in, 31–43; South Side, 32, 34–37, 39–42, 239; West Town, 35–36
Chicago Commission on Race Relations, 35
Chicana critical studies, 7
Cisneros, Sandra: antiwar activism, 6, 113–114, 209–210; archives, 36, 119, 168, 224, 227; Before Columbus Foundation Book Award granted to, 4; childhood and education, 2, 237–239; color of Guenther Street house, 221, 234; critical reception, 7; diaries of, 31–32, 36–41, 44, 119, 120, 124–125; early education, 123–127, 239–241; father of, 2, 6, 124, 126, 137–138, 227; grants awarded to, 3–4, 129, 191n31; Illinois Arts Council artist in residence, 3, 175; at Iowa Writers' Workshop, 2–3, 9, 126–127, 130, 147, 159–161, 206, 238–239; as *la maestra*, 11; at Latino Youth Alternative High School, 3, 182; literature director at Guadalupe Cultural Arts Center, 4, 176, 184–187, *186*; at Loyola University, 2, 3, 126; MacArthur Foundation Fellowship awarded to, 1, 5, 247; MFA thesis, 3; mother of, 2, 128, 227–233; National Medal of Arts awarded to, 1, 6, 220; NLGJA 1995 keynote address, 112–113, 126–127, 146–147; PEN/Nabokov Award granted to, 1; portrait painted by Ángel Rodríguez-Díaz, 144–146, *145*, 227; pseudonym "Katarina Kremidis" used by, 182–183; public readings by, 3, 4, 5, 175, 199, 201, 207–208; visiting professorships, 4–5, 142–143; Women's Caucus for Art 1995 keynote, 165
Cisneros, Sandra, views of: on abandoned projects, 247–248; on *animalitos*, 244; on brothers, 237–239; on *Caramelo*, 243, 246–247; on collaboration, 244–245; on early poetry, 239–240; on *Have You Seen Marie?*, 243; on *The House on Mango Street*, 243–244, 245; on influential books and authors, 242–243; on inner critics and censors, 238–239, 243, 245, 247–248; on interior design and decorating, 240–241; on living in Mexico, 243; on *Loose Woman*, 247; on *Martita, I Remember You*, 246; on #MeToo movement, 244; on *My Wicked Wicked Ways*, 243; on wanting to be a writer in youth, 240–241
Cisneros, Sandra, works of. *See individual book and essay titles*
Cisneros Del Moral, Alfredo, 2, 6, 124, 126, 137–138, 227
citizenship, 82, 87, 92, 94–95, 109
colonialism: acquisition of, 72; colors of, 221;

INDEX

counternarratives to, 68, 122–123; decolonial imaginary, 82, 85, 93, 102–104; decolonial mapping, 81–87, 91, 93–95; decolonization, 83, 102; erotic decoloniality, 105; exoticism of, 53; mestizo women and, 70–71; scale and, 16–18, 19, 21–22, 23, 24–25
colorism, 23, 75
colors and patterns, 218–223
Comanche Wars, 91
Combahee River Collective, 187
conocimiento, 9, 101–102, 105, 110–114
Cordero Anguiano, Elvira, 2, 128, 227–233
Cortés, Hernán, 17
costumbrismo and costumbrista tradition, 15–19, 22, 23, 25, 28
Crenshaw, Kimberlé, 187–188
criminality, 112, 137
critical race narratology, 8, 65–66
cultural geographies, 81–82, 85

Daley, Richard J., 37, 39
Dávila, Luis, 175
decolonialism. *See* colonialism
de Hoyos, Angela, 185
demastery, 105–107
desire: bodies and, 48–60, 101–114; creation and, 163–164; demastered, 105–107; erotic conocimiento and, 9, 101–114; girlhood friendships and, 138; liminality and, 156; same-sex, 138, 139; telenovela feeling and, 48–60
despatialization, 83, 85
detribalization, 23–24
development, government, 33–34
developmentalism, discourse of, 22
diasporic communities, 21, 53
diasporic narratives, 81, 82, 95n4
Dickinson, Emily, 159
disidentification, 28, 51–52, 139
Doble, Flora, 143
Donahue, James J., 65–66
Dove, Rita, 3, 126, 160
Dowling, David, 160–161

empire: imperial violence, 15, 18, 209; *Interior de una pulquería* (Arrieta) and, 15–16; scale as ideological tool, 16–18, 19, 21–22, 23, 24–25. *See also* colonialism
erotic conocimiento, 9, 101–102, 105, 110–114
Escobar, Arturo, 22
Esquibel, Catrióna Rueda, 138
essentialism, 51, 149

Estill, Adriana, 8, 69–70, 107
excess, aesthetics of, 8, 47–52, 54, 57–58, 60
exclusion: American Dream and, 90; in *Caramelo*, 21, 72; of Chicana writers, 93–94, 129, 173; in *The House on Mango Street*, 31–32, 41–44; space and, 93–94; of Spanish colonialism, 21

Fernández, Lilia, 35, 36
Fetta, Stephanie, 122
Frederick, Joan, 5
Freinkel, Lisa, 106
Frías, Carlos, 134
Friedman, Susan Stanford, 158

Galindo, Mary Sue, 185, 186, *186*
Gano, Geneva M., 50, 248
Garcia Lopez, Christina, 122–123
Garduño, Flor, 227
gay men, Latino, 137–151
gender: aesthetic of excess and, 20, 51–60; coloniality of, 20, 102; education and, 126–127; expectations and norms, 51–52, 54, 56, 73–74, 77, 137, 138, 142, 200–201; fluidity, 147–148; in *The House on Mango Street*, 32–33, 44–45; identity and, 32–33, 44–45, 73, 77; racialized, 63–65, 70, 73, 77; shame and, 70, 120; solidarity, 114; storytelling and, 63–66. *See also* intersectionality
gendered bodies, 52, 57–60, 65, 77, 90, 183
genital geography, 108
genitalia, female, 101–104, 108–109; clitoris, 108; hymen and antihymeneal poetry, 58, 60, 108–109; vagina, 102, 103–104, 116n33
geographic locations and distances, 84, 88, 105–106, 139–140, 195, 196
geographics, 82–83, 86, 90–91, 95
Glück, Louise, 2
Goeman, Mushuana, 85
Gomez, Marsha, *186*
Gonzales, Martha R., 122
Gonzáles-Berry, Erlinda, 7
González, Christopher, 65, 68
Gonzalez, Ralfka, 143
Goodman, Audrey, 9–10
Graf, Amara, 47
Grau, Julie, 5
Greenberg, Linda Margarita, 10
Greene, Leslie, 6
Grosz, Elizabeth, 102
Guadalupe Cultural Arts Center: Cisneros as

259

INDEX

literature director of, 4, 176, 184–185, 186; public reading at, 199, 212n5; *Tonantzín* (journal), 4, 184–187
"Guadalupe the Sex Goddess," 103–104, 139, 188
Gutiérrez Revuelta, Pedro, 7
Gutiérrez y Muhs, Gabriella, 7
Guzmán, Georgina, 9

Hairs/Pelitos (Cisneros), 5, 207, 212n15
Harjo, Joy, 3, 9, 126, 155–168; *Crazy Brave*, 165; "I Give You Back," 165–166; *Poet Warrior*, 159–160, 162, 167; "Running," 157, 166; "Speaking Tree," 167–168
Have You Seen Marie? (Cisneros), 6, 83, 217, 229, 243
Hayles, N. Katherine, 65
Hemingway, Ernest, 127, 135n8
Heredia, Juanita, 33
Hernández, Ellie D., 187
Hernández, Ester, 5, 6, 142–143, 229
Hernandez, Jillian, 48, 50
Hernández, Macarena, 10–11
Hernández, Teresa, 8–9
Herrera, Olga L., 8, 245
Herrera-Sobek, María, 7, 197
Herrera y Lozano, Lorenzo, 9, 149–151
hierarchies, class and racial, 16–19, 22, 23, 25, 51, 75, 123
Hinojosa, Rolando, 4, 185
Ho, Jennifer Ann, 65
homogenization: *casta* system and, 17–18, 22, 25; of Latina writers, 181, 183
hooks, bell, 120, 123, 125, 132
House of My Own, A (Cisneros), 6, 128, 130, 166, 201
House on Mango Street, The (Cisneros): Cisneros on, 243–244, 245; color used in, 218–219; "The Family of Little Feet," 42, 43; "The First Job," 42; "Geraldo No Last Name," 37; "Gil's Furniture Bought & Sold," 42–44; "Louie, His Cousin & His Other Cousin," 37; minimalist aesthetics in, 127–129; "Our Good Day," 37, 41, 42, 43; publication of, 4; racial exclusion in, 41–45; racialized space in, 41–45; scholarship on, 32–34; shame and, 120–121, 125–126, 127–129, 131, 132; "A Smart Cookie," 37, 128–129; "Those Who Don't," 36, 41, 44–45; Vintage edition, 5, 197, 245; writing of, 3–4
Huerta, Dolores, 5
Hurtado, Aída, 121
Hymen (Greek god), 108

hymen and antihymeneal poetry, 58, 60, 108–109

imaginaries: colonial imaginary, 15, 17–19, 24, 25, 27–28, 93; decolonial imaginary, 82, 85, 93, 104; racialized imaginary, 18, 19, 21–23, 28; scalar imaginary, 16–19, 24, 25, 27–28; spatial imaginary, 81–82, 85, 89, 92
in-betweenness, racial, 44
Indigeneity, *Caramelo* and, 17–18, 20–25, 28, 70–75, 77
Indigenous knowledge, 102, 123
Indigenous scholars, 83, 85
Indigenous teaching methods, 162
installations, art. *See* visual art and installations
interconnection, 11, 25, 86, 114, 178, 189, 209
Interior de una pulquería (Arrieta), 15–17, 16, 19, 28
intersectionality, 32, 126, 182–183, 187–188
Iowa Writers' Workshop, 2–3, 9, 126–127, 130, 147, 159–161, 206, 238–239
Iraq war, 6
Isabella Stewart Gardner Museum (Boston), 224–225

Jump-Start Theater, 5
Justice, Donald, 2, 161, 170n30

Kanellos, Nicolás, 174, 175, 197
Karaula, Jasna, 6, 113–114, 227
Kaup, Monika, 33
Kim, Sue J., 65
King, Martin Luther, Jr., 32, 37, 38, 39, 40
kinship: castagories and, 18; normative relations of, 137–138; raciality and, 27–28; telenovelas and, 54; unmappability of, 88; writers and, 159, 175, 182, 188–189
Kitchen Table Press, 162, 171n37
Koshy, Susan, 28
Kuribayashi, Tomoko, 33

Lanser, Susan, 65
Lara, Agustín, 131
Lara, Irene, 102, 104
Lefebvre, Henri, 33
"lesbian," use of the term, 138
lesbians, 138, 142–143, 146–147, 205
literary geographies, 81, 82, 85, 87, 94–95
Loose Woman (Cisneros): affective grammar of, 48–49, 50; "After Everything," 57; Cisneros on, 247; colors used in, 220; cover of, 143;

INDEX

gendered body and, 57–60; "Heart, My Lovely Hobo," 57, 58; "I Am So in Love I Grow a New Hymen," 58–60, 106–108; "I Awake in the Middle of the Night and Wonder If You've Been Taken," 113–114; "I Don't Like Being in Love," 55; "Little Clown, My Heart," 57–58; "A Little Grief like Gouache," 220; "Loose Woman," 48, 49–50, 56, 163; mariachi and *gritos* in, 48, 53, 56–57; museums and art in, 223–224; "My Nemesis Arrives after a Long Hiatus," 220; "Old Maids," 55, 108–109; "Original Sin," 55; publication of, 5, 48; "Pumpkin Eater," 56; "Small Madness," 57; "Still-Life with Potatoes, Pearls, Raw Meat, Rhinestones, Lard, and Horse Hooves," 148, 155–157, 164–165, 166; telenovelas and, 47–60; "Vino Tinto," 163–164; "You Bring Out the Mexican in Me," 50–55, 56–57, 148–151, 220
López de Gómara, Francisco, 17
López Lozano, Danny, 5
Lopez Perez, Margarita, 178, 185
Lorde, Audre, 102, 156, 159, 160, 178, 189
Los MacArturos, 5
Lowden, Frank, 35
Lugones, María, 20, 111

Macondo Foundation, 5–6
Macondo Writers Workshop, 157–158
Madonna (singer), 58
Mango Publications, 197
Manzanas Calvo, Ana María, 33
mapping: in Cisneros's diaries, 37, 39; decolonial, 81–95
Marcus, Sharon, 108
marginalization: aesthetic of marginality, 129; cross-identification and, 142; in institutional settings, 123–126, 132, 162; minimalist aesthetic to critique, 127–129; of mistresses, 101, 102–103, 109–110, 114; in publication, 196–197; shame and, 123–126, 132
Martín-Barbero, Jesús, 48, 52, 54
Martínez, César, 226
Martita, I Remember You / Martita, te recuerdo (Cisneros), 6–7, 243, 246
Massey, Doreen, 33, 82
Mathis, Dennis, 3
Matthews, Bill, 2
McCracken, Ellen, 68, 69
McMahon, Marci, 33
Medina, Lara, 122
Mellinger, Lisa, 5

memorialization, 19
memory: color and, 221–222; embodied, 75–76; geographics and, 81–82, 88–89, 95; truth and, 67
Mesa-Bains, Amalia, 121–122, 132–133
mestizaje, 18–19, 23, 25, 70, 127, 222
metaphor: body and, 49; in love poetry, 106–108; rebozo as, 63, 66–75
#MeToo movement, 114, 244
middle class, 52, 110
Milligan, Bryce, 4, 186
mistresses, 101–103, 107–114
modernity, 48, 89
Mondini-Ruiz, Franco, 5, 142–143, 226
Mora, Pat, 4, 185
Moraga, Cherríe, 4, 142, 185, *186*, 188–189
Moreno, Cesáreo, 233–234
Morgan, Shaun, 65
Moriuchi, Mey-Yen, 18
Mormando, Garrett, 5
Movimiento Artístico Chicano (MARCH), 3
Mujeres Latinas en Acción, 3
Mulholland, Mary-Lee, 56
Muñoz, José Esteban, 51, 139
Muñoz, Sonia, 48, 52, 53, 54
Murphy, Kaitlin M., 88
museums, 10, 223–225
My Wicked Wicked Ways (Cisneros), 3, 48; "The Blue Dress," 219; "By Way of Explanation," 107–108; Cisneros on, 243; colors used in, 219; "Curtains," 219; epigraph to, 159; "His Story," 137–138; mistresses in, 103, 107–108, 110–111; museums and art in, 223–224; "New Year's Eve," 111; "Poem as Preface" (introduction), 162–163; publication of, 4, 187, 197; "Rodrigo Poems, The" (Cisneros), 110–111; "Tantas Cosas Asustan, Tantas," 159; "A Woman Cutting Celery," 110–111, 176

Nahuatl language, 25, 102
narratology, 8, 65–66
National Hispanic Cultural Center (Albuquerque), 229–233
nationalism: *Caramelo* and, 22; Chicana, 188; Cisneros's narrators and, 84; costumbrismo and, 18; limits and trappings of, 81–82, 92, 94–95
National Lesbian and Gay Journalists Association (NLGJA), 112–113, 146–147
neoliberalism, 101, 103
niño, raúl, 3

INDEX

nostalgia, 20, 25, 88
Nunn, Tey Marianna, 10

Obama, Barack, 6, 220
Obejas, Achy, 187
Olivares, Julián, 7
orgasm, 59, 101, 112
otherness, 42, 45, 51, 60, 126, 137, 147, 149

panocha, 102, 104
panocha conocimientos, 102
Paz, Octavio, 85
Pennel, Craig, 5
peonage system, 21–22, 23–24
Pérez, Emma, 82, 93
Pérez, Gina M., 36
Pérez, Laura E., 102
Pineda-Madrid, Nancy, 102, 104, 110
Pitts, Andrea J., 111–112
Poetics of Space, The (Bachelard), 31, 33
Portillo, Lourdes, 5, 142
Pratt, Mary Louise, 158
Protagonist of an Endless Story, The (Rodríguez-Díaz), 144–146, 145, 227
pulquería, 15–16, 16
Puro Amor (Cisneros), 6–7, 244

queer cross-identification, 137–142, 146–148, 150–151
queer studies, 9, 89

racialization: of bodies, 65, 69, 77; *casta* art and, 18–19; of Chicago's space, 31–43; class mobility and, 90; ethnic labels and, 181–182; of gender identity, 63–65, 70, 73, 77; of imaginaries, 18, 19, 21–23, 28; of norms, 73–74, 77; of sexuality, 101, 105; shame and, 122; of trauma, 72
Ramírez, Martín, 226
Ramírez, Sara A., 10
Ramos-Zayas, Ana Y., 36
rasquachismo, 121–122, 129–133, 217, 229
Rebolledo, Tey Diana, 7, 187
rebozos, 20, 27, 63, 66–75, 133, 222–223
Retka, Janelle, 119–120
Rich, Adrienne, 162, 191n20
Rincón, Belinda Linn, 9
Riojas Clark, Ellen, 5
Ríos, Alberto, 4
Rios, Katherine, 138–139
Rivera, Salima, 174, 178
Rivera-Barrera, José Luis, 226

Rocha, Rina, 182
Rodriguez, Carmen, *186*
Rodriguez, Cristina, 33
Rodríguez, Luis J., 203, 204, 205, 213n19
Rodriguez, Ralph E., 152n13
Rodríguez, Richard T., 9
Rodríguez-Díaz, Ángel, 5; Cisneros's first meeting of, 143–144; *The Protagonist of an Endless Story, The* (portrait of Cisneros), 144–146, *145*, 227
Roediger, David, 44
Rojas, Maythee G., 110
Romo, Ito, 5, 227
Room of Her Own, A (Cisneros), 227, 229–234, *230*, *231*, *232*

Saldívar-Hull, Sonia, 51–52, 56, 203–204, 248
Salinas, Luis Omar, 4, 185, 226
Salinas, Shanna M., 8
Santos, John Phillip, 4, 185
scale, 16–18, 19, 21–22, 23, 24–25
segregation, racial, 31–32, 34–36, 40–41, 44–45
self-knowledge, 109–112
shame: bell hooks on, 120, 123, 125; scholarship, 122–123; school-inflicted, 119–134; *sin vergüenza* aesthetics, 120–123, 130, 131, 133–134; storytelling and, 63–64, 66, 70–74, 77
Shuru, Xochitl Estrada, 51
Silko, Leslie Marmon, 161
Singh, Julietta, 105
"Sir James South Side" (Cisneros), 3
slavery, 21–22, 72
"Smith's Supermarket, Taos, New Mexico, at the Fifteen Items or Less Checkout Line" (Cisneros), 163–165
So, Richard Jean, 173
Soja, Edward W., 33
Solís, Diana, 3, 142, 173–174, 178, 181, 190n3
Soto, Gary, 3
Soto, Sandra K., 105
Spivak, Gayatri, 83
Stavans, Ilan, 68, 149
sucia love, 9, 101, 103, 104, 109–114
Szeghi, Tereza M., 69

Tabuenca Córdoba, María Socorro, 93
Tapia, Elena, 106
Tejanx communities, 91, 93–94
telenovela, 8, 47–60, 130
Tenayuca, Emma, 5
testimoniar, 6

INDEX

Texas-Indian Wars, 91
Texas Small Press Book Fair, 4, 185, 186
Third Woman (journal), 10, 142, 173–174, 180–182, 184–186, 187, 192n40
Third Woman Collective, 178, 191n14, 191n30
Third Woman Press, 173–174, 184–185, 187; founding of, 10, 194, 197, 212n4, 237; titles, 4, 197
Third World feminism, 3
Three of Cups Tarot card, 178
Tia Chucha Press, 204, 205, 213n19
Tienda Guadalupe, 5
Tlazolteotl, 104, 151
Tobin, Claudia, 157
Tomkin, Silvan, 122
Tonantzín (journal), 4, 184–187
Torquemada, Fray Juan, 104
Torres, Belkys, 47
Triumph of Bacchus, The (Velázquez), 15–16, *16*
Tuana, Nancy, 103
Tuck, Eve, 83, 85
types and typicality, 16–21, 23, 25, 27

vagina, 102, 103–104, 116n33
Vargas, Deborah, 101, 103, 110
Velázquez, Diego, 15–16, *16*
Villa, Raúl Homero, 83–84
Vinson, Ben, 23
Vintage Cisneros, 6
Viramontes, Helena María, 4, 10, 122–123, 185, 195–211; archives, 197; "The Cariboo Cafe," 209–210; *The Moths and Other Stories*, 197, 199; on Proposition 187, 208–209; *Their Dogs Came with Them*, 196, 197; *Under the Feet of Jesus*, 196, 197, 199–200, 206, 207;
Virgen de Guadalupe, La, 84–86, 104, 133, 139, 222
visual art and installations, 217–234; colors and patterns used by Cisneros, 218–223; *The House on Mango Street: Artists Interpret Community* (Cisneros-related exhibit), 233; museums and art in works by Cisneros, 223–225; notebook visualizations by Cisneros, 227–228; paintings by Cisneros, 228; *A Room of Her Own* (installation), 227, 229–234, *230*, *231*, *232*

Warhol, Andy, 224
Warhol, Robyn, 65
whiteness, 42–43, 44, 53–54, 55, 110, 111
Williams, Eugene, 35
Wilson, Jeff, 142
Wittliff Collections (Texas State University), 36, 119, 168, 224, 227
Woman Hollering Creek and Other Stories (Cisneros), 5, 129–130, 138–139, 144; Alarcón's influence on, 188; "*Bien* Pretty," 221–222, 228; colors used in, 220, 221–222; community cartography in, 81–95; cultural geographies and, 81–82, 85; "Eleven," 119, 129, 221–222; "Eyes of Zapata" (Cisneros), 101, 144, 146; geographics and, 81–83, 86, 90–91, 95; La Llorona, 146; literary geographies and, 81–82, 85, 87, 94–95; "Little Miracles, Kept Promises," 139–140, 225; "The Marlboro Man," 139, 141–143; maximalist aesthetics in, 129–130; museums and art in, 225; "Never Marry a Mexican," 101, 110, 111, 224; publication of, 5, 197; "Salvador Late or Early," 220; styles and themes in, 81–83, 84, 93–94, 129–130, 134, 138–139; "Tepeyac," 82, 83–89, 90, 93, 96n17; "Woman Hollering Creek," 56, 82, 89–94, 138–139
"Woman of No Consequence, A" (Cisneros), 112–113, 126–127, 146–147
Woman without Shame / Mujer sin vergüenza (Cisneros), 7, 120, 133, 135, 157; Joy Harjo's blurb for, 157

Yang, K. Wayne, 83, 85
Yarbro-Bejarano, Yvonne, 7, 187
Ybáñez, Terry, 5, 207, 227
Ybarra-Frausto, Tomás, 121
Young, Kevin, 155, 156
Young, Reggie, 3